T0204550

2 Angels

And I

Myself

God's

Alien 1

Alien 2

Me

GOD'S
ME, MYSELF, AND I

THE TRUTH

AND ULTIMATE TRUTH

ABOUT THE TRINITY

CONSPIRACY

PART 1

BY GOD'S SHEEPDOG

God's Me, Myself, and I The Truth and Ultimate
Truth about the Trinity Conspiracy

Part 1
God's Me - The Mystery of Christ

Written by God's Sheepdog

In Dedication to:
Apostle Paul Crouch and First Lady Jan Crouch

I dedicate this body of work to Apostle Paul and First Lady Jan Crouch. I call him "Apostle" because he, through God, created a network that housed many preachers within it, and it brought millions, including myself, through our hard times. They are responsible for saving millions of souls, yet Brother Paul caught a lot of hate when it came to the truth about the Trinity. Some of us had forgotten that he was a man used by God, but yet a man—a man whom some of us thought should know everything. So we hated on him when he did not have the answer no one in the entire world had and has not had for over 2000 years.

Although Apostle Paul did not have the answer, he never stopped looking for it. Therefore, this body of work is dedicated in his hands, as he gives to you the final truth about the Trinity that will put an end to the debates forever about who the true God is and who Jesus Christ is whom He sent.

One thing about Brother Paul was he never backed down from a spiritual fight. It did not matter who was wrong or right but that the truth came out of the fight. This truth, although it is different from the Trinity we know, put to rest the fight about the Trinity forever.

To Apostle Paul Crouch and First Lady Jan Crouch, thank you for having hearts of love and souls that were steadfast and did not waver but sorted out truth.

Rest in peace, for your God has spoken for you!

God's Sheepdog

7

Table of Contents

Part 1: God's Me - The Mystery of Christ

Introduction

In today's world, as in times past, we have come so open to all kinds of religions, when all the while it has not been about religion at all. I know many of you know that it is about the relationship and not the religion," but whom is the relationship with?" In addition, with Oneness, Unitarians, Trinitarians, Jews, and Muslims, all seeing God differently, "How do we know who is the True God?" Still to this day, we have many questions such as this. Who is it that we are to live by? How can we live by a man? Is Jesus a man or God? Did God create us? When and how did God create us? Is it true that we evolved? If we did evolve, how then could God have created us? Who is the Father? Why are we here on earth? Is God three persons in a Godhead? If so, won't that mean that God is just a Godhead?

Question after question have we to ask. You see, just as you, I too had many questions I needed answers too. Therefore, I started seeking God for myself. I had enough of men trying to tell me their opinions instead of what God's Word says. Therefore, I did as Matt. 6:33 states: "But seek ye first the kingdom of God and His righteousness; and all these things shall be added unto you."

After years of feeling lost, angry, hurt, misunderstood, frustrated, and unworthy of life—I was not suicidal, just tired of the life I was living—I started praying, fasting, and seeking God's face. Then one day God told me, I was His Sheepdog. Then I said to God, "Okay, God, if you are real, I want to see a miracle." God told me I was going to be a miracle. I did not understand at the time, but now, some years later, I do. After God gave me this work to do, I could not believe that, out of every one in the world, God chose me. Then one day, I just could not stop thinking about it. I just could not stop saying "Me, God Me, Me, God, Me?" Then after saying, this for a while, it hit me. "Wow, God, Me God!" Then God said, "Yep, it is a miracle, Roland, that I chose you out of everyone in the world to bring this work

11

forth unto my people. Then, at that moment, I realized, I am a miracle!

TO GOD BE THE GLORY!
John 17:3
And this is life eternal, that they might know thee the only True God, and Jesus Christ, whom thou hast sent!"

CHAPTER 1

Our Christian Theology of the Trinity

G enesis 1:1 – "In the beginning God created the heavens and the earth." In the beginning, God created "God," and He wants us to know Him, and He wants us to know Him as He truly is. Many of us have been taught the concept of the Trinity—that there is one Godhead with three persons in it. Well, that is not true; a part of God was manifested in only one person. Manifested— according to Webster's college dictionary—means in verb form, "to make clear or evident to the eye, or the understanding; to manifest approval or disapproval."

1 Timothy 3:16 states, "And without controversy great is the mystery of godliness: God was manifest in the flesh, justified in the spirit, seen of angels, preached unto the Gentiles, believed on in the world, received up into glory." Now, in this portion of Scripture, manifest was used as a verb. "Person" means "a human being, a man, woman, or child; (2) A human being as distinguished from an animal or thing." With that definition, we can understand that just as we humans are "flesh," people, God was manifest in the flesh—remember the Word became flesh. You can go through the whole Bible and you will not find God being manifest in any other person this way. Also through this process we will learn, that God is not a person, or a substance, but a Spirit, and that through God's Spirit, God manifests Himself. The same with the Holy Spirit—it is not a person, it is the Spirit of God, manifest in us through faith in God's Word, His Son, Jesus the Christ, our God, who is also Spirit. We also have been led to believe that the Lord Jesus Christ, our God, is to return in bodily form as a man. Well

13

again, that is not true, and to find the truth, we need to know more about the spiritual body and the natural body, which we will learn more about in part two.

God does not want anyone to be confused or misled, which leads individuals to go astray and become lost. Up until the age of thirty-three years, I have always had a confrontational relationship with God because of some things that I had to go through in my life. What I was led to believe just did not feel right to me. I felt that there had to be more to help me understand my life as well as whom God really is. Thus began my journey to understanding God's purpose for me in this life. I started seeking God's face all day and all night. I hardly slept at night with so many questions.

Because God knew my heart was truly seeking His Wisdom, His Knowledge, and His Understanding, God showed me my purposes in this life, as He called me His Sheepdog. After God called me His Sheepdog, I really started fasting, sowing seeds, and praying. All I asked from God was that He gives me His Wisdom, His Knowledge, and His Understanding. Once God was pleased with me, He gave me this work to do. This work is to reveal in God's Word who God the Father truly is.

I am God's Sheepdog, and as such, He has called me to go out into the pastures of this world and proclaim the truth about Him to His lost and confused sheep that there shall be one Fold with one Shepherd.

To God Be The Glory!

Matthew 6:24-34 – "No man can serve two masters: for either he will hate the one, and love the other; or else he will hold to the one, and despise the other. Ye cannot serve God and mammon. Therefore, I say unto you, Take no thought for your life, what ye shall eat, or what ye shall drink; nor yet for your body, what ye shall put on. Is not the life more than meat, and the body than raiment? Behold the fowls of the air: for they sow not, neither do they reap, nor gather into barns; yet your heavenly Father feedeth them. Are

14

ye not much better than they? Which of you by taking thought can add one cubit unto his stature? And why take ye thought for raiment? Consider the lilies of the field, how they grow; they toil not, neither do they spin: And yet I say unto you, That even Solomon in all his glory was not arrayed like one of these. Wherefore, if God so clothe the grass of the field, which to day is, and to morrow is cast into the oven, shall he not much more clothe you, O ye of little faith? Therefore take no thought, saying, What shall we eat? or, What shall we drink? or, Wherewithal shall we be clothed? (For after all these things do the Gentiles seek): for your heavenly Father knoweth that ye have need of all these things. But seek ye first the kingdom of God, and his righteousness; and all these things shall be added unto you. Take therefore no thought for the morrow: for the morrow shall take thought for the things of itself. Sufficient unto the day is the evil thereof."

Unless otherwise stated, all scriptures are taken from the King James Version.

Genesis 1:1 –"In the beginning God created the heavens and the earth." Therefore, in the beginning, God created; God created first. Please keep this in mind as you read each chapter. In addition, how God created everything is very important. Genesis 1:1-31 and Proverbs 8:1-31 will not only let us know how God created everything, but they will also start somewhat revealing the true God, God's Me, Myself, and I, which will be made more clear in the chapters to come. Once we learn more about God's Me, Myself, and I, then the purpose of the Bible becomes more apparent.

God's Me, Myself, and I, are very important for us to know, because once we learn this, the mystery of the Bible itself will becomes open unto us. No matter how old we are or how long we have been believers, our faith in God's Word, through His Christ, will become 100% convicted. The things we once thought we could get away with we will never want to do again. In addition, when faced with trials, we will

15

be able to rejoice as we go through them, because we will know whom God really is and will have no doubt in that knowledge. We will know when we call on the name of Jesus exactly who we are talking to and why we call on the name of Jesus. These are the end times, and Christ is soon to return. If you have noticed, many preachers who we once thought were men of God have now been revealed not to be so—just wolves in sheep's clothing. The Bible speaks of all this falseness "that will come to light" at the end of time.

Through this work, God is calling all the confused, lost, and stray sheep back to His fold. This work will be the light for all those who remain in the darkness. God is revealing Himself through this work to the wise and to the simple. The Trinity taught as it is, is the biggest reason why many of God's people are still in the dark. Not only does it keep His people in the dark, it also teaches heresy, because the Trinity is not teaching who God Truly is.

Okay, the Greek word "Trinity" was first used in Christian Theology by Theophilus of Antioch in about 170 AD but not as a divine Trinity; he wrote, "*In like manner also the three days which were before the luminaries, are types of the Trinity [Τριάδος], of God, and His Word, and His Wisdom. And the fourth is the type of man, who needs light, that so there may be God, the Word, Wisdom, man.*" Then, around the third century, a Latin Theologian by the name of Quintus Septimius Florens Tertullianus (Tertullian) was credited for using the words "*Trinity,*" "*person,*" *and* "*substance*" *to try to explain that the Father, the Son, and the Holy Spirit are one in essence but not in persons. He states that they are three in persons, but not in substance.*

Now, Tertullian was a prolific Christian author and a Berber—an indigenous person of North Africa. Being conservative, Tertullian did originate and advance new theology to the early church. He is most famous for being the oldest extant Latin Writer to use the term "Trinity" and for presenting the oldest extant formal exposition of a Trinitarian theology. Other formulations that appears in his work are "three persons and "one substance." It is important for us to understand at this moment that Tertullian was a writer, a Christian Apologist, which is the field of Christian theology that aims to present a rational basic for the Christian faith, defend the faith against objections, and expose the perceived flaws of other worldviews.

Understanding theology, what it means, is very important. Theology is the study of a god or, more generally, the study of religious faith, practice, and experience or of spirituality. Please take note of the word "study." Tertullian studied, which means he used his own knowledge from his studying. As with most of us writers, we first study the subject that we want, and then write about it. Once we have studied, we used our own thoughts and intellect to explain the notes from our studies. Here is what God say about our thoughts compared to His thoughts, though. Isaiah 55:9: "For as the heavens are higher than the earth, so are my ways higher than your ways, and my thoughts than your thoughts."

Tertullian, the founder of Latin Christianity, in a book called *Ante-Nicene Fathers*, volume 3; chapter III- Sundry Popular Fears and Prejudices. The Doctrine of the Trinity in Unity, Rescued from These Misapprehensions.
Listen to what he said closely," The Doctrine of the Trinity in Unity, in Unity," remember the word Unity—mean to join or unite. He writes:

The simple, indeed, (I will not call them unwise and unlearned,) who always constitute the majority of believers, are startled at the dispensation (of the three in one), on the ground that their very rule of faith withdraws them from the world's plurality of gods to the one only true God; not understanding that, although He is the one only God, He must yet be believed in with His own οἰκονομία, (The,Grc-Latin, word is Oikonomia, "which means," management of a household or stewardship, "also called Divine Economy.")

17

*The numerical order and distribution of the Trinity they
assume to be a division of the Unity; whereas the Unity
which derives the Trinity out of its own self is so far from
being destroyed, that it is actually supported by it. They are
constantly throwing out against us that we are preachers of
two gods and three gods, while they take to themselves pre-
eminently the credit of being worshippers of the one God;
just as if the Unity itself with irrational deductions did not
produce heresy, and the Trinity rationally considered
constitute the Truth. We, say they, maintain the Monarchy
(or, sole government of God). And so, as far as the sound
goes, do even Latin's (and ignorant ones too) pronounce the
word in such a way that you would suppose their
understanding of the μοναρχία (or Monarchy) was as
complete as their pronunciation of the term. Well, then
Latin's take pains to pronounce the μοναρχία (or Monarchy),
while Greeks actually refuse to understand the οἰκονομία, or
Dispensation (of the three in one). As for myself, however, if I
have gleaned any knowledge of either language, I am sure
that μοναρχία (or Monarchy) has no other meaning than
single and individual rule; but for all that, this monarchy
does not, because it is the government of one, preclude him
whose government it is, either from having a son, or from
having made himself actually a son to himself, or from
ministering his own monarchy by whatever agents he will.
Nay more, I contend that no dominion so belongs to one only,
as his own, or is in such a sense singular, or is in such a
sense a monarchy, as not also to be administered through
other persons most closely connected with it, and whom it
has itself provided as officials to itself. If, moreover, there be
a son belonging to him whose monarchy it is, it does not
forthwith become divided and cease to be a monarchy, if the
son also be taken as a sharer in it; but it is as to its origin
equally his, by whom it is communicated to the son; and
being his, it is quite as much a monarchy (or sole empire),
since it is held together by two who are so inseparable.
Therefore, inasmuch as the Divine Monarchy also is
administered by so many legions and hosts of angels,*

18

according as it is written, "Thousand thousands ministered unto Him, and ten thousand times ten thousand stood before Him and since it has not from this circumstance ceased to be the rule of one (so as no longer to be a monarchy), because it is administered by so many thousands of powers; how comes it to pass that God should be thought to suffer division and severance in the Son and in the Holy Ghost, who have the second and the third places assigned to them, and who are so closely joined with the Father in His substance, when He suffers no such (division and severance) in the multitude of so many angels? Do you really suppose that Those, who are naturally members of the Father's own substance, pledges of His love, instruments of His might, nay, His power itself and the entire system of His monarchy, are the overthrow and destruction thereof? You are not right in so thinking. I prefer your exercising yourself on the meaning of the thing rather than on the sound of the word. Now you must understand the overthrow of a monarchy to be this, when another dominion, which has a framework and a state peculiar to itself (and is therefore a rival), is brought in over and above it: when, e.g., some other god is introduced in opposition to the Creator, as in the opinions of Marcion; or when many gods are introduced, according to your Valentinuses and your Prodicuses. Then it amounts to an overthrow of the Monarchy, since it involves the destruction of the Creator.

    This is Tertullian's explanation of how he invented the Trinity in God as to a triune God. You can see that he relied on his own intellect and not God's Spirit. You also get a sense of his arrogance. While I was reading how he explained his invention—the Trinity—I could not help but to notice, he did not rely on the Spirit of God to teach him the truth. Nor did he use God's Word to explain the truth, "but heresy, "and, consequently, for years he had caused many people to teach this heresy.

    This is sad, being that he was a Polemicist against heresy. In truth, the Trinity is in us and not God; God is not a triune God. The Trinity in us is what gives us our free will.

First, I would like to go back through Tertullian's explanation to point out some very important things. Looking at the first sentence stopping at "believes," Tertullian makes it clear that his intellect is more superior than theirs—the Greeks. However, Proverbs 2:7 says, "Be not wise in thine own eyes; fear the Lord, and depart from evil." Had Tertullian truly feared the Lord, He would have used God's Spirit and not his own intellect. If he had used God's Word through God's Spirit, he would have learned that the Trinity—the Unity—is in us and not God. Then, the heresy of the Trinity—as it is taught—would have never departed from evil—through Tertullian's own intellect.

Listen to what Tertullian states as heresy:

They are constantly throwing out against us that we are preachers of two gods and three gods, while they take to themselves pre-eminently the credit of being worshippers of the one God; just as if the Unity itself [the Unity itself] *with irrational deductions* [taking away the Son and Holy Spirit from the union] *did not produce heresy, and the Trinity rationally considered constitute the Truth* [wrong, it constitutes Heresy].

Well, first, there is no unity of the three in God, because God's "Me, Myself, and I" are one Spirit, one God! The Father does not need to unite within Himself to form unity, because He is the Holy Spirit that divides Himself, as he will. "God is all in all!"

The word "unity" derives from the root "unit." "Unit" means "a single entity; one person or thing." Therefore, in order for the Trinity to form unity, each one person of the three must agree—each must unite. "Unite" means "to join, combine, or incorporate, so as to form a single whole or unit." In the case of the Trinity, each of the three persons agrees to become united, and then and only then can they form unity. Unity, the way Tertullian is using it, means "oneness of mind, feeling, as among a number of persons;

20

concord, harmony." Therefore, unity as he is using it first implies separation, and that, my beloved, is heresy!

Here is how Noah Webster's Dictionary explains the Trinity in God: "the union of three persons—the Father, the Son, and the Holy Spirit—in one Godhead so that all the three are one God as to substance but three persons as to individuality."

Tell me, is that not separation? These three individuals had to agree to come under the one Godhead first if each of the three has individuality.

According to the Easton's Bible Dictionary, the Father is a distinct divine person (hypostasis, subsistentia, persona, suppositum, intellectuale) distinct from the Son and the Holy Spirit. That Jesus Christ was truly God, and yet was a person, distinct from the Father and the Holy Spirit, that the Holy Spirit is also a distinct person.

All of this, my beloved, is false teaching and a form of heresy. Think, if the three were in one Godhead, wouldn't it be instead three Godheads in one Godhead with equal power? Because, in order to have a union of three—as Tertullian explains it—they had to agree to unite first. That means three individual heads agreeing to become one head, correct? However, when Paul was speaking to the Gentiles in Roman 1:19- 20, he made it clear that it is God's single Godhead. Paul writes, "Because that which may be known of God is manifest—or made clear—in them—the gentiles—for God hath shewed it unto them. For the invisible things—His Word and His Wisdom—of him—God—from the creation of the world are clearly seen, being understood by the things that are made, even his—God's, not the Son's or the Holy Spirit's, but God's—eternal power and Godhead; so that they are without excuse."

Well, if God's eternal power and Godhead can be understood by the things He made, this lets us know that God's Godhead is not the three in one Godhead, because we know, by the Bible, everything that was made was made by God's Word and God's Wisdom. John 1:1-3 states, "In the beginning was the Word, and the Word was with God, and the Word was God. The same was in the beginning with God; All things were made by him; and without him was not any thing made that was made." Moreover, everything that was made by the Word of God was made by God's Wisdom as well. Jeremiah 51:15 states, "He hath made the earth by his power, he hath established the world by his Wisdom, and hath stretched out the heaven by his understanding."

So what is God's Godhead? Well, God's Godhead is just that: God's head. God's Godhead consists of (1) His Brain, (2) His Wisdom and His Understanding—or His Mind,—which produces (3) His Word, "His Son." John 1:14 states, "And the Word was made flesh, and dwelt among us, (and we beheld his glory, the glory as of the only begotten of the Father,) full of grace and truth." And the spoken Word of God was made flesh, and we know that God's spoken Word, which made everything, was developed from God's Wisdom and understanding, because the Word was Jesus and Jesus is the Christ of God. Luke 9: 20 says similarly, "He—Jesus— said unto them, But whom say ye that I am? Peter answering said, 'The Christ of God.'" In addition, the Christ of God is the Wisdom of God and the power of God, according to 1 Corinthians. 1 Cor 1:24 says, "But unto them which are called, both Jews and Greeks, Christ the power of God, and the Wisdom of God." This clearly establishes that God's eternal power is His Knowledge, because, as we know, knowledge is power, and His Wisdom and Understanding, "the Christ," is the power of His Godhead. It is summed up this way in Eph 3: 9-11: "And to make all men see what is the fellowship of the mystery, which from the beginning of the world hath been hid in God, who created all things by Jesus Christ—God's Word and Wisdom. To the intent that now unto the principalities and powers in heavenly places might be known by the church the manifold Wisdom of God, According to the eternal purpose which He purposed in Christ Jesus our Lord."

This is why in Christ Jesus Emmanuel dwelleth all the fullness of the Godhead, bodily, because God's Word and God's Christ in the Word was made clear in the flesh. God's

Word—His Son—and God's Christ—His Wisdom—was the Lord Christ—the fullness—within Jesus Emmanuel. Jesus Emmanuel did not get to be Lord and Christ until after his crucifixion. Acts 2:36 reads, "Therefore let all the house of Israel know assuredly, that God hath made that same Jesus, whom you ye have crucified, both Lord and Christ." Understand, Jesus Emmanuel did not become Lord and Christ until after he was crucified. "But The Word from the beginning was our Christ Lord, our Lord God. God's spoken Word—Lord—and God's Wisdom—Christ—are the God Head within Jesus Emmanuel and us. This we will also learn more about in part two of this work.

See, we have the mind of Christ Jesus Emmanuel, but neither he nor we have the complete Mind of the Lord our God. 1 Cor 2:16 reads, "For who hath known the mind of the Lord—God—that he may instruct him? But we have the mind of Christ—Jesus Emmanuel." There is no Trinity in the Father, the Begotten Son, and the Holy Spirit as to three in a Godhead, but these three are one, as we are one with them.

Our and God's spoken Word displays our wisdom and understanding, because we can only speak what we know or don't know. Our knowledge is based on our developed wisdom and understanding. Therefore, what is in your head all the time—thoughts, thoughts, and more thoughts—are nothing but words—our son—a conversation between our spiritual mind, our natural mind, our soul's mind, and our brain. Colossians 2: 8-9 states, "Beware lest any man spoil you through philosophy and vain deceit—which is what Tertullian did with his invention, the Trinity in God—after the tradition of men, after the rudiments—or first principles—of the world—which is what been happening for thousands of years—and not after Christ. For in Him—Christ Jesus Emmanuel—dwelleth all the fullness—God's Word, Wisdom, and power—of the Godhead bodily." So, for in Him—Christ Jesus Emmanuel—should dwelleth all the fullness of God's head: God's Word, God's Wisdom, God's understanding, and God's power, bodily. Now, if all the fullness of God's head should dwell in Him—Jesus

Emmanuel—wouldn't that mean he is not in that fullness of God's Head if it dwells in him from God, as the fullness of God's head? Also, since Christ was—supposedly—a third of the Godhead, as the concept of the Trinity explains it— remember, the Father, the Son, and the Holy Spirit in one Godhead, so that all three are one God as to substance—why did Christ Jesus Emmanuel need the Father to send the Spirit of Truth in His name? Could not Christ Jesus Emmanuel, being equal as a third in the Godhead, just have left the Spirit of Truth with them instead? John 14: 26 states, "But the Comforter—the Spirit of Truth—which is the Holy Spirit— or the Father's Spirit in motion or action—whom the Father will send in my name, he shall teach you all things, and bring all things to your remembrance, whatsoever I have said unto you." Christ Jesus Emmanuel could not; the Father had to send the Spirit of Truth from within Himself, using His Word by which the Spirit of Truth came, because He—Christ Jesus Emmanuel—is only the natural body and soul of the Father's Word—the Lord Jesus Christ—the spiritual body, the divided Spirit of God the Father. John 15:26 reads, "But when the Comforter—the Spirit of Truth—Is come, whom I—the Word—will send unto you from the Father, even the Spirit of Truth, which proceedeth from the Father, he shall testify of me—the Lord our God, the Word." Please get this, Jesus Emmanuel said in John 14:26, "the Comforter which is the Holy Spirit—the Father—whom the Father will send—whom the Father—who is His Word—will send, Father will send— In my name, but on the other hand the Lord Jesus Christ our God, "the Father's Word just said, "when the Comforter—the Spirit of Truth—is come, whom I—the Word, the Lord Jesus Christ our God—will send unto you from the Father, even the Spirit of Truth, which proceedeth from the Father." Got it? God's Word sent back the Spirit of Truth from within the Father, which is Himself; the Spirit of Truth proceeded from the Father as the Word sent Him back from Himself, because The Word, which is the Word of Truth, proceeded from the Father Himself, and they are one. God the Father is the God of truth: Ps 31:5 "Into thine hand I commit my spirit: thou hast redeemed me, O LORD God of truth." The Spirit of Truth is the truth of God's Spirit, and this Truth of God in motion or action is the Holy Spirit, or God's body in action. It is God's Holy Spirit because the Holy Spirit is the Spirit of the Holy God in action, which makes God the Father that one dividing Spirit that gives to all, in us all. 1 Thessalonians 4:7-8 reads, "For God—His Word, Wisdom, and Truth—hath not called us unto uncleanness, but unto holiness—His Word, Wisdom, and Truth—He therefore that despiseth, despiseth not man, but God, who hath also given unto us his Holy Spirit—The Fullness of God Himself."

You see, when we use the Father's Word through His Spirit to explain His Me, Myself, and I, Tertullian's theology—his invention of the Trinity in God—starts to look like foolishness.

Therefore, so that the Godhead in Christ Jesus Emmanuel is clearly understood let us go through it this way. First, the Word became flesh, and His name was Jesus Christ—the Spirit-produced Son of God before Christ Jesus Emmanuel, the natural "begotten" son, was born. Hereby know ye the Spirit of God: Every Spirit that confesseth that Jesus Christ is come in the flesh is of God—1 John 4:2. The flesh that the Word came in was King David's—Jesus Emmanuel's Father—Rom 1:3, "Concerning his Son Jesus Christ—Emmanuel—our Lord, which was made of the seed of David according to the flesh."

Second, Jesus—The Word—is the Christ. 1 John 5:1 reads, "Whosoever believeth that Jesus is the Christ is born of God: and every one that loveth him that begat loveth him also that is begotten of him."

Third, the Christ—in the Word—is the Wisdom and power of God the Father. "But unto them which are called, both Jews and Greeks, Christ the power of God, and the Wisdom of God"—1 Cor. 1:24.

Thus, being that all is one Spirit, the one Father God, who is the Holy Spirit in action dividing the things of Himself into our lives, our worship of one God. Mr. Tertullian, is not irrational—without logic—that we take to

25

ourselves pre-eminently the credit of being worshippers of the one God. We are not deducting from God. How can one deduct God's Word, God's Wisdom, or God's Spirit of Truth away from God's body? One cannot, because Christ Jesus Emmanuel himself said, "the Lord our God, the Lord is one": "And Jesus answered him, 'The first of all the commandments is, Hear, O Israel; the Lord our God, the Lord is one'—Mark 12:29. Now, when Christ Jesus Emmanuel said this, he was not talking about himself—son of man—because he was not yet gloried as Lord, being that he had not suffered and died yet according to Hebrews. Hebrew 2 9-10 "But we see Jesus—Christ Jesus Emmanuel—who was made a little lower than the angels—just like us—for the suffering of death, crowned with glory and honor; that he, by the grace of God should taste death for every man. For it—death—became Him—The Lord Jesus Christ our God—for whom are all things, and by whom are all things, in bring many sons unto glory, to make the captain—Christ Jesus Emmanuel—of their salvation perfect through suffering." Luke 24:26, reads "Ought not Christ—Jesus Emmanuel—to suffered these things and to enter onto his glory—becoming Lord, & Christ."

Tertullian also states, *"And the Trinity rationally [or with logic] considered, constitute the truth."* Again, rationally or irrationally, with or without logic, "He is still relying on human Wisdom and not God's Wisdom." The Trinity rationally considered does not constitute the truth. The Trinity rationally considered—the way Tertullian invented it in God—have, and will always," constitutes false teaching, which is a form of heresy.

With it now clear, what Tertullian called heresy and what he said is the truth; let us look at more of Tertullian's explanation for his invention, shall we? So that we could get a clear sense of where Tertullian's head was at, I skipped the first sentence of his explanation. I had to point out first what Tertullian called heresy before we dealt with the rest of his explanation. So now, let us look at the first sentence.

The first sentence states, *"The simple, indeed [I will not call them unwise and unlearned], who always constitute the majority of believers, are startled at the dispensation [of the three in one] on the ground that their very rule of faith withdraws them from the world's plurality of gods to the one only true God; not understanding that, although He is the one only God, He must yet be believed in with His own οἰκονομία [The Grc-Latin, word is Oikonomia, which means 'management of a household or stewardship,' also called 'divine economy']."*

When we look at Tertullian's three chosen words and their meanings, we see that he makes it clear that God cannot be God without help: (1) Dispensation – a certain order, system, or arrangement; administration or management. (2) Plurality – more than half of a whole; the majority or a number greater than one. (3) Oikovouia (The Grc-Latin, word is Oikonomia) – management of a household or stewardship [administration].

For me, Tertullian makes it clear with terms like "arrangement," "administration," "management of a household," "plurality," and "a number greater than one that God needs help and that without help God can't do what He said He can do. Tertullian either forgotten or did not understand that in the Old Testament, God's Me, Myself, and I, did exactly what God said He could do. In the Old Testament, God's Me, Myself, and I was one God, and He performed everything with His Brain and Mind—His Me—His Word—His Myself—and His spiritual body—His I. He did the same thing in the Old Testament, the same way He did it in the New Testament. He just used different people. In the Old Testament, He spoke to our ancestors with His Word using prophets, and in the New Testament, He spoke to us directly with His Word and by His Word, which He spoke through His Begotten Son. That is the only differences as to

27

God Himself. In the Old and New Testaments, God used His Me, His Myself and, His I, "so to say that God's Me, Myself, and I, are an administration, an arrangement, or a plurality of gods shows Tertullian's lack of God's Spirit in him to guide him."

In addition, in Ephesians, Paul tells us that Jesus Emmanuel has a God—Eph 1:3 "Blessed be the God and Father of our Lord Jesus Christ—Emmanuel—who—God the Father—hath blessed us with all Spiritual blessings in heavenly places in Christ—His Wisdom and power." Now, if Jesus—Emmanuel—is a third of the Godhead as the Trinity is explained, why does He need a God if he is a God himself in a Godhead with God? Understand now, that it was God, who gave us all spiritual blessing in His Wisdom and Power, through His Word. Therefore, to make this clear, God gave all spiritual blessing to us in His Wisdom, His Understanding, and His Power through His Word. God's Word, Wisdom, and Understanding are His Spirit. Ephesians 1:17 states, "That the God of our Lord Jesus Christ, the Father of glory, may give unto you the spirit of wisdom and revelation in the knowledge of Him." Thus, we now know that God is God all by Himself; that God's Me, Myself, and I are not an administration or arrangement; and that God is not a plurality of gods, but that God, His Word, and His body in action is Himself, the Holy Spirit in motion, who gives us Himself.

Please, search the Spirit of God in these things that He has had me to write unto you! "In the beginning was the Word—Me—and the Word was with God—Myself—and the Word was God—I.—John 1:1. To illustrate this verse, imagine you have two rooms closed off by a door. In room one, you have two people—Tom and Sally—and in room two, you have one person—God. Remember, the rooms are closed off; room 1 and room 2 cannot see each other. Then God in room 2 speaks, and the two in room 1 cannot see who spoke, they can only hear His Word. Therefore, Tom goes and opens the door, and then he sees that the word was God. By seeing that the word was God, Tom now knows that the word they heard was with God. Then Sally asks Tom whose Word it was that they heard, and then Tom tells her that the word was God. Got it?

You see, Tertullian would have you to think that God's spoken Word is bounded or is not sufficient without an administration of three in a Godhead. Well, that is not the truth. God's Word is not bounded or limited. Hebrews 4:12 "For the word of God is quick and powerful, and sharper than any two edge sword, piercing even to the dividing asunder of soul and spirit, and of the joints and marrow, and is a discerner of the thoughts and intents of the heart—mind." God's Word is not limited because He is Spirit within God the Father. 2 Timothy 2:9 "Where in I suffer trouble, as a evil doer, even unto bonds, But the Word of God is not bound."

CHAPTER 2

The Glory of the One Spirit of God

Note: I am a Minster of God's, and I am God's Sheepdog who is being led by the Spirit of God to reveal to the world who is the true God, and as God's Sheepdog, I can only do this through God's Word. Therefore, throughout this work, I will be using many scriptures—God's Word—to explain the truth and the ultimate truth about the Trinity Conspiracy.

It is important to know that in sundry times, God used prophets to speak with us, but in these last days, He used His Spirit-produced Son, His Word, to speak to us through His Begotten Son. Heb 1:1-2 reads, "God, who at sundry times and in diverse manners spoke in time past unto the fathers by the prophets, Hath in these last days spoken unto us by his Son, whom he hath appointed heir of all things, by whom also he made the worlds." This was because the Begotten Son was full of God's head bodily, which is God's Word—His Son—His Wisdom, and the five other Spirits within Her—the Christ—and this through God's Spirit is what gives Christ Jesus and us our power to overcome with faith in the Word. However, the Trinitarians would have you to believe that the Godhead is all three persons in one Godhead. They say Christ Jesus Emmanuel was fully God the Father, bodily, which we can see is not true, because if Christ Jesus Emmanuel was fully the Father, bodily, who then was Jesus Emmanuel praying to—Himself? No! You see, he was not fully God bodily, but God was fully in him bodily. In addition, if Jesus Emmanuel was fully God bodily, why did not he have the same mind as God? 1 Cor 2:16 states, "For who hath known the mind of the Lord, that he may instruct him? But we have the mind of Christ." Jesus Emmanuel himself backs this up when He said in John 14:24, "He that loveth me not, keepeth not my sayings, and the Word which ye hear is not mine, but the Father's which sent me." Moreover, in John, Jesus Emmanuel tells us in John 12:49 -50, "for I have not spoken of myself; but the Father which sent me, He gave me a commandment, what I should say, and what I should speak. And I know His commandment is life everlasting: whatsoever I speak therefore, even as the Father said unto me, so I speak." Therefore, Jesus says that he speaks as the Father says to speak. Why? Because God's Brain and Mind—His Wisdom, Power, and Understanding—God's Me—which produces God's Word—God's Myself—controls God's Holy Spirit—His I, His body—and God's Word gives Jesus Emmanuel what he should speak and say. The same with us and our brain and mind, which produces our word, controls our bodies, and gives our vocal cord the words that it should speak and say.

God's Me, Myself, and I are all Spirit—God the Father, the Holy Spirit Himself, that one Spirit that divides as He will. John 4:24 tells us, "God is spirit: and they that worship Him must worship Him in spirit and truth." God, His Word, His Wisdom, and His Understanding in action are God Himself, the Holy Spirit in motion, not the Trinity in the Father as to a triune God.

The Holy Spirit of God's Me, Myself, and I are not a third of the Godhead, as the teaching of the Trinity would have you to believe. If the Holy Spirit is an equal third in the Godhead, why did it need to wait until Jesus Christ had been glorified back to the Father? John 16:7 reads, "Nevertheless I—the Word—tell you the truth; it is expedient for you that I go away: for if I go not away, the comforter will not come unto you; but if I—the Word—depart, I—the Word—will send Him—the Spirit of Truth—unto you. Also see John 7:39; Luke 11:13. In addition, this third equal in the Godhead could not even speak on Himself. It could only speak to our Spirit what it heard God's Brain and Mind agree upon in their

32

discussion as to what should be said. Listen to John 7:13 "Howbeit when He, the Spirit of Truth, is come, He will guide you into all truth: for He shall not speak of himself; but whatsoever He shall hear, that shall he speak: and He will shew you things to come."

Please hear, the Spirit of Truth is only a part of the Holy Spirit. For the Spirit of God wants us to know clearly, who is the True God and Father. The Holy Spirit is God's spiritual body, and God, being the Father of spirits, can divide His Holy Spirit among whom He pleases. 1 Thessalonians 4:7- 8 – "For God hath not called us unto uncleanness, but unto Holiness, He therefore that despiseth, despiseth not man, but God, who hath also given unto us his Holy Spirit."

God's Me, Myself and I are one Spirit. God's Brain, Mind, Word, and Spirit are the Holy Spirit, God the Father Himself. I want to drive this home in us so very much! Once God's Me, Myself and I are completely revealed to the world through this work, then people will start understanding and seeing God as He truly is. They then will be able to have a real relationship with the true God. This, Beloved, will mean more—more than your pastor telling you to just hold on, or to have faith—because you will know that you have the Power of the True God within.

Please, please, beware when this starts to happen, Satan is not going to be happy! He will be losing all those who are in the dark! Oh yes, He will lose them because this work is truth and the truth shall set us free.

The One and only True God, He is not so limited, or weak that He could not be God alone. Nevertheless, according to the Trinity, the only way God can be God is within a Godhead, with other persons, in an Oikovouia or Oikonomia—management or administration. John tells us, though, that God is a Spirit, and God, being Spirit, can only give, divide, or process through what He is—which is Spirit.

God has so many different spiritual gifts and blessings that He divides among His people, and each of those gifts and blessings are of God's Spirit. God gives these gifts through His body being in action, through Himself, the Holy Spirit! In 1 Corinthians 12:8-10, Paul talks about the different gifts and blessings, but we should focus on 1 Corinthians 12:4- 6. The terms used in these scriptures, like "same Spirit," "same Lord," "same God," "administration," and "operations," are what must have confused Tertullian. So that we are not confused, though, let us look at the same scripture: "Now there are diversities of gifts, but the same Spirit—God Himself—1 Corinthians 12:4." It is God's Spirit through God Himself, God gives, according to His own will. Hebrews 2:4 states, "God also bearing them witness, both with signs and wonders and with divers miracles, and gifts of the Holy Spirit—and gifts of the Holy Spirit—according to his—God—own will." In addition, let us look at the same Lord. 1 Corinthians 12:5 states, "and there are differences of administrations, but the same Lord—God's Word, God Himself." So, understand that this administration is not in God, but was developed through God's Word, the same Lord. The Lord is Jesus; Jesus is the Christ. The Christ is the Wisdom, Understanding, and Power of God, which displays God's Word—the Son—because the Word became flesh. We are that administration—every one of us who believes and lives according to God's Word. We through faith in God's Word developed an administration in the body of Christ. As members, we trust 100% in God's Wisdom, Understanding, and Power, which is God's Word, because faith cometh by hearing and hearing by the Word of God. Therefore, because of our faith and obedience in God's Word, we become an administration in God's Wisdom and Power, the Christ.

Examples of the administrations are in 1 Corinthians 12: 27-28, which states, "Now ye are the body of Christ and members in particular. And God hath set some in the Church, first apostles, secondarily prophets, thirdly teachers, after that, miracles, then gifts of healing, helps, governments, diversities of tongues."

Therefore, you see, God's Me, Myself, and I, are not an administration within God, but it is God all by Himself. We who believe and do the will of God, living according to

His Word, become a part of the operation of God on this earth. Being a part of the operation of God makes us the Church—the body—and God's Wisdom, Understanding, and Power, which display His Word, are the head. This is the operation, of the administration; God develops in us through Himself, His Wisdom and Understanding, God's Christ within God's Word within us. This development makes us God's Children adopted through the Lord Jesus Christ, God's Word and Wisdom.

As you can see, there is no plurality among God, His Brain—the Male—His Wisdom—the Female—and His Word—the Son—nor is their plurality among God—His Brain, Mind, Wisdom—His Word—His Spirit-produced Son—and the Holy Spirit—His spiritual body—which are God's Me, Myself and I—one Spirit, God Himself. John 4:24 tells us, "God is spirit, and they that worship him must worship him in spirit and truth."

Now, because we—the church—are many, we have many different works. However, it is God, through His Word, that same Lord, who gives all through His Holy Spirit, that same Spirit, Himself, God's body/Spirit in motion or action. Here, lets look at the same God in 1 Corinthians 12:6, which states, "And there are diversities—differences—of operations—works—but it is the same God which worketh all in all." That same God which worketh, does what? He worketh. In who?—In all of us. This same Spirit, same Lord, and same God, are God the Father of all spirits, dividing Himself unto us all as He will.

All of this clarification of God's Holy Spirit comes down to this: He gives to us from Himself that we may profit spiritually in all things. 1 Cor 12:7-11 reads, "But the manifestation of the Spirit is given to every man to profit withal. For to one is given by the Spirit the word of wisdom; to another the word of knowledge by the same Spirit; To another faith by the same Spirit; to another the gifts of healing by the same Spirit. To another the working of miracles; to another prophecy; to another discerning of spirits; to another divers kinds of tongues; to another the interpretation of tongues: But all these worketh that one and the selfsame Spirit, dividing to every man severally as he will."

Let's recall Tertullian's statement: *"we should be startled at the dispensation [of the three persons in one] on the grounds that our very rule of faith withdraws us from the worlds plurality of gods, to the one only true God; not understanding that, although He is the one only God, He must be believed in with His own Oikovouia or administration."*

I do not know about you, but for me, after hearing God's Word, I am more than startled at this claim. I am sadden, afraid, and hurt for all those who have been misled by this heresy teaching of the Trinity being in God the Father as to a triune God. For in God's Me, Myself and I, there are not three persons in one Godhead, because the four—God's Brain, Mind, Word, and Spirit—are one—that same one Spirit, God Himself.

Therefore, yes, our very rule of faith does withdraw us from the world's plurality of gods. Our rule of faith comes from God's Word, and God's Word says that God's Me, Myself and I are one God all by Himself. Moreover, we understand that He is the one and only true God, and He is believed in by His own developed Oikovouia—administration—which was developed by His Word of Life through His Spirit. However, we can no longer believe in the dispensation of the three person in one Godhead that puts God in an oikovouia—administration—within Himself.

God is a Spirit, the one and only true Holy Spirit, and God uses that same Spirit that He divides among us to do His work. 1 Corinthians 12:11-13 sums it up this way: "But all these worketh that one and selfsame Spirit, dividing to every man severally as he will. For as the body is one, and hath many members, and all members of that one body, being many, are one body: so also is Christ. For by one Spirit—

36

God's Holy Spirit—are we all baptized into one body—
God's Word—whether we be Jews or Gentiles, whether we
be bond or free; and have been all made to drink into one
Spirit—God's Me, Myself and I; God Himself." Remember
too John 4:24. God is a Spirit, and God's Word is life and
Spirit as well. John 6:63 says, "it is the spirit that quicketh;
the flesh profiteth nothing." Why? Because, the words that I
speak unto you—they are Spirit, and they are life. That life in
the Spirit of the Word, through faith, is what makes us free. 2
Corinthians 3:17 reads, "Now the Lord is that Spirit, and
where the Spirit of the Lord is, there is Liberty—freedom."
That liberty or freedom is given to us through God's holiness
of Spirit. 1 Thessalonians 4:7-8 further says of the Spirit,
"For God hath not called us unto uncleanness, but unto
Holiness. He therefore despiseth, despiseth not man, but God,
Who hath also given unto us His Holy Spirit." His what?—
His Holy Spirit.

Well, there you have it, God is Spirit, God's Me—
Wisdom—is Spirit, God's Myself—His Word—is Spirit, and
God's I—His Holy Spirit—is Spirit—God The Father,
Himself, one Spirit, one God, the Father who divides His
Spirit among whom He pleases.

Again, to show us that God's Me, Myself, and I are
one Spirit is this. God is in us, the Son—the Word—is in us,
and the Holy Spirit is in us and we ourselves are still one—
lets look at 1 John 4:15, which states, "Whosoever shall
confess that Jesus is Son of God, God dwelleth in him, and
he in God." The Son—the Word—Is in us as well according
to John 14: 23: "Jesus—the Word—answered and said unto
him, If a man love me, he will keep my words: and my Father
will love him, and we will come unto him, and make our
abode—home—with him." We will make our abode with
him because of John 10: 30: "I and the Father are one,"
How?—because the Lord Jesus is God's Word that God
made flesh. Remember, Philip asked the Lord, "show us the
Father," and Jesus said to him in John 14:9, "Have I been so
long time with you, and yet hast thou not known me, Philip?

He that hath seen me hath seen the Father: and how sayest thou then, Show us the Father?" Now, when Jesus said he that hath seen me hath seen the Father, He was not talking about seeing with the natural eyes or seeing Him physically, we know they saw Him in that way. He was talking about seeing Him with their spiritual eyes, with the Spirit—they that worship must worship in Spirit, because we walk by faith and not by sight—thereby seeing with the Spirit, through Christ Jesus Emmanuel, and seeing Him, The Lord Jesus Christ our God—God's Word, Wisdom, and Understanding, God's Power—within Jesus Emmanuel. The Word of God is the Father that we should see when we look at Jesus Emmanuel. He said himself, "it is not me who do the work but the Father within, He doeth the work." This is why the Lord said, hast thou not known me all this time, Philip? In addition, John 14:10 says, "Believest thou not, that I am in the Father and the Father in me?"—which means, I am the Father's Word, and the Word that the Father speaks is I. The words that I—Jesus Emmanuel—speak unto you, I speak not of myself: but the Father that dwelleth in me, He doeth the works."

Now if God is in Jesus Emmanuel doing all the work, than this is our proof that Jesus Emmanuel is not in an Godhead with God if only God is doing the work from within his.

The Holy Spirit is in us too according to 1 Corinthians 3:16: "Know ye not that ye are the temple of God, and that the Spirit of God dwelleth in you?" This Spirit of God that dwells in us is God Himself, His Holy Spirit in motion within us, the temple of the Holy Spirit. 1 Cor 6:19-20 reads, "What? Know ye not that your body is the temple of the Holy Ghost which is in you, which ye have of God—your body is the temple of the Holy Ghost which is in you, which ye have of God and not "which ye have a part of God—and ye are not your own? For ye are bought with a price: therefore glorify God in your body, and in your spirit, which are God's." Got it? All three of these Spirits of God, plus His Wisdom, are within us; God, His Wisdom, His Word, and His Holy Spirit are in us as one Spirit."

So, if all three are in us, and we ourselves are one, tell me, how can there be three individual persons in a Godhead? It can't be, because God's Me, Myself, and I, are one God and one Spirit—the Father of all Spirits Himself."

Again, that one Spirit of God is God the Father dividing Himself among us as He pleases. So being that there is one Spirit for believers of God means that there should be only one body, one faith, one Lord, and, yes, one God who is in us all. Nevertheless, early Christian theology has turned this relationship with one into a religion of many different faiths and beliefs. This has led to a separation of that one body. Of oneness, Ephesians 4: 4-6 states, "There is one body, and one Spirit, even as ye are called in to one hope of the calling; one Lord, one faith, one baptism, one God and Father of all, who is above all, and through all, and in you all."

CHAPTER 3

The Ripping of God's Spirit

The cost of all the different faiths and beliefs by the early theologian has not only separated the body of Christ but has ripped it apart by leading many of God's people to go astray. Here's how it was done according to Ephesians 4:11-15: "and he gave some, apostles, and some, prophets, and some, evangelists; and some, pastors and teachers—Notice that Paul said 'some.' He said 'some' because not all who do these things know who God or the Lord truly is, and, therefore they are not called by God—for the perfecting of the saints for the work of the ministry, for the edifying of the body of Christ. Till we all come in the unity of the faith, and of the Knowledge of the Son of God, unto a perfect man, unto the measure of the stature of the fullness of Christ. That we henceforth—or from now on—be no more children, tossed to and fro, and carried about with every wind of doctrine, by the sleight of men, and cunning craftiness, whereby they lie in wait to deceive. But speaking the truth in love, that we may grow up into him in all things, which is the head, even Christ." There is only one Father and His sole Word for us. We must not be deceived, for there are many different gods and lord just waiting to lead us astray through manmade doctrines. 1 Corinthians 8:5-6 reads, "for though there be that, that are called gods, whether in heaven or in earth, [as there be gods many, and lords many]. But to us, is but one God the Father—Male, Female, Son, and body—of whom are all things, and we in Him; and one Lord Jesus Christ—our God, The Word of Life—by whom are all things and we by Him." Not every man has the true knowledge of this, because the god of this world has blinded their minds. 1

Corinthians 8:7 sums it up this way: "Howbeit there is not in every man that knowledge: for some with conscience of the idol—unbeliever—unto this hour, eat it as a thing offered unto an idol; and their conscience being weak, is defiled."

Therefore, it is important for us to understand where God's Me, Myself, and I are in us and how He works in us. God's Me—His Male—His Brain—and Female—His Wisdom—God's Myself—His Son, His Word—and I—His spiritual body—In us as His Spirit of Truth is our conscience. That right, God in our conscience is the Spirit of Truth. Our conscience is our righteous meter; it is what lets us know right from wrong, good from evil, love from hate, despite how this world treats us. This is why Paul appealed to our consciences as he wrote in 2nd Corinthians: "Therefore seeing that we have this ministry—all of us are of that ministry with the Spirit of God in us as our conscience—as we have received mercy, we faint not. But have renounced the hidden things of dishonesty, not walking in craftiness, nor handling the word of God deceitfully; but by manifestation—clarification—of the truth, commending ourselves, to every man's conscience, in the sight of God—2 Cor 4:1-2.

Some might say if God's Spirit in us is our conscience, how can some people kill and commit sin without feeling guilty? They can do it because of what 2 Corinthians 4:3-4a says: "but, if our gospel—God's Word of Truth—be hid, it is hid to them that are lost. Why to those who are lost, because they do not believe in the Truth. (4a) In whom—unbelievers—the god of this world hath blinded the minds—please notice the word "minds"—of them which believe not." Therefore, a blinded mind is a mind that believes Satan lies—a mind that refuses to accept the truth of God's Word—the Gospel of God. This is different from a person who loses his or her mind; this person is out of his or her own mind. Being out of mind, one cannot understand the soul mind, the spiritual mind, or the carnal mind."

Now, these deceivers of the blinded minds can only defile that which is pure or holy in our minds, which is the

42

Spirit of Life, God's law in us. So what is the law of the Spirit of Life in us? It is God's Word, Wisdom, Understanding, and Power, which is the Lord Jesus Christ our God, and this is what sets us free from the law of sin and death. I know what you are thinking. If the law of God's Spirit is in us, how can it be weakened and defiled? Romans 8:2-4 answers: "for the law of the Spirit of life—the Lord Jesus Christ our God—in Christ Jesus—Emmanuel—hath made us free from the law of sin and death. For what the law—the Ten Commandments—could not do in that it was weak through the flesh, God sending His own Son, in the likeness of sinful flesh—You see, the Word was God's Son before God sent Him in the likeness of man—and for sin condemned sin in the flesh.

Our conscience/soul, God's Spirit, that creature in us was weak through the flesh." I know, how was God's Spirit weakened in us through the flesh? Romans 8:20 tells us, "for the creature—the Spirit—was made subject to vanity—or worthlessness—not willingly, but by reason of Him who hath subjected the same, in hope." The reason God did all this can be found in Romans 8:4: "That the righteousness of the law—His Word, His Wisdom, His Understanding, and His Power—might be fulfilled in us, who walk not after the flesh, but after the Spirit."

Therefore, understanding, God's Me, Myself, and I, are a must for us. Until we understand this, we will never come into that unity of that one faith, nor will we come into the unity of the knowledge of the Son of God. For this and other reasons, God is been revealed through this work to the world. For the time is soon to come, and many of us are yet lost'

This brings us to how God works in us. Please keep this scripture in mind, as we understand God's Spirit working in us: "for they that are after the flesh do mind the things of the flesh; but they that are after the Spirit, the things of the Spirit"—Romans 8:5. Our carnal mind is constantly at war with our spiritual mind and our conscience/soul—God's home—because to want after the flesh is to be carnal-minded—Satan's home. God's Spirit of Truth in us, our conscience, works this way: every decision we make is made by our soul's mind, which is influenced by either our spiritual mind—the head of our conscience, God's home—or our carnal mind—the head of our flesh, Satan's home. It is Satan's home because God has only one enemy: Satan, the devil. Romans 8:6-7 reads, "For to be carnally minded is death; but to be spiritually minded is life and peace. Because the carnal mind is enmity against God: for it is not subject to the law of God, neither indeed can be." So, the one we listen to the most is the one in us that we grow or develop. For example, "If we grow or develop our Spirit mind—the head of the conscience, God's home—then God's spoken Word in us becomes God's living Word in us, because we are wanting after the Spirit of God that dwelleth in us and not the flesh." The more we grow or develop in God's spiritual mind in us, the less power our carnal mind has over our soul's mind. This means the more we listen to God's Word, Wisdom, and Understanding and do what it says, the more power our soul's mind have over our carnal mind—the head of the flesh Satan home. In turn, the more power we have over our carnal mind, the easier it is for us to be transformed through the renewing of our—Soul's—mind, and for this reason, Satan is after our Soul's minds. Satan would love us to stay after the flesh, and as long as we stay after the flesh, he knows we cannot please God. However, because we are after the Spirit, the Spirit of Christ dwells in us. Romans 8:10 tells us: "if Christ be in you, the body is dead because of sin; but the Spirit is life because of righteousness—belief in God Word and Wisdom."

Therefore, God's Me, Myself, and I, in us work to help us do what Romans 12:2 says, which is, "be not conformed to this world: but be ye transformed by the renewing of your mind, that ye may prove what is that good, and acceptable, and perfect, will of God." It is the mind—that carnal mind—that Satan tries to use in wearing us down to sin. Understand, when we say no to sin, Satan doesn't stop there; again and again he brings to our remembrance the good old feeling of that sin he tempts us with. He knows if he can only turn that thought in our carnal minds into lust, he will have us. Because after lust comes enticement, and when lust is conceived it brings forth sin and sin when it is finished, it brings forth death. James 1:14-16 says, "But every man is tempted, when he is drawn away of his own lust—drawn away of his own lust—and enticed. Then when lust hath conceived, it bringeth forth sin: and sin, when it is finished, bringeth forth death. Do not err, my beloved brethren." This is how God works in us if we obey or disobey our conscience, the Spirit of Truth.

It is very important that we obey our conscience—our righteous meter. To obey our conscience is to be steadfast in our Spirit mind, and in doing so, we again are renewing our whole mind, and to constantly renew our minds, means we faint not when faced with many trails. Hebrews 12:2- 3 tells us, "looking unto Jesus—Christ Emmanuel—the author and finisher of our faith; who for the joy that was set before him endured the cross, despising the shame, and is set down at the right hand of the throne of God. For consider him that endured such contradiction of sinners against himself, lest ye be wearied and faint in your minds."

Now, for unbelievers who were blinded by Satan, they cannot grow or develop their God's Me, Myself and I in themselves, because they are of the ones who became weary and fainted in their minds. And by doing this, they submitted their God's Me, Myself, and I and their consciences to their carnal mind—the flesh. The more they listen to their carnal minds, the less they listen to their spiritual minds to grow and develop in the Truth of God's Word, and this leaves them wanting after the flesh and not after the Spirit. The Bible tells us that they who are after the flesh cannot please God, and neither are they of God. It also tells us that after sin come death. 1 Corinthians 3:16 -17 puts it this way: "know ye not that ye are the temple of God, that the Spirit of God dwelleth in you? If any man defiled the temple of God, him shall God destroy; for the temple is holy, which temple ye are?"

45

To truly know God's Me, Myself, and I, and where He dwells in us will also start to help us see that the Trinity—as to a triune God—is not in God but is in us. The Trinity is one of the tools Satan uses to keep the minds of those in the dark blinded. He uses the Trinity in God, of three persons in one Godhead, to keep those who are lost confused. We know that God is not a God of confusion but of peace. Therefore, until the truth about the Trinity is revealed, the churches—Christ's body—will never come in unity of the faith. Churches to this day are still confused, wannabe believers with this heresy teaching of the Trinity being in God as a triune God and not in us, as to the three that must agree in one.

We will see several conspiracies to hide the truth and ultimate truth about the Trinity by the time this work is done! The first conspiracy—the mystery of the Father, the mystery of God, and the mystery of Christ—that we are going to learn about is being hidden in more than ten so-called Bibles. The true answer to these mysteries—which is hidden—will prove that God is more than a triune God if you want to count Spirits. The Trinity is in us and not God. To God be the glory! If you look at the shield of the Trinity, you can see it teaches heresy!

Now, when we look at this shield and read it as it is, we have to ask ourselves, how can this be?

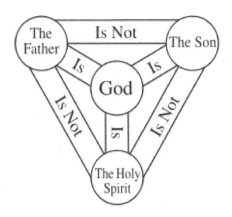

It says The Father, Son, and Holy Spirit are one God, but that they are not each other, Really? It says that the Father is not the Son and the Son is not the Father. This is so wrong, because the Son of God, the Lord Jesus Christ our God, is the Father's Word. But if our word is not us, than this shield is correct. This shield is talking about Christ Jesus Emmanuel—son of man—the flesh and soul of God's Word—the Lord Jesus Christ, God's spiritual Son—and not the Word Himself. They misunderstood in their understanding of the Son; they did not understand that even though He was One while on earth, He is two: the Spirit-produced Son and the begotten son. The Spirit-produced Son—the Word—he is God. This is why Jesus said in John 10:30, "I and the my Father are one."

This shield also says that the Father is not the Holy Spirit and the Holy Spirit is not the Father. Again, so wrong, because John 4:24, tells us that God is a Spirit, and there's only one Spirit for all who believe 1 Corinthians 12:13: "For by one Spirit are we all baptized into one body, whether we be Jews or Gentiles, whether we be bond or free; and have been all—again, all—made to drink into one Spirit—God Himself."

The shield also says that the Son is not the Holy Spirit and that the Holy Spirit is not the Son. Wrong! Wrong!

47

Wrong! Again, wrong! Because the Holy Spirit is the Father and the Father's Word is Him! They both are God, and they both are our comforters. John 14:16 says, "And I pray the Father, and He shall give you another—give you what?— another comforter." They are both the same; God's Word is Spirit, and God's Spirit of Truth is Spirit—God, the Holy Spirit, our comforter. 2 Cor 1:3-4 reads, "Blessed be God, even the Father of our Lord Jesus Christ, the Father of mercies, and the God of all comfort; Who comforteth us in all our tribulation, that we may be able to comfort them which are in any trouble, by the comfort wherewith we ourselves are comforted of God." The Father—His Male— the Brain—and Female—His Wisdom—the Mind—His Son—the Word—and His Holy Spirit—the body in action— are all one God! Again, how can one take or separate God's Brain from His Mind and Word or the three—His Brain, Mind, and Word—from the fourth—God's Holy body, the Holy Spirit? How?

Now we see that this teaching of the Trinity in God, as to a triune God, is false and that teaching it is heresy, because 1 John 5:7b tells us that the Father—the Male and Female—the Word—the Son—and the Holy Spirit—the body—are one. Oh, by the way, this scripture has been taken out of every Bible except two or three. This is one of the conspiracies that hid the truth about the Trinity being in us and not in God the Father, as to a triune God!

But listen to what our Trinitarian shield says, which is that the Father, the Son, and the Holy Spirit are not each other but that they are all God. Come on! Are they for real? Think about this with your spiritual mind: what sense does this make, because if they all are one God—the Father of all spirits, the Holy Spirit, that one Spirit that divides as He— The Father—pleases—aren't they each other?

Therefore, this proof from God's Word is starting to make the rest of Tertullian's chapter III look like foolishnesss when compared to Theophilus of Antioch's understanding of God's Wisdom. Just to quote Theophilus again, he writes, "*In like manner also the three days which were before the luminaries, are types of the Trinity [Τριάδος], of God, and His Word, and His Wisdom. And the fourth is the type of man, who needs light, that so there may be God, the Word, Wisdom, man."*

It is important to know that Tertullian—Quintus Septimius Florens Tertullianus—was an early Christian Apologist. Christians apologetics is a field of Christian theology that presents a national basis for the Christian faith, defending the faith against objections and exposing the perceived flaws of other worldsviews. Please Note: Apologists have based their defense of Christianity on historical evidence, philosophical argumenta, scientific investigations, and other disciplines. So now you understand that Tertullian's job was to defend the idea he came up with of the Trinity. He was defending the faith—of the three in one Godhead—without the Spirit of the Father to guide him. There's more to the mystery of the Father than the Father, the Son, and the Holy Spirit, and the second chapter of Colossians makes this clear. Colossians 2:2-4 states, "That their hearts might be comformed, being knit together in love—here it is here—and unto—or attain—all riches of the full assurance—or promise—of understanding—and the full promise of understanding is—to the acknowledgement—or recognition of the existence of truth—of the mystery of God, and of the Father, and of Christ; In whom—the answer to this mystery—are hid all the treatures of wisdom and knowledge. And this I say, lest any man should beguile—to influence by guile; mislead; delude or to take away from by cheating or deceiving—you with enticing words." This is what Tertullian did with his invention of the Trinity—as to a triune God—being in God and not us. He was so caught up in the names and timing of the three, and because of this, he concluded that they must be three individuals. In chapter III of Tertullian's explanation for his invention, he says that he is not talking about separation, but in chapter IV that is exactly what he says. And he's defending the faith—which is wrong—and not the Word. If—and it is—the Word is true, then the faith needs no defending, because faith cometh by hearing, and hearing by the Word of the Father.

CHAPTER 4

Wisdom The Power of God Within

To make sure we understand God's Me, Myself, and I, clearly—God the Father—the Male, His Brain—God's Word of Life—the Son, His Word—and God's Wisdom of Life—the Female, His Wisdom, His Mind—let's go back to the beginning, back to the Old Testament. Genesis 1:1 says, "In the beginning God created the heaven and the earth. God created heaven and earth," and He used His spoken Word—His Word of Life—and His Holy Spirit—His spiritual Body—no Trinity, just God all by Himself! Genesis 1:2 further reads, "And the Spirit of God moved over the face of the waters." So now that we know God's Me, Myself and I, are a spirit and that there is only one Spirit for us—believers—the Father Himself—we know that Genesis 1:2 means, "and God moved over the face of the waters." Verse 3 continues, "And God said let there be light and there was light." The spoken Word, God the Father, just spoke it, and there it was. You see, the Father's Word has Wisdom behind it—Wisdom to know that there needed to be light. The Father's Word has power also—power to just speak light into existence. Remember "in the beginning was the Word, and the Word was with God, and the Word was God." So when God said let there be light, God spoke what His Christ—the Wisdom of God—thought would be best for the earth. Then, His Christ—the power of God—made happen, through God's Holy Spirit, His holy body, what God had spoken with His Word of Life. Again, no Trinity is involved, just God activating His Wisdom in His Spoken Word through His Brain to put His body, His Holy Spirit, into action. It's just God in motion. This is why John 1:2-3 states, "The same was in the beginning with God. All things were made by Him; and without Him was not any thing made that was made." Here's how it works, for God to speak it into existence, His Mind—His Wisdom, Understanding, and Power—had to think of it first. Then, once His Mind thought of it, His Brain, which is attached to His spiritual body, had to be used to bring it into existence by speaking His Word—the Spirit of God moved over the face of the waters. Without God's Wisdom using God's Word to give God's Brain Knowledge, God's Spirit could not have spoken God's Word and nothing that was made would have been made.

For example, if I think of an idea, this idea will not come into existence unless it first goes through my brain, because my brain sends the correct signal to my body to bring into existence that idea. Our brains control our bodies, and our minds influence our brains to act. You see, the Father's Word—the Lord our God—has Wisdom and power—the Christ of the Father—behind, within, or as a part of Him. This is why faith cometh by hearing and hearing by the Word of God the Father, whether listening or reading, either way we are hearing the Word, which is also God's Wisdom and power. The Father's Word is the Father Himself—His Brain of His Spirit—the Male—His Mind of His Spirit—Wisdom, the Female—His spoken Word of His Spirit—the Son—and the Father in action is God the Father of all spirits, the Holy Spirit Himself in motion. Yes, God's Brain—the Male—His Mind—Wisdom, the Female—His Word—the Son—and His body—His Holy Spirit—is Spirit! Remember, God made us in His own image, and we have a brain, a mind, and a word, and they are the activators of our body.

Therefore, this being true means that once we've decided to obey either our spiritual mind—God's Wisdom— or our carnal mind—Satan's wisdom—that decision was first discussed with our brain, our male, using our word, our son, to communicate with our minds, "God's wisdom, our female, our spiritual mind and Satan's wisdom our natural mind and the one we obey will determine if we sin or not. Please understand, it had to be discussed with the brain first, in order for the brain to send the right signal to the body, to carry out that decision that was made. Indeed, our minds can come up with a lot of thoughts, but without the brain to send the correct signal to the body, those thoughts in our mind will never be acted upon. Remember we are made in God's image and after His likeness."

Therefore, this brings us to Gen 1:26-27: "And God said, let us made man in our image, after our likeness. So God created man in his own image, in the image of God created he him; male and female created he them." Okay, okay, I hear you. "Let us make, in our image, after our likeness" is not two or three but God himself. It is God Himself: His Brain—the Male—using His Spoken Word—the Son—to discuss with His Mind, His Wisdom, His Understanding, and His Power—the Female, Christ—within His body—the Holy Spirit—what they should do with man. In addition, when God said this, He was not talking about the flesh or soul—as to His image—because the flesh came from the dust, and then afterward the living soul was blown within man after the Lord God formed man. See Gen 2:7. What God was saying was, "Let us make man—who is spirit at this stage of creation—like us, after our likeness, with a connected brain and a mind, so that he may produce word to worship and communicate with me, and to grow in the knowledge of Me, that we may have fellowship and that he may choose to love and serve Me, his Creator." Deut 11:13 reads, "And it shall come to pass, if you shall hearken diligently unto my commandment—God's Word, Wisdom, and Power—which I command you this day, to love the Lord thy God, and to serve Him with all your heart—or mind—and all your Soul." Paul writes in Rom 7:25, "I thank God through Jesus Christ our lord. So then, with the mind I myself serve the law of God; but with the flesh, the law of sin."

The Father equipped us with a spiritual mind like His, and when the Lord God formed that spirit within man made from the dust, we were equipped with a carnal mind like Satan adopted. Then the Lord God blew in between the

53

two—Man, the created Spirit-filled creature created in God's image—the spiritual mind and brain—and the formed dead body from the dust of the ground—the carnal mind—and created our living soul, the soul's mind. For this reason, we—our souls—are now to choose whom we are going to serve: God—the Spirit mind—or Satan—the carnal mind. Joshua 24:15 puts it this way: "And if it seem evil unto you to serve the Lord, choose you this day whom you will serve; whether the gods—Satan—which your Fathers served that were on the other side of the flood, or the gods—Satan—of the Amorites, in whose land ye dwell: but as for me and my house, we will serve the Lord."

God also made man—which was spirit first—in His own image, after His likeness—with a brain and mind, which have the ability to produce word—so that man could have dominion over the fish of the sea, over the fowl of the air, over the cattle, over all the earth, and over every creeping thing that creepeth upon the earth.

I told you earlier when God said, "let us make, in our image, and after our likeness," He was not talking about two or three individuals but God Himself. Our proof of that is Genesis 1:27, which states, "So God—God—created man in His own image—Created in what? His own image—in the image of God created He—Who? He, God—him—him, not they, but him, who? Adam—male and female, created He—God—them—the Brain—Male—and the Spiritual Mind—the Female—which produced Word, the Son." God is one, Male and Female, which produced the Son through the use of the Spirit/ body. "Let us" and "after our likeness" is one God—the Male, Female, Son and Spirit, God the Holy Spirit—the image in which we were made. Gen 5:1-2 reads, "This is the book of the generations of Adam. In the day that God created man, in the likeness of God made he—God—him—Adam—Male and female created he them—the Brain—Male—and the spiritual Mind—Female—which produced Word, the Son—and blessed them—the Brain—Male—and the spiritual Mind—the Female—which produced Word, the Son—and called their—the Brain—Male—and the spiritual Mind—

Female—which produced Word, the Son—name Adam in the day when they—the Brain—Male—and the spiritual Mind—Female—which produced Word, the Son—were created."

God's Me, Myself, and I, are the Father—His Male—and His Wisdom—His Female—His Word—His Spirit-produced Son—and His Holy Spirit—His Body—and they are all one Spirit within one—God the one Father, God the one Christ, God the one Word—or Lord God—and God the one Spirit. It is God the Father Himself.

Think, Tertullian or Theophilus? Which is closer to the truth? If God's Son existed as His Word or Lord God in the Old Testament without the use of Mary the virgin, how could He have a Son—or Word—without a Female—or Wisdom?"

Now, in a more in-depth understanding, God the Father is going to give us the truth and the ultimate truth about the Trinity Conspiracy through His Own Word.

First let us stop here, and prepare your soul's mind!

We need to prepare our minds to allow the Father's Spirit to teach us this truth. We are to prepare by fasting and praying before we continue to read the rest of this work. However, before we start, we need to let go of all strife and un-forgiveness. Then, pray and ask the Father how long you should fast. Ask Him to give you His Wisdom, His Understanding, and His Knowledge. In doing this, we are showing God how serious we are about seeking His Kingdom and all of His righteousness, so that all these things, whatsoever we need, will be added unto us: The truth and the ultimate truth about the Trinity Conspiracy.

Welcome Back! Here's my prayer for you!

Dear Heavenly Father God, I thank thee for those who are truly seeking you. I thank you for what you're about to do in their lives by revealing the truth and ultimate truth about the Trinity Conspiracy to your people. God, as I have prayed and fasted during this work I now pray for all whom been taught, and led astray, because of this heresy teaching of the Trinity being in you, and not us. I pray that you would reveal the truth to them as you did your Sheepdog, that each one, after receiving this truth, commits his or her mind, body, and soul back to you in Spirit and in all truth, that they would take this truth and witness to others who are lost and don't know you. I pray also for those who have unknowingly and those who have knowingly taught and led your people astray with this heresy teaching. I pray that you forgive them and have mercy on their souls. I pray that once they receive this truth, that they put aside their pride and start preaching the truth. I thank you God in advance for answering this prayer as I ask it in Jesus' name. Amen and Amen!

CHAPTER 5

The Conspiracy to Hide the Truth about God's Wisdom

Now, what God is about to reveal to us about Himself—who He is—His Son—who He is—His Spirit—who He is—and us—who we are—should and will change your life and soul forever!

Please take note that there has been, and still are, conspiracies to keep this truth from the children of God the Father. These conspiracies have added and taken away from the Father's Word. They have even changed the meaning of the Father's Word to fit the heresy invention and teaching of the Trinity being in the Father—as a triune God—instead of us—as the three that must agree in one. This conspiracy has been carried out through the publishing of different so-called Bibles. For us to hear and understand the Father's Word clearly, we should use the authorized King James version of the Bible. This Bible and one or two others did not change God's Word, but others like the NIV and Living bible have added and/or taken away from God's Word to keep this truth hidden. One of the most important scriptures in the Bible, which reveals that Father God is more than a triune God, has been changed and/or omitted. It has been changed to keep us from knowing the truth about God's Me, Myself, and I and to keep us doubting God's Word in the true Bible—KJV. It is nothing but confusion! In turn, this confusion keeps us lost, and it promotes the heresy teaching of the Trinity being in God as to a triune God. Please understand you cannot just dismiss God's Wisdom within His head or put Her as low as a character or attribute of God—even though She's God's Power. The reason being is that She is the Lord our righteousness. Jeremiah 33:14-16 says, "Behold, the days come, saith the LORD, that I will perform that good thing which I have promised unto the house of Israel and to the house of Judah. In those days, and at that time, will I cause the Branch of righteousness to grow up unto David; and he shall execute judgment and righteousness in the land. In those days shall Judah be saved, and Jerusalem shall dwell safely: and this *is the name* wherewith she shall be called— she shall be called, She Wisdom—The LORD our righteousness."

Many of these so-bibles have left the word "She"— God's Wisdom—out of God's head and are teaching others to do the same as well by the changing of these scriptures. They changed God's Female from a "She" to an "it" when they changed the word "SHE" to the word "IT." Some are even saying "they or Jerusalem" is the LORD our righteousness instead of God's Wisdom.

Jeremiah 33:16—Also read v. 14 and 15—of these same Bibles:
Parallel Verses

New International Version
In those days Judah will be saved and Jerusalem will live in safety. This is the name by which it will be called: The LORD Our Righteous Savior.'

New Living Translation
In that day Judah will be saved, and Jerusalem will live in safety. And this will be its name: 'The LORD Is Our Righteousness.'

English Standard Version
In those days Judah will be saved, and Jerusalem will dwell securely. And this is the name by which it will be called: 'The LORD is our righteousness.'

New American Standard Bible

In those days Judah will be saved and Jerusalem will dwell in
safety; and this is the name by which She will be called: the
LORD is our righteousness.'

In those days shall Judah be saved, and Jerusalem shall dwell
safely: and this *is the name* wherewith She shall be called,
The LORD our righteousness.

In those days Judah will be saved, and Jerusalem will dwell
securely, and this is what She will be named: Yahweh Our
Righteousness.

International Standard Version
At that time Judah will be delivered and Jerusalem will dwell
in safety. And this is the name people will call it, "The
LORD is Our Righteousness."'

NET Bible
Under his rule Judah will enjoy safety and Jerusalem will live
in security. At that time Jerusalem will be called "The LORD
has provided us with justice."

GOD'S WORD® Translation
In those days Judah will be saved and Jerusalem will live
securely. Jerusalem will be called The LORD Our
Righteousness.

In those days shall Judah be saved, And Jerusalem shall
dwell safely; And this is the name whereby She shall be
called, The LORD is our righteousness.

'In those days Judah shall be saved, and Jerusalem shall
dwell in safety; and this is *the name* by which She shall be
called: the LORD is our righteousness.'

Jubilee Bible 2000

In those days shall Judah be saved, and Jerusalem shall dwell safely; and this is the name with which She shall be called, The LORD our righteousness.

King James 2000 Bible

In those days shall Judah be saved, and Jerusalem shall dwell safely: and this is the name by which it shall be called, The LORD our righteousness.

American King James Version

In those days shall Judah be saved, and Jerusalem shall dwell safely: and this is the name with which She shall be called, The LORD our righteousness.

American Standard Version

In those days shall Judah be saved, and Jerusalem shall dwell safely; and this is the name whereby She shall be called: Jehovah our righteousness.

Douay-Rheims Bible

In those days shall Juda be saved, and Jerusalem shall dwell securely: and this is the name that they shall call him, The Lord our just one.

Darby Bible Translation

In those days shall Judah be saved, and Jerusalem shall dwell in safety. And this is the name wherewith She shall be called: Jehovah our Righteousness.

English Revised Version

In those days shall Judah be saved, and Jerusalem shall dwell safely: and this is the name whereby She shall be called, The LORD is our righteousness.

Webster's Bible Translation

In those days shall Judah be saved, and Jerusalem shall dwell in safety: and this is the name by which She shall be called, JEHOVAH our righteousness.

In those days shall Judah be saved, and Jerusalem shall dwell safely; and this is [the name] by which She shall be called: Yahweh our righteousness.

Young's Literal Translation
In those days is Judah saved, And Jerusalem doth dwell confidently, And this is he whom Jehovah proclaimeth to her: 'Our Righteousness.'

Only the bibles in gray kept the original word. So, you tell me, is this a conspiracy or just some honest overlooked mistakes? Before you answer, read a little more. Colossians 2:2 is another one of the most important scriptures that proves that God's Wisdom helped God produce their Word, their Son, within God's head, and it too has been changed from the King James Version. The King James Version of Colossians 2:2 states, "That their hearts might be comforted, being knit together in love, and unto all riches of the full assurance of understanding, to the acknowledgment of the mystery of God, and of the Father, and of Christ." Out of more than twenty bibles, only the four in gray kept the true meaning of the scripture. They are AKJV, NKJV, KJV, and Webster's Bible translation. All the rest changed the Words of God, which changes the meaning of what God was trying to teach us.

TAKE A LOOK!

New International Version
My goal is that they may be encouraged in heart and united in love, so that they may have the full riches of complete understanding, in order that they may know the mystery of God, namely, Christ.

New Living Translation
I want them to be encouraged and knit together by strong ties of love. I want them to have complete confidence that they understand God's mysterious plan, which is Christ himself.

English Standard Version
that their hearts may be encouraged, being knit together in love, to reach all the riches of full assurance of understanding and the knowledge of God's mystery, which is Christ.

New American Standard Bible
that their hearts may be encouraged, having been knit together in love, and attaining to all the wealth that comes from the full assurance of understanding, resulting in a true knowledge of God's mystery, that is, Christ Himself.

King James Bible
That their hearts might be comforted, being knit together in love, and unto all riches of the full assurance of understanding, to the acknowledgement of the mystery of God, and of the Father, and of Christ.

Holman Christian Standard Bible
I want their hearts to be encouraged and joined together in love, so that they may have all the riches of assured understanding and have the knowledge of God's mystery—Christ.

International Standard Version
Because they are united in love, I pray that their hearts may be encouraged by all the riches that come from a complete understanding of the full knowledge of the Messiah, who is the mystery of God.

NET Bible
My goal is that their hearts, having been knit together in love, may be encouraged, and that they may have all the riches that

assurance brings in their understanding of the knowledge of the mystery of God, namely, Christ.

Aramaic Bible in Plain English
And that their hearts may be comforted and that they may approach by love all the wealth of assurance and understanding of the knowledge of the mystery of God The Father and of The Messiah.

GOD'S WORD® Translation
Because they are united in love, I work so that they may be encouraged by all the riches that come from a complete understanding of Christ. He is the mystery of God.

Jubilee Bible 2000
that their hearts might be comforted, being knit together in charity and in all the riches of the fulfilled understanding to know the mystery of the God and Father and of the Christ.

King James 2000 Bible
That their hearts might be comforted, being knit together in love, and unto all riches of the full assurance of understanding, to the acknowledgment of the mystery of God, and of the Father, and of Christ.

American King James Version
That their hearts might be comforted, being knit together in love, and to all riches of the full assurance of understanding, to the acknowledgment of the mystery of God, and of the Father, and of Christ.

American Standard Version
that their hearts may be comforted, they being knit together in love, and unto all riches of the full assurance of understanding, that they may know the mystery of God, even Christ.

Douay-Rheims Bible

63

That their hearts may be comforted, being instructed in charity, and unto all riches of fulness of understanding, unto the knowledge of the mystery of God the Father and of Christ Jesus.

Darby Bible Translation
to the end that their hearts may be encouraged, being united together in love, and unto all riches of the full assurance of understanding, to [the] full knowledge of the mystery of God.

English Revised Version
that their hearts may be comforted, they being knit together in love, and unto all riches of the full assurance of understanding, that they may know the mystery of God, even Christ.

Webster's Bible Translation
That their hearts may be comforted, being knit together in love, and to all riches of the full assurance of understanding to the acknowledgment of the mystery of God, and of the Father, and of Christ.

Weymouth New Testament
in order that their hearts may be cheered, they themselves being welded together in love and enjoying all the advantages of a reasonable certainty, till at last they attain the full knowledge of God's Truth, which is Christ Himself.

World English Bible
that their hearts may be comforted, they being knit together in love, and gaining all riches of the full assurance of understanding, that they may know the mystery of God, both of the Father and of Christ.

Young's Literal Translation
that their hearts may be comforted, being united in love, and to all riches of the full assurance of the understanding, to the

full knowledge of the secret of the God and Father, and of the Christ.

The conspiracy in all of these bibles, in the way they added and took from the Word of God, has caused many of God's people to be in a confused state of mind as to the truth and ultimate truth about the Trinity. The true answer to this mystery of the three—of God and of the Father and of Christ—is our proof that God the Father of all spirits is not a triune God. The King James Version of the Bible states, And unto all riches of the full assurance of understanding," Now, the riches of the full assurance—or promise—of understanding is to the acknowledgement— acknowledgement means 'recognition of existence, truth or validity of something, to admit or acknowledge—of the Mystery of God and of the Father and of Christ." What this scripture means for the children of God the Father is "the riches—the benefits, favor, hope, help, or blessings—of the full assurance—full promise, pledge, guaranty, or surety—of understanding—knowing who the Father truly is—to the acknowledgement—is just to admit the existence of these three mysteries—of God (1), and of the Father (2), and of Christ (3)." Because once we do this, we will start truly seeking God's Kingdom and all of His righteousness, and this will give us all the riches of the promise from God that add all things unto us. Now, the other seventeen Bibles have changed the word "acknowledgement" to the word "knowledge." Knowledge means, "to know, familiarity or certain mental apprehension." This meaning is very different from acknowledgement. Some of the Bibles have even left out words like "Christ," "assurance," and "the Father," trying to make the mystery of the three about Christ alone. However, the scripture states that the mystery is in each one of them: the mystery of God, the mystery of the Father, and the mystery of Christ. Here we have three—God, the Father, and Christ—so tell me, if the mystery is in each one of three, why did not Tertullian use these three in his invention of the Trinity being in God the Father as to a triune God?

Again, by their—those who changed the Bible—changing the meaning of scripture, the readers—children of God the Father—will never come into all riches, because he or she will not acknowledge the truth of the three, which means he or she will not get to know the truth and ultimate truth about the Trinity Conspiracy.

You see, those who are at work to keep this truth hidden know that this mystery in these three and the true answer to it will prove that the heresy teaching of the Trinity—as to a triune God—being in the Father is false. Because the true answer to this mystery will reveal the truth about God's Me, Myself, and I. So for this reason, Matthews 7:22- 23 states, "many will say to me in that day, Lord, Lord, have we not prophesied in thy name? And in thy name have cast out devils? And in thy name done many wonderful works? And then will I profess unto them, I never knew you, depart from me, ye that work iniquity."

Here, the Lord is not talking to the church members only but to some of the priests, preachers, pastors, false prophets, evangelists, and bishops. Because these are the people who would be doing this kind of work—casting out devils, etc—in the world. It is clear by these scriptures that they—the pastors, etc—thought they knew who the Lord really was and that they were doing right, because they said, "Lord, Lord, look at what we did in your name." This also makes it clear that some of these heads of the churches are leaders who are working iniquity—or wickedness—by knowingly teaching this heresy of the Trinity being in the Father and not in us, and others unknowingly, because they chose to follow after the tradition of man—Tertullian's invention of the Trinity. Instead of seeking the Kingdom of the Father and His righteousness for themselves, by using God's Holy Spirit to guide them, they allow man to teach them, which is why 1 John 2:26-27 says, "these things have I written unto you concerning them that seduce you. But the anointing—God's Spirit of Truth—which ye have received of him—God the Father—abideth in you, and ye need not that any man teach you: but the same anointing—the Father Holy

Spirit of Truth—teacheth you of all things, and is truth, and is no lie, and even as it—the Spirit of Truth—hath taught you, ye shall abide in Him—the Father's Word." Because, Jesus said in John 15:7, "If ye abide in me—because I'm the Father's Word—and my word—which is the Father—abide in you—by crucifying the flesh daily and living holy—ye shall ask what ye will, and it shall be done unto you." This is why Jesus said in John 14:23 & 26, "If a man love me, he will keep my words: and my Father will love him, and we will come unto him, and make our abode in him. But the Comforter, which is the Holy Ghost/Father, whom the Father will send in my name, he shall teach you all things, and bring all things to your remembrance, whatsoever I have said unto you."

Now do not get confused and think, "See, there is the three right there: (1) the Father, (2) in my name—the Word—and (3) the Holy Ghost." John makes it clear that Jesus was the Father's Word before the world began and that is He is the Father's Word—the Son—right at this present moment. Remember, in the beginning was the Word, and the Word was made flesh! Look at what Jesus said in John 17: 4-5, "I have glorified thee on the earth: I have finished the work which thou gavest me to do. And now, O Father, glorify thou, me with thine own self, with the glory I had with thee before the world was," which was the Father's Word of Wisdom.

CHAPTER 6

The Dividing of God the Father's Holy Spirit

Jesus also wants us to know that the Father is the Holy Ghost—that one Spirit that we are all baptized in and made to drink from. In John 4: 23-24, Jesus said, "But the hour cometh, and now is, when the true worshippers shall worship the Father in spirit and in truth: for the Father seeketh such to worship him. God is a spirit: and they that worship Him must worship Him in spirit and in truth." For those of us who could not understand that easily, Jesus made sure we would have no doubt about the Father being the Holy Spirit. He spoke in John 15:26, "But when the Comforter is come, whom I—the Spirit of Life—will send unto you from the Father, even the Spirit of Truth—proof it came from the Father—which proceedeth from the Father, he shall testify of me."

Therefore, the Spirit of Truth, the Comforter, is the Holy Ghost, God the Father Himself. John 14:26 reads, "But the Comforter—the Spirit of Truth—which is the Holy Ghost—the Truth of the Father's Spirit, His holiness within His Spirit, for God is Spirit the Holy Ghost Himself—whom the Father will send in my name, he shall teach you all things, and bring all things to your remembrance, whatsoever I have said unto you."

In addition, the Spirit, which came from the Father to help our soul, is the Spirit of Truth sent to make us free from Satan and his lies. John 8:32 says, "And ye shall know the truth, and the truth shall make you free." God's Spirit of Truth is the Truth in God the Father—the Holy Spirit that makes Himself and us holy.

You see, the Comforter—the Truth of the Father's Spirit, God's holiness of Spirit—proceedeth from the Father, and His Word, the Son, also proceedeth from the Him. The word "proceed" means, "originate;" so the Spirit of Truth and the Son both originated from the Father. In addition, "originate" means "to have origin, arise from, or to give origin." Moreover, "origin" means "source or something from which anything is derived. And "derived" means "to attain from a source or origin, and to attain something is to possess it;" it's your, it is your possession. God the Father also possessed His Wisdom Proverbs 8:22 – "the Lord possessed me—Wisdom—in the beginning of His way, before his work of old." The Father is Wisdom, Lord, because the Father is the owner of His Wisdom. "Possess" means "to have as belonging to or own." Understand now? The Father possessed His Wisdom, which is His Spirit of Wisdom. In addition, He possessed His Word, which is His Word of Life. Moreover, He possessed His Truth which is His Spirit of Truth, which is a part of His Holy Spirit sent for man's soul so that man may know the truth. They all are spirits—spirits that derived from God the Father, the Holy Spirit. Got it? There is not three persons in a Godhead as to a triune God as we been falsely taught!

God can—and did—divide His Spirit how he pleases: "But all these—Spirits—worketh that one and selfsame Spirit—God, the Holy Spirit—dividing to every man severally as He will. For by one Spirit—God, Himself—are we all baptized into one body—God's Word, Wisdom, and Power—whether we be Jews or Gentiles, whether we be bond or free; and have been all made to drink into one Spirit—the Father God Himself—1 Corinthians 12:11 & 13. Tertullian was caught up in the names, in his own intellect, to the point that he did not seek God's Spirit to reveal whom these names represented within the Father.

You see, all these Spirits proceeded from the Father because the Father God is the Father of all spirits and life! In addition, God's Wisdom that processes from Him, She is Spirit and life. Prov 3:13-20 reads, "Happy is the man that findeth Wisdom, and the man that getteth understanding. For the merchandise of it is better than the merchandise of silver, and the gain thereof than fine gold. She is more precious than rubies: and all the things thou canst desire are not to be compared unto her. Length of days is in her right hand; and in her left hand riches and honour. Her ways are ways of pleasantness, and all her paths are peace. She is a tree of life to them that lay hold upon her: and happy is every one that retaineth her. The LORD by Wisdom hath founded the earth; by understanding hath he established the heavens. By his knowledge the depths are broken up, and the clouds drop down the dew." The same with His Word; He is Spirit and life sent to quicken our spirits—the creature that was subjected to vanity—because "quicken," means, "to restore life to or revive." John 6:63 says, "It is the spirit that—or 'that is'—quickeneth; the flesh profiteth nothing—Why?—the Words that I speaketh unto you, they are spirit, and they are life." Understand now, it is the Father dividing His Holy Spirit as He pleases. He can do this because He is the Father of spirits and life! Hebrews 12:9 charges, "Furthermore we have had fathers of our flesh which corrected us, and we gave them reverence: shall we not much rather be in subjection unto the Father of spirits, and live [to be given eternal life]?

Now that we understand this, means, our spirits are now ready to receive the rest of the mystery of Colossians 2:2. Particularly the mystery of God, the mystery of the Father, and the mystery of Christ: "That our hearts might be comforted, being knit together in love, and unto all riches of the full assurance of understanding, to the acknowledgment of the mystery of God, and of the Father, and of Christ"—Colossians 2:2.

CHAPTER 7

The Truth about the Mystery of Colossians 2:2

Please, as we go through these mysteries, we need to use Jesus' thought pattern in Matthew 5:20: "For I say unto you, That except your righteousness—our belief in God's Wisdom, Word, and Truth—shall exceed the righteousness of the scribes—scholars or teachers of the Jewish law and tradition—and Pharisees—a sanctimonious, self-righteous or hypocritical, person—ye shall in no case enter into the Kingdom of Heaven."

Being that we have already started to understand some of the mystery of the Father, let us finish it. First, I think it would be best that I tell you the answers to each mystery and then explain them.

The mystery of the Father is that He is Male—the Brain—and Female—Wisdom, the Mind—and when these two communicate, they use their Son, the Word, and the three in motion are the fourth—the Holy Spirit—or the Father's body in action—making the four one, the Father of all spirits who gives us life.

The mystery of God is that He is the Spirit-produced Son of the Father's Male and Female, making Him the Lord Our God—the Father's Word, Our Lord God—because the Lord Our God is the Word of life—Our God who made us and gave us Life.

The mystery of Christ is that She is the Female of the Father—His Wisdom, Understanding, and Power, the Holy Spiritual Mind of the Father. She too, being our tree of life, gives us life, and She is our Spiritual Mother just as God the Father is our Spiritual Father, because Wisdom is justified by Her Children.

Now, let us finish the mystery of the Father. I have shown you above that the Father is the Holy Spirit. So, knowing that there is one Spirit and that He, God the Father, is Spirit—John 4:24—we can understand that when Moses said in Genesis 1:2b, "And the Spirit of God moved upon the face of the waters," he was saying that the Father God moved over the face of the waters. This is clear also because Father God's path is in the waters and the beams of His chambers are in the waters. Psalm 77:19 – "Thy way is in the sea, and thy path in the great waters, and thy footsteps are not known." Psalm 104:3 – "Who layeth the beams of His chambers in the waters: who maketh the clouds His chariot: who walketh upon the wings of the wind." The Father's path is in the waters, and He layeth the beams of His chambers in the waters. The Father God moved upon the face of the waters, and the waters saw Him. Psalm 77:16 – "The waters saw thee, O God, the waters saw thee; they were afraid: the depths also were troubled." See how excited David was? The waters saw thee, O God; the waters saw thee!

See, our two comforters, the Lord Jesus—the Father's Word, His Spirit of life—and the Father's Truth—His Spirit of Truth—are both spirits. (1) The Word was sent to give us eternal life through faith because He is the Spirit of Life. (2) The Truth of God, who shall teach us all things, was sent to guide us into all truth to make us free by bringing all things to our remembrance—whatever the Word has said to us—to help us receive eternal life through faith in the Word and obedience to the Spirit of Truth. Both proceeded from the Father who is Spirit—that one Spirit, the Holy Spirit. John 14:26 puts it this way: "But the Comforter [the Spirit of Truth], which is the Holy Ghost—or Father in motion— whom the Father—the Holy Spirit in action—will send in my name. He—the Spirit of Truth—shall teach you all things and bring all things to your remembrance, whatsoever I—the Word, the Spirit of Life—have said unto you."

Last, but not least, after Christ Jesus Emmanuel—the soul and body of the Father's Word—was baptized, He was led of the Spirit to be tempted in Matthews: "Then was Jesus led up of the Spirit into the wilderness to be tempted of the devil"—Matt 4:1. Proof that the Father is that Spirit that leads him/us to be tempted of Satan—but not the tempter himself—is when Jesus showed us how we should pray in Matthews 6:13, which states, "And lead us not into temptation—and lead us not into temptation—but deliver us from evil." Understand now, it was the Father God Himself, the Holy Spirit, who led Christ Jesus to be tempted. It was the Spirit that led Jesus, but if the Son—Jesus Emmanuel—is the second in charge and the Holy Spirit is the third in charge in the Godhead—according to the invention of the Trinity in The Father—how then can the third in charge—supposedly the Holy Spirit—turn and take charge over the second—supposedly the begotten son—and lead Him? It cannot be, because there is no second or third in the Godhead, no Trinity in the Father as to a triune God! The Father is the Holy Spirit who divides His Spirit as He pleases! This is why Jesus Christ—the Father's Spirit-produced Son—put the Holy Spirit—the Father—above Christ Jesus—the Father's natural begotten Son—and why Jesus Christ used "Son of Man" instead of "Son of God." Matthews 12:31-32 tells us, "wherefore I say unto you, all manner of sin and blasphemy shall be forgiven unto men: but the blasphemy against the Holy Ghost—the Father—shall not be forgiven unto men. And whosoever speaketh a word against the Son of man—Christ Jesus Emmanuel our raised Lord—the soul and body of the Father's Word—it shall be forgiven him: but whosoever speaketh against the Holy Ghost—the Father—it shall not be forgiven him, neither in this world, neither in the world to come." You know why now, because the Holy Ghost/Spirit is the Father Himself, and the reason why Jesus Christ used "Son of Man" and not "Son of God" is because He is the Lord Jesus Christ our God—the Word, Wisdom, Understanding, and Power of the Father. He is the Spirit of Life in the Holy Spirit/Ghost—the Father Himself! For this is the reason why Jesus—the Word—put the Holy Spirit over the Son of Man—the begotten Son—and why He prohibited speaking blasphemy against the Holy Spirit, which is

Himself! We will learn more about God's I—the Holy Spirit—in part three of this work, but for now, let's finish learning about the mystery of the Father—his Male and Female of His Holy Spirit, or the Brain and Mind of the Father's body.

As I said earlier, the Father is Male—the Brain—and Female—Wisdom, the Mind—and when these two communicate, they use their Son—the Word—and the three in motion is the fourth—the Holy Spirit—or the Father's body in action—making the four one—the one Father of all spirits who gives us life.

The Father's Brain, the Male of the Spirit, is connected to His holy spiritual body, just like us. Our brains are connected to our bodies; our brains—or the male in us—tell our bodies what to do, when to move, and how to move. The same is true of the Father's Brain of His Spirit—or the Male in Him—it tells His Holy Spirit—His holy body—what to do, who to abide in, or when to move. Remember, the Father made us in His own image—Genesis 1: 26-27—and if we have a brain and a mind—the connected male and female—in us, then the same is true of the Father.

Therefore, to prove that the Male in the Father is His Brain, we need to know who the Female in Him is. First, we need to understand that the Father is both Male and Female. To do this, we will start with Genesis 1:27: "So God—the Father—created man in His own image, in the image of God—the Father—created He—God—him—Adam—male and female created He—God—them—the connected spiritual brain and mind within the formed earthly man."

It is important to note at this point that this is the second transformation of man. Before man was formed from the dust and put on the earth—the third transformation—he went through two other transformations or stages. The first was the spirit-filled creature who was brought forth in the waters above the heavens. Proof that this is the second transformation of man and that man was truly created at this point in the image and likeness of God, male and female, is

76

Gen 5:1-2: "This is the book of the generations of Adam. In the day that God created man, in the likeness of God—the Father—made he—God—him—Adam—male and female created he—God—them—the connected spiritual male/brain and the spiritual female/mind within Adam—and blessed them—the connected spiritual male/brain and the spiritual female/mind within Adam—and called their—the connected spiritual male/brain and the spiritual female/mind within Adam—name Adam, in the day when they—the connected spiritual male/brain and the spiritual female/mind within Adam—were created." This means the Father God, who is Male and Female, created man—Adam/us—in His own image—after His own likeness—and after He created them— the connected spiritual male/brain and the spiritual female/mind within Adam—He named them Adam, and He blessed Adam when He created Him. This is true because we know Eve was not yet made from Adam's rib bone. In addition, her being female and being made from Adam's bone is our proof also, because Adam's rib bone is not female nor the image or likeness—the connected spiritual male and female—of God the Father. It came from the dust of the ground and can not be fruitful—or reproduce!

Okay, the Father is Male and Female, and I told you that the Brain of the Spirit is the Male of the Father God Himself. I know, I know! Just because the Father is Male and Female that does not prove that, the Male is the Brain of the Holy Spirit. This is the mystery of the father. The only way to prove that the Male is the Brain is to first show you who the Female is in the Father and how the spiritual Son—the Lord Jesus Christ our God, the Father's Word of life—was produced from the Father. Then it will be clear that the Brain of the Spirit is the Male of the Father.

The mystery of Christ: I told you earlier that the mystery of the Christ was that She, Wisdom, is the Female in the Father—His Mind. Well, here is your proof that the Christ is the Wisdom and Power of God the Father. God's Christ is the developed Knowledge from the Father's Understanding of His sound Wisdom—the Power of God and the Father's spoken Word. Without Wisdom, there is no Understanding; without Understanding, there is no Knowledge; without Knowledge, there is no Word; without Word, there is no spiritual Power; without spiritual Power, there is no Christ; and without Christ, there is no hope. God's Female, Wisdom, is the Power and Christ of God. 1 Cor 1: 24 says, "But unto them which are called, both Jews and Greeks, Christ the Power of God—the Father—and the Wisdom of God—the Father." The Father's Wisdom tells us in Solomon's Proverbs that She is Counsel and sound Wisdom—Her Knowledge—which makes Her Understanding and gives Her strength—or Power/Might. Prov 8:14 reads, "Counsel is mine—Wisdom—and sound wisdom, I—Wisdom—am understanding, I—Wisdom—have strength—Might." Solomon also lets us know that Christ's Power, the Father's Knowledge, is the Father's Wisdom and Understanding, and they are Female.

First, Wisdom is Female: "Wisdom crieth without; she uttereth her voice in the streets: She crieth in the chief place of concourse, in the openings of the gates: in the city she uttereth her words, saying, How long, ye simple ones, will ye love simplicity? And the scorners delight in their scorning, and fools hate knowledge—Prov 1:20-22.

Ask yourself, when God's Wisdom put forth Her voice, who was She speaking, other than God's Word, their Son?

Second, Understanding is Female: "Doth not Wisdom cry? and understanding put forth her voice? She—Understanding—standeth in the top of high places, by the way in the places of the paths. She—Understanding—crieth at the gates, at the entry of the city, at the coming in at the doors. Unto you, O men, I call; and my voice is to the sons of man. O ye simple, understand Wisdom: and, ye fools, be ye of an understanding heart—mind.—Prov 8:1-5

Again, ask yourself, when God's Understanding put forth Her voice, who was She speaking, other than God's Word, their Son?

Likewise, when God's Word of Understanding

speaks, whom is She speaking to other than God's Wisdom? Then still, when God's Word of Wisdom—God's Word and Wisdom, which is God's Understanding—speaks, who are They speaking to other than God the Father, the Holy Spirit Himself?

So that we are clear that this Wisdom and Understanding belongs to the Father, let us read Proverbs 8:6-36: "Hear; for I—Wisdom—will speak of excellent things; and the opening of my lips shall be right things. For my—Wisdom—mouth shall speak truth; and wickedness is an abomination to my lips. All the words of my—Wisdom—mouth are in righteousness; there is nothing froward or perverse in them. They are all plain to him that understandeth, and right to them that find knowledge. Receive my—Wisdom—instruction, and not silver; and knowledge rather than choice gold. For—I—Wisdom is better than rubies; and all the things that may be desired are not to be compared to it. I Wisdom dwell with prudence, and find out knowledge of witty inventions. The fear of the LORD is to hate evil: pride, and arrogancy, and the evil way, and the froward mouth, do I hate.

Tell me, if God's Wisdom is just a characteristic of God and not God, "how can She hate, hate evil: pride, and arrogancy, and the evil way, and the froward mouth?" Or how could She, being just a characteristic of God's hate anything?

Counsel is mine—Wisdom—and sound Wisdom: I—Wisdom—am understanding; I—Wisdom—have strength—Might. By me kings reign, and princes decree justice. By me princes rule, and nobles, even all the judges of the earth. I love them that love me—Wisdom can love—and those that seek me early shall find me. Riches and honour are with me; yea, durable riches and righteousness. My fruit is better than gold, yea, than fine gold; and my revenue than choice silver. I lead in the way of righteousness, in the midst of the paths of judgment: That I may cause those that love me to inherit substance; and I will fill their treasures. The LORD possessed me in the beginning of his way, before his works of old—cavemen. I was set up from everlasting, from the beginning, or ever the earth was. When there were no depths, I was brought forth; when there were no fountains abounding with water. Before the mountains were settled, before the hills was I brought forth: While, as yet he had not, made the earth, nor the fields, nor the highest part of the dust of the world. When he prepared the heavens, I was there: when he set a compass upon the face of the depth; When he established the clouds above: when he strengthened the fountains of the deep. When he gave to the sea his decree, that the waters should not pass his commandment: when he appointed the foundations of the earth; Then I was by him, as one brought up with him—Then I was by him, as one brought up with him—as one brought up with him—and I was daily his delight, rejoicing always before him. Rejoicing in the habitable part of his earth; and my delights were with the sons of men. Now therefore hearken unto me, O ye children: for blessed are they that keep my ways. Hear instruction, and be wise, and refuse it not, Blessed is the man that heareth me, watching daily at my gates, waiting at the posts of my doors. For whoso findeth me findeth life, and shall obtain favour of the LORD. But he that sinneth against me—Did you know you could sin against Wisdom?—wrongeth his own soul: all they that hate me love death." Got it?

Just so that we are clear that this Wisdom of God's is the Female of God and that She is God, the LORD our righteousness, let's take a look at what Jeremiah 33:14-16 said about Her: "Behold, the days come, saith the LORD, that I will perform that good thing which I have promised unto the house of Israel and to the house of Judah. In those days, and at that time, will I cause the Branch of righteousness to grow up unto David; and he shall execute judgment and righteousness in the land. In those days shall Judah be saved, and Jerusalem shall dwell safely: and this *is the name* wherewith she—Her, God's Wisdom, the Christ of God—

shall be called, the LORD our righteousness." This Wisdom, the LORD our righteousness is the Female/Mind of God the Father, and if we sin against Her, we sin against the Father and wrong our own souls. Yes, just like we sin against the Father, we sin against Wisdom, and that, my beloved, is death. If we sin against Wisdom, we love death, but if we find Wisdom, we find life. Now, for us to sin against God's Wisdom and for Her to give us life, She has to be God within God. God possessed Her in the beginning of His ways, She was brought forth before His works of old, as one by His side who also was the one brought up with him rejoicing always before Him. Now the Father's Wisdom, Understanding, and Knowledge, which are the Mind of the His Holy Spirit/body, are Female, the Father Himself. The same is true of us; our wisdom, and our understanding—our knowledge—are also Female, and they are the making of our minds. I also said in order to prove that the Male in the Father is His Brain I needed to show who the Female was and how the spiritual Son—the Word—was produced. I've shown you the Female in the Father is His Mind, and proof that His Brain is the Male is how—between the two—the Brain and Mind—the spiritual Son—the Word—was produced. You see, the way that the spiritual Son—our God—the Father's Word, was produced, was by God's Brain and Mind, the Male and Female of the Holy Spirit.

It works this way. God's Mind, the Female in the Father—His Wisdom, Understanding, and Power—has a thought or idea or knows something needs to be done. The Mind, the Female, then discusses or talks it over with the Brain, the Male, in the Father—God's Spirit-controller—using their Son—their Word—to communicate with each other, and whatever the two decide on produces the spoken Word—their spiritual-produced Son—that brings that decision forth. The same is true of us. As we think, our minds talk things over with our brains using our word—our son—to communicate between the two before we speak or act on that decision. Moreover, whatever we speak, those words—our sons—are produced from, our female and male. The two discuss our thoughts and decide what would be best. The thought process and the answer to that conversation between the two produce our words.

God's Me is His Wisdom and Power, which is His Mind, and this is the mystery of Christ—the Female of the Father, the one of the two that are side by side as two brought up with each other as one before the Father's works of old. By seeing that Wisdom is Female—the Mind of the Father—which, together with the Father's Male—His Brain—produced their Son—the Word—we should also see that the Male of the Father is His Brain, because the Brain is dead without the Mind. God's Brain and our brains cannot do anything without the Mind. Wisdom, Understanding, and Knowledge are our Counsel and Might that give us the same Fear as God's—to hate evil, pride, and arrogance—and together they gives us the Power of God, which is God's Word, our Lord God. God's Me—His Female, His Power, His Mind, the LORD our righteousness, the Christ of God—is the mystery of the Christ within God the Father, and we're going to learn even more about Her in parts two and three.

This brings us to the mystery of God—our God, the Lord God—the Father's Word, which is the Word of life. He is the Spirit that gave our souls life; He is the Spirit of Life that proceeded from the Father as His Word with the Father's Wisdom, Understanding, and Power within Him, making Him God's Word of Truth, the Lord Jesus Christ our God! The Lord our God is the Father's Word of life, which, after God the Father rested on the seventh day, took charge over everything on the eight day that the Us had made, which allowed Him, the Word of life, God's spoken Word, to rule over life, to give life, and to become Lord over life, the Lord our God. The Father's Word became our Lord God because at the time and now, He was and is the only law or rule for our ancestors—believers—and us to live by. The Father's Word, according to St. John, made us, and without Him we would not be here. John 1:3-4 reads, "All things were made by Him, and without Him was not any thing made that was

made. In Him was Life and the Life was the light of men."
Therefore, because God's Word made us, He is our Lord, and
being our Lord, which proceeded from the Father God,
makes Him our Lord God. From the New Unger's Bible
Dictionary, "Lord" means "he to whom a person or thing
belongs, the master, the one having disposition of men, as the
owner." He—the Lord—owns us. Being that He has
ownership over us, He is our Lord God! This is why Moses
started using "Lord God" in Genesis chapter two and
throughout his books: "And God blessed the seventh day, and
sanctified it: because that in it he had rested from all his work
which God created and made. These are the generations of
the heavens and of the earth when they were created, in the
day that the LORD God—the Word; John 1:1-4—made the
earth and the heavens—Gen 2:3-4. The Father allowed His
Word of life, the Lord our God to continue to rule over us
until the Father spoke to Him the words of Ps 110: 1: "The
LORD said unto my Lord, Sit thou at my right hand, until I
make thine enemies thy footstool."

You see, we all know that the Lord is the Father's
Word who was made flesh: "And the Word was made flesh,
and dwelt among us, (and we beheld his glory, the glory as of
the only begotten of the Father,) full of grace and truth—John
1:14. The Word—Jesus Christ—was made flesh, and Jesus
Christ is Lord. Phil 2:11 reads, "And that every tongue
should confess that Jesus Christ is Lord, to the glory of God
the Father." In the book of Romans, Paul tells us the Lord
owns us: "For whether we live, we live unto the Lord; and
whether we die, we die unto the Lord: whether we live
therefore, or die, we are the Lord's—Romans 14:8. Okay, the
Lord is Jesus, and Jesus is the Word, and in the book of Acts
we are told, "The word which God sent unto the children of
Israel, preaching peace by Jesus Christ—Emmanuel—(He is
Lord of all)—Acts 10:36. Therefore, the Word—the Spirit-
produced Son—that the Father sent unto Israel is our Lord,
our Lord God, and He came preaching peace by, or through,
Jesus Emmanuel—the begotten son, he who delivered unto
us all God's spoken Word of life, the Gospel of God, God's

Word of Truth. Acts 10:37-38 reads, "That word [I say], ye know, which was published throughout all Judaea, and began from Galilee, after the baptism which John preached; How God anointed Jesus of Nazareth—the begotten son—with the Holy Ghost and with power: who went about doing good, and healing all that were oppressed of the devil; for God was with him." Tell me, if the begotten son is God, why did God need to be with him? If Jesus Emmanuel is God, why did God need to anoint with Himself—the Holy Ghost and with Power? In addition, if the begotten son is God, why did God need to anoint him with the Holy Spirit and with Power at all?

It's the Word, the Father's Word of life, that is our God. John 1:1 tells us, "In the beginning was the Word—the Spirit-produced Son—and the Word was with God—the Father—and the Word—the Spirit-produced Son—was God—the Father." This is why Jesus said that He and the Father are one. Notice, Jesus didn't say "the Father, the Holy Spirit, and I are one" but "I and my Father are one—John 10:30—because the Father and He are the One Holy Spirit. Now when Jesus said this, He was not talking about Christ Jesus—the son of man—but Himself—the Father's Word, Jesus Christ our God, the Son of God, and the Spirit of Life that proceeded from the Father. Listen, Jesus Emmanuel—the son of man, the soul and body of God's Word—tells us that it is the Father's Word in him—Jesus Christ our God—and not him—Christ Jesus our Rised Lord—that is doing the work. This comes from John 14:10, which says, "Believest thou not that I am in the Father—as the soul and body of God's Word—and the Father in me—as His Word of life? the words that I speak unto you I speak not of myself: but the Father that dwelleth in me, he doeth the works."

Understand now, it is the Father within Christ Jesus Emmanuel that doeth the work in him and us through His Word, the Lord Jesus Christ our God. So this scripture means, "Philip, as long as I've been with you, ye do not know me. He who has seen me—the work that I do—has seen the Father, so how can you say show us the Father?

Believest thou not that I am the soul and body of the Father's Word and that the Father's Word in me is the Father Himself within this flesh of mine that you see? How sayeth you show us the Father? The Word you hear from me—Christ Jesus Emmanuel—as the soul and body of the Father's Word is the Father which speaks His Myself, His Word. They are the one Spirit that doeth the work of me—Jesus Emmanuel—that you see." So it is the Father that dwelleth in Jesus Emmanuel— the son of man/us—that doeth the work. Our proof that this is true is this: when Jesus said "ye had not known me," he was not talking about the physical him but the spiritual Him, because the spiritual Him—the Lord Jesus Christ our God, the Word—is the Father within him who we should see when we look at the work that the son of man is doing. Furthermore, we know they saw him physically; therefore, he was not talking about seeing him physically but seeing Him spiritually as the Word of God within the flesh that they do see. Got it?

It's the Word—the Father's Word—that is our God. I AM THAT I AM, I AM THE FATHER'S WORD, THAT I AM, THE LORD THY GOD! Again, He is our God, because the Father's Word is our life—our Eternal Life. He is the result of the Male and Female in the Father's Holy Spirit— the Brain and Mind in the Father—that was produced by and proceeded from the Father to give us Himself as the Word of Life! 1 John 1:1-3: tells us, "That which was from the beginning—the Word of life—which we have heard, which we have seen with our eyes, which we have looked upon, and our hands have handled, of the Word of life; For the life was manifested—made clear—and we have seen it, and bear witness, and shew unto you that eternal life, which was with the Father, and was manifested—made clear—unto us; That which we have seen and heard declare we unto you, that ye also may have fellowship with us: and truly our fellowship is with the Father, and with his Son Jesus Christ—our God the Word of life."

The Father gave His Son—the Word—life within Himself, so if we abide in His Word—the Son—we abide in life. Listen to the words of Moses in Matt 4:4: "But he—Jesus Emmanuel—answered and said, 'It is written, Man shall not live by bread alone, but by every word that proceedeth out of the mouth of God." The Word that Christ Jesus spoke is life, and because He proceeded from the Father, He is Spirit, making the Father's Word of life the Spirit of Life. John 6:63 says, "It is the spirit that quickeneth—restored to life or revived or give life—the flesh profiteth nothing: the words that I speak unto you, they are spirit, and they are life." See, the Word is Spirit and life—the Spirit of Life."

This Word of Life or Spirit of Life is our God, because without Him, who is our Life, we will surely perish. He's the one who is faithful and true—the one who is fighting for the lost souls in the end times. Rev 19:11-16 reads, "And I saw heaven opened, and behold a white horse; and he that sat upon him was called Faithful and True, and in righteousness he doth judge and make war. His eyes were as a flame of fire, and on his head were many crowns; and he had a name written, that no man knew, but he himself. And he was clothed with a vesture dipped in blood: and his name is called The Word of God. And the armies which were in heaven followed him upon white horses, clothed in fine linen, white and clean. And out of his mouth goeth a sharp sword, that with it he should smite the nations: and he shall rule them with a rod of iron: and he treadeth the winepress of the fierceness and wrath of Almighty God. And he hath on his vesture and on his thigh a name written, KING OF KINGS, AND LORD OF LORDS." The Father's Word is our God; in the beginning He gave us life on earth. Also, for us who believe and live by Him—the Word—He gives us eternal life through Himself, the Spirit of Life, which is the Father's Spirit-produced Son." This is the mystery of God, the Father's Word—the Son, Man-Child—who was produced by and proceeded from the mystery of the Father—the Brain, the Male—and the two together are the mystery of Christ, which is Wisdom—the Mind, the Female—the Power of God the Father.

Now this is the mystery of God, the mystery of the Father, and the mystery of Christ in Colossians 2:2, and the changing of the meaning of this scripture by other so-called Bibles is heresy, and it shows us that someone is trying to hide the truth and ultimate truth about the Trinity Conspiracy. The answer to the mystery of these three has been revealed to us by God's Me—God's Wisdom, His Female. She is the one who has uncovered this conspiracy by other Bibles to hide who God truly is.

Again I ask, is there a conspiracy to hide who God is or is it just some honest mistake with these other Bibles that has changed God's Word? Wait. Don't answer now, for there is more that we should read before we answer this question.

This is not the only conspiracy to hide the truth. God's Me, Myself, and I are God's Brain—His Male—God's Mind and Wisdom—God's Female—and God's Word—His Son, the Spirit-produced Son—and the three in action are one—the Holy Spirit at work—which is God's body in motion working within us and the things that we do. Ask yourself, when you are reading God's Word, what are you reading other than God's Wisdom, and when you are reading God's Wisdom, who are you reading other than God's Mind, which is God, the Father Himself? Remember, it is God's Me—His Wisdom, His Female—that has uncovered this conspiracy to hide the truth and ultimate truth about the Trinity not being in God the Father as to a triune God.

CHAPTER 8

The Conspriacies and The Cost to Pay For Those Conspiracies

The truth and uncovering of these conspiracies—no Trinity in God as to a triune God and the hiding of the truth about the mystery of God, the mystery of the Father, and the mystery of Christ—has uncovered another conspiracy by these same so-called Bibles to hide the truth about God's Me, Myself, and I, being one. Only the King James, American King James, Jubilee Bible 2000, and Webster's Bible Translation kept it revealed. In fact, these same so-called Bibles that have changed Colossians 2:2 have omitted and changed the TWO MOST IMPORTANT VERSES in the Bible that prove that the Trinity is not in the Father as to a triune God but in us, as to the three, that must agree within one. These two most important verses are the seventh and eighth verses of 1 John 5, which read, "For there are three that bear record in heaven, the Father, the Word, and the Holy Ghost: and these three are one; And there are three that bear witness in earth, the Spirit, and the water, and the blood: and these three agree in one."

Take a Look!

New International Version (©1984)

(7) For there are three that testify: (8) the Spirit, the water and the blood; and the three are in agreement.

New Living Translation (©2007)

(7) So we have these three witnesses-(8) - the Spirit, the water, and the blood--and all three agree.

89

English Standard Version (©2001)
(7) For there are three that testify: (8) the Spirit and the water and the blood; and these three agree.

New American Standard Bible (©1995)
(7) For there are three that testify: (8) the Spirit and the water and the blood; and the three are in agreement.

International Standard Version (©2008)
(7) For there are three witnesses- (8) the Spirit, the water, and the blood-and these three are one.

GOD'S WORD® Translation (©1995)
(7) There are three witnesses (8) the Spirit, the water, and the blood. These three witnesses agree.

King James Bible
(7) For there are three that bear record in heaven, the Father, the Word, and the Holy Ghost: and these three are one. (8) And there are three that bear witness in earth, the Spirit, and the water, and the blood: and these three agree in one.

American King James Version
(7) For there are three that bear record in heaven, the Father, the Word, and the Holy Ghost: and these three are one. (8) And there are three that bear witness in earth, the Spirit, and the water, and the blood: and these three agree in one.

American Standard Version
(7) And it is the Spirit that beareth witness, because the Spirit is the truth. (8) For there are three who bear witness, the Spirit, and the water, and the blood: and the three agree in one.

Bible in Basic English
(7) And the Spirit is the witness, because the Spirit is true (8). There are three witnesses, the Spirit, the water, and the blood:

and all three are in agreement.

Douay-Rheims Bible
(7) And there are three who give testimony in heaven, the
Father, the Word, and the Holy Ghost. And these three are
one. (8) And there are three that give testimony on earth: the
Spirit, and the water, and the blood: and these three are one.

Darby Bible Translation
(7) For they that bear witness are three: (8) the Spirit, and the
water, and the blood; and the three agree in one.

English Revised Version
(7) And it is the Spirit that beareth witness, because the Spirit
is the truth. (8) For there are three who bear witness, the
Spirit, and the water, and the blood: and the three agree in
one.

Webster's Bible Translation
(7) For there are three that bear testimony in heaven, the
Father, the Word, and the Holy Spirit, and these three are one.
(8) And there are three that bear testimony on earth, the Spirit,
and the water, and the blood: and these three agree in one.

Weymouth New Testament
(7) For there are three that give testimony—the Spirit, the
water, and the blood; (8) and there is complete agreement
between these three.

Berean Study Bible
(7) For there are three that testify: (8) the Spirit, the water,
and the blood--and these three are in agreement.

Berean Literal Bible
(7) For there are three bearing testimony: (8) the Spirit and
the water, and the blood--and these are three in one.

Holman Christian Standard Bible

(7) For there are three that testify: (8) the Spirit, the water, and the blood--and these three are in agreement.
NET Bible
(7) For there are three that testify, (8) the Spirit and the water and the blood, and these three are in agreement.

Aramaic Bible in Plain English
(7) And The Spirit testifies because The Spirit is the truth. (8) The Spirit and the water and the blood, and the three of them are in one.

New American Standard 1977
(7) And it is the Spirit who bears witness, because the Spirit is the truth. (8) For there are three that bear witness, the Spirit and the water and the blood; and the three are in agreement.

Jubilee Bible 2000
(7) For there are three that bear witness in heaven, the Father, the Word, and the Holy Spirit; and these three are one. (8) And there are three that bear witness on earth, the Spirit and the water and the blood; and these three agree in one.

World English Bible
(7) For there are three who testify: (8) the Spirit, the water, and the blood; and the three agree as one.

Young's Literal Translation
(7) because three are who are testifying in the heaven, the Father, the Word, and the Holy Spirit, and these -- the three -- are one; (8) and three are who are testifying in the earth, the Spirit, and the water, and the blood, and the three are into the one.

As you have read, out of these twenty-four Bibles, twenty have changed and omitted the true Word of God to fit the trinitarian terms of the Godhead. Ask yourself, are these bibles trying to hide something? Does the way these Bible have changed and omitted these two most important verses in the bible prove that the Trinity of the three Persons in the Godhead must agree to form unity or that God is one? If these so-called Bibles are not trying to hide anything, why did they take out all of verse seven that proves that God is one? Verse 7 states, "For there are three that bear record in heaven, the Father, the Word, and the Holy Ghost: and these three are one."

One of these Bibles, the New International Version, has omitted all these other scriptures.

Here take a look!

The following verses have been taken completely out of the New International Version:

Matthew 17:21—Gone
"Howbeit this kind goeth not out but by prayer and fasting."

Matthew 18:11—Gone
"For the Son of man is come to save that which was lost."

Matthew 23:14—Gone
"Woe unto you, scribes and Pharisees, hypocrites! for ye devour widows' houses, and for a pretence make long prayer: therefore ye shall receive the greater damnation."

Mark 7:16—Gone
"If any man have ears to hear, let him hear."

Mark 9:44—Gone
"Where their worm dieth not, and the fire is not quenched."

Mark 9:46—Gone
"Where their worm dieth not, and the fire is not quenched."

Mark 11:26—Gone
"But if ye do not forgive, neither will your Father which is in heaven forgive your trespasses."

Mark 15:28—Gone
"And the scripture was fulfilled, which saith, And he was numbered with the transgressors."

Luke 17:36—Gone
"two men shall be in the field; the one shall be taken, and the other left."

Luke 23:17—Gone
For of necessity he must release one unto them at the feast.

John 5:4—Gone
"For an angel went down at a certain season into the pool, and troubled the water: whosoever then first after the troubling of the water stepped in was made whole of whatsoever disease he had."

Acts 8:37—Gone
"And Philip said, If thou believest with all thine heart, thou mayest. And he answered and said, I believe that Jesus Christ is the Son of God."

Acts 15:34—Gone
"Notwithstanding it pleased Silas to abide there still."

Acts 24:7—Gone
"But the chief captain Lysias came upon us, and with great violence took him away out of our hands,"

Acts 28:29—Gone
"And when he had said these words, the Jews departed, and had great reasoning among themselves."

"May the grace of our Lord Jesus Christ be with you all. Amen."

Wow. If changing and removing the scriptures changes the meaning of God's intended Word and Wisdom in His Word, and if the scriptures are changed and removed knowingly and taught accordingly, doesn't this then show that one is trying to hide something? Again, the two most important scriptures that prove the truth and ultimate truth about the Trinity Conspiracy are removed and changed! The New International Version of 1 John 5:7-8 reads, "For there are three that testify: the Spirit, the water and the blood; and the three are in agreement."

Now, the King James Version—which is the true Bible—of **1 John 5:7-8** alternatively reads, "For there are three that bear record in heaven, the Father, the Word, and the Holy Ghost: and these three are one. And there are three that bear witness in earth, the Spirit, and the water, and the blood: and these three agree in one."

Now here is what God says the cost to pay is for taking away or adding to His Word:

Proverbs 30:5-6: "Every word of God is pure: he is a shield unto them that put their trust in him. Add thou not unto his words, lest he reprove thee, and thou be found a liar."

Revelation 22:18-20: "For I testify unto every man that heareth the words of the prophecy of this book, If any man shall add unto these things, God shall add unto him the plagues that are written in this book. And if any man shall take away from the words of the book of this prophecy, God shall take away his part out of the book of life, and out of the holy city, and from the things which are written in this book. He which testifieth these things saith, Surely I come quickly. Amen. Even so, come, Lord

Jesus."

1 John 5: 7-8, the two most important verses have been removed and changed—changed to fit Tertullian's invention of the three agreeing in a Godhead, because there is no three in a Godhead as to a triune God. When we try to add Christ Jesus Emmanuel within God's head, we see that it cannot be. If within Christ Jesus Emmanuel—the soul and body of the Father's Word, the Lord Jesus Christ our God, the Spirit of Life—had dwelled all the fullness of the Godhead bodily, how than can He be within the Godhead when the full Godhead is within him? Spirit can enter flesh, but flesh cannot enter spirit, and if flesh cannot enter spirit, Christ Jesus Emmanuel our Lord—who is flesh and bones—cannot enter into God's head. But God's head--His Word, Wisdom, etc—see Isa 11:1-2—can and did enter into him bodily!

Therefore, by changing and omitting 1 John 5: 7-8, these so-called Bibles have misled the children of God the Father to believe in Tertullian's invention of the Trinity being in the Father as to a triune God. We are misled, because of the way they put verses 7 and 8 together.

As I pointed out to you earlier in this part, if the three are individuals in a Godhead—without God's Wisdom, the Female—they would have had to agree first to come together in one in order to have unity if they are individuals. In addition, if they are individuals they could not come together or form unity without Wisdom, God's Female. Moreover, when we read verses 7 and 8, the way these other so-called Bibles have put them together, the three have to agree to join as one in order to become one, and that's exactly what these so-called Bibles have mislead us into believing.

The New International version of 1 John 5:7-8 reads, "For there are three that testify: the Spirit, the water and the blood; and the three are in agreement." But again, when we read the King James Version of 1 John 5:7-8, we see that it reads differently: "For there are three that bear record in heaven, the Father, the Word, and the Holy Ghost: and these three are one. And there are three that bear witness in earth, the Spirit, and the water, and the blood: and these three agree in one."

Thus, it is clear that the Father, His Word, His Wisdom, and His spiritual body—the Holy Ghost/Spirit—are one Spirit—the Father God Himself who divides within us as He will—and that the Trinity is not in Him but in us. Tell me, how can one separate his/her brain and mind, word, and body to be individuals? One cannot. So how is the Trinity in us you ask? It is in us because 1. the Spirit—our brain, our conscience, the Spirit of Truth within us, and our soul—which is God's Holy Spirit divided within us. 2. The water—God's Wisdom, God's Word, God's Truth, and God's Power—that dwells within us, and 3. The blood—our natural mind, our flesh, our members, and our body—which is the covering of the Spirit, the temple of the living God within us. These three—the Spirit, water, and blood—have to agree in one (us) in order for us to be able to live as one with God from within. These three—the Trinity within us—will either choose to live a life of sin—by the blood—the body, the flesh—influencing the Spirit— the soul's mind, our conscience, the Spirit of Truth and our soul—making the two in disagreement with the Water—God's Wisdom, God's Word, God's Truth, and God's Power—or they will empower us to live according to God's Me, Myself and I—by the blood agreeing with or being subdued by the two—and that choice to unify or to form unity from within is the transforming power of God within us—the power that renews our minds and gives us strength to present our bodies—the temple of God—as living sacrifices, holy and acceptable unto God, just as Romans 12:1-2 states: "I beseech you therefore, brethren, by the mercies of God, that ye present your bodies a living sacrifice, holy, acceptable unto God, which is your reasonable service. And be not conformed to this world: but be ye transformed by the renewing of your mind, that ye may prove what is that good, and acceptable, and perfect, will of God."

You cannot say that the Father, who is Male and

Female—His Brain/Male and Mind and Wisdom/Female—who produced the Word—their Spirit-produced Son—and the Holy Ghost—the Father's body in action—are three distinct persons in a Godhead and just leave out Wisdom who alone with the Male produced the Son. Understand, neither God nor we can produce a word to speak without first having the wisdom within to speak or produce that word. Our words come from our wisdom or lack of wisdom. As to a triune God, there is no Trinity in God the Father, and the two most important scriptures in the Bible that prove this have been removed and changed in over ten different Bibles. When we look at the King James Version of verse 7 of 1 John 5, we see, "For there are three that bear record in heaven, the Father—Male/Brain and Female Wisdom/Mind—the Word—the Spirit-produced Son, not the begotten son—and the Holy Ghost—God's holy body—and these three are one." God's Male, Female, Son, and Truth in action—or God's Brain, Mind, Word, and Truth working in our lives—is God's holy body—His Holy Spirit in motion. It is the Power of God that makes things or gets things done, whatsoever He—the body—hears from Him—the Brain—that He do, for He is the body of the Spirit that is God the Father. The Father, Word, and Holy Spirit are the one Spirit that bears witness of the begotten son. These three bear record in Heaven and in us as well. Got it now? You cannot say that the Father—His Brain the Male and Mind His Wisdom the Female—the Word—His Son—and the Holy Ghost—the Father's body—are three distinct persons in a Godhead and leave out God's Wisdom being a part of that Godhead. Moreover, the same is true of us; our brains and minds, our word and our body, are not distinguishable from ourselves, and we cannot leave out our Wisdom as a part of our fullness of the Godhead. They are one in us, as they are one in the Father, and the reason why the three bear record in Heaven of the begotten son and us is this: the Father bears record/witness because He is that One Spirit and we are created in His image, after His likeness. Genesis 1:26a-27 reads, "And God said, Let us make man in our image, after

98

our likeness…So God created man in his own image, in the image of God created he him; male and female created he them."

The Father also bear record because the words of Isaiah 55:10-11says: "For as the rain cometh down, and the snow from heaven, and returneth not thither, but watereth the earth, and maketh it bring forth and bud, that it may give seed to the sower, and bread to the eater: So shall my word be that goeth forth out of my mouth: it shall not return unto me void, but it shall accomplish that which I please, and it shall prosper in the thing whereto I sent it."

The Word bears record/witness because of the words of Hebrews 4:12-13: "For the word of God is quick, and powerful, and sharper than any twoedged sword, piercing even to the dividing asunder of soul and spirit, and of the joints and marrow, and is a discerner of the thoughts and intents of the heart. Neither is there any creature that is not manifest in his sight: but all things are naked and opened unto the eyes of him with whom we have to do."

God's Word—the Lord Jesus Christ our God—bears record/witness also because He is true. John 8:14 records, "Jesus answered and said unto them, 'Though I bear record—witness—of myself, *yet* my record is true: for I know whence I came, and whither I go; but ye cannot tell whence I come, and whither I go.'" He is also Truth: "Sanctify them through thy truth: thy word is truth—John 17:17.

Also keep in mind that the begotten son—Christ Jesus Emmanuel our risen Lord—cannot bear record/witness of himself according to John 5:30-31: "I can of mine own self do nothing: as I hear, I judge: and my judgment is just; because I seek not mine own will, but the will of the Father which hath sent me. If I bear witness of myself, my witness is not true."

The Holy Ghost bears record/witness also because of the words of Romans 8:14-16: "For as many as are led by the Spirit of God, they are the sons of God. For ye have not received the spirit of bondage again to fear; but ye have received the spirit of adoption, whereby we cry, Abba,

Father. The Spirit itself beareth witness—record—with our spirit, that we are the children of God—the Father."

Understand, the Father—His Male and Female—Son, and Body are Spirit. Being that His Brain, Mind, Word, and body are Spirit and that they are one tells me that God the Father is that one Spirit that divides unto us as He pleases. However, because of the heresy teaching of the Trinity—the conspiracy to hide the truth about the Trinity—many of us do not know the Father. The one scripture that can prove that they are one has been changed and removed. The King James Version gives us the proof that the three are one in 1 John 5:7: "For there are three that bear record in heaven, the Father, the Word, and the Holy Ghost: and these three are one." In addition, the other second most important scripture proves that the Trinity—as Tertullian explains it—is in us in 1 John 5:8: "And there are three that bear witness in earth, the Spirit, and the water, and the blood: and these three agree in one."

We now understand that the Father is Spirit, that His Word is Spirit, that His body is the Holy Spirit, and that He divides Himself within us for the souls of humankind. 1 Corinthians 12:11-13 tells us that there is only one Spirit for believers, and that one Spirit divides to every man as He will. Again, God the Father is Spirit, He is holy, and His name is Holy, He divides His Spirit as He will, which means the Father is the Holy Spirit, which makes Him the Father of Spirit and life for all holiness of Spirit.

Heb 12:9-10 reads, "Furthermore we have had fathers of our flesh which corrected us, and we gave them reverence: shall we not much rather be in subjection unto the Father of spirits, and live? For they verily for a few days chastened us after their own pleasure; but he for our profit, that we might be partakers of his holiness."

Knowing that God the Father—the Male and Female—the Word—the Spirit-produced Son—and the Holy Spirit—His spiritual body in action—are one Spirit is our proof that some one is trying to hide this truth and ultimate truth about the Trinity not being in God as to a triune God.

100

The truth about this heresy teaching of the Trinity being in God has been hidden from God's children for a long time. This conspiracy to keep this truth hidden has caused some to sell their souls—those who knowingly changed and omitted or added and took from the Word of God the Father. Again, here is what God says about His Word and what the cost is to pay for him who adds or takes away from His Word:

Proverbs 30:5-6: "Every word of God is pure: he is a shield unto them that put their trust in him. Add thou not unto his words, lest he reprove thee, and thou be found a liar."

Revelation 22:18-20: "For I testify unto every man that heareth the words of the prophecy of this book, If any man shall add unto these things, God shall add unto him the plagues that are written in this book. And if any man shall take away from the words of the book of this prophecy, God shall take away his part out of the book of life, and out of the holy city, and from the things which are written in this book. He which testifieth these things saith, Surely I come quickly. Amen. Even so, come, Lord Jesus."

CHAPTER 9

Our Trinitarian Understanding of the Trinity Shield

Now, therefore, to every man/woman of the Father, if you have read this work and still teach the doctrine of the Trinity being in God as to a triune God and not us, BE YE WARNED! YOU ARE TEACHING HERESY AND LEADING SOULS, INCLUDING YOUR OWN, TO HELL! Matthew 7:22-23 says, "Many will say to me in that day, Lord, Lord, have we not prophesied in thy name? And in thy name have cast out devils? And in thy name done many wonderful works? And then will I profess unto them, I never knew you: depart from me, ye that work iniquity."

Now, is this shield right, or wrong, in the sight of God?

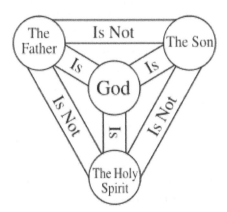

Well, now that we have Tertullian's word of how he invented the unity of the Trinity in the Godhead—remember his title of his third chapter: "The Doctrine of the Trinity in Unity"—and we have God the Father's Word that the Trinity is in us and not within Him as to a Godhead of three. So tell me, is this shield right or wrong in the sight of God the Father?"

Now, let us look at the people who made Tertullian's invention doctrine.

Wikipedia states, "*About a century after Tertullian came up with his invention, the First Council of Nicaea in 325 A.D. established the doctrine of the Trinity in the Godhead as orthodoxy (right or true) and adopted the Nicene Creed (which is the creed or profession of faith).*

It is also important to know that according to Wikipedia *Quintus Septimius Florens Tertullianus anglicised as Tertullian wrote his trinitarian formula*—his invention— *after he became a Montanist, which was an early Christian movement that speared rapidly, although Orthodox Nicene Christianity prevailed against Montanism within a few generations, labeling it a heresy. The sect persisted, which means that in spite of opposition or criticism, they pushed forward his idea, this heresy, in some isolated places into the 6th century. His ideas*—the Trinity in the Godhead—*were at first rejected as heresy by the church at large but later accepted as Christian orthodoxy.*

Montanism, known by its adherents as the New Prophecy, was an early Christian movement of the late 2nd century, later referred to by the name of its founder, Montanus. The movement held similar views about the basic tenets of Christian doctrine to those of the wider church, although the possibility of new revelations and ecstasies was not accepted by the wider church. The Bishop of Rome ultimately condemned the movement as heretical and excommunicated its adherents. It was a prophetic movement that called for a reliance on the spontaneity of the Holy Spirit and a more conservative personal ethic. Parallels have been drawn between Montanism and modern-day movements such as Pentecostalism, the charismatic movement, and the New

Now, couple all this with some of the earlier beliefs of the First Coucil of Nicaea. I challenge you to read some of the earlier beliefs of the First Council of Nicaea, then you tell me who is right, the First Council of Nicaea, which adopted Tetullian's invention—the trinitarian formula—or Theophilus of Antioch who somewhat understood God's Word.

God the Father said His image is Male—Brain—and Female—Mind, Wisdom—with the ability to produce a Son—their Word—within His Holy Spirit—the one Spirit that divides Himself as He will, because He is the Father of Spirit, the Holy Spirit. You choose who is right; the choice is yours! But don't make up mind now, wait until you have read all three parts and then tell me who is right, "God's Word or Telltullian's word?"

As for me, I'm with Joshua as he states in Joshua 24:15 – "And if it seem evil unto you to serve the LORD, choose you this day whom ye will serve; whether the gods which your fathers served that were on the other side of the flood, or the gods of the Amorites, in whose land ye dwell: but as for me and my house, we will serve the LORD."

Okay, now ask yourself again, who is closer to the truth about the Trinity: Theophilus of Antioch *(the Trinity [Τριάδος] of God, and His Word, and His Wisdom. And the fourth is the type of man, who needs light, that so there may be God, the Word, Wisdom, Man)* or Tertullian *(the first to use the Latin words "Trinity," "person," and "substance" to explain that the Father, Son, and Holy Spirit are one in essence, not one in person).*

There you have it: God's Me—the Father, the Male and Female—Myself—the Son, their Word—and I—the body, the Holy Spirit—the truth and ultimate truth about the Trinity not being in God as to a triune God but is within us as the three that must agree as one.

As we enter into part two, we will learn all we need to know about God's Myself—His Word of life, our Lord God, the Lord Jesus Christ our God. In six days, the Father created all things with His Word of life, and afterward He rested on the seventh day and placed all authority under His Word of life—the Lord God, His Son, the Lord Jesus Christ our God, the Father's Word. Yes, the Father's Word of life. The Lord God had the name Jesus Christ before He came into the flesh. 1 John 4:1-2 reads, "Beloved, believe not every spirit, but try the spirits whether they are of God: because many false prophets are gone out into the world. Hereby know ye the Spirit of God: Every spirit that confesseth that Jesus Christ—the Word—is come in the flesh—sinful cavemen or natural flesh—is of God" See also 1 John 4:3 & 2 John 1:7.

Now, please understand, not only did God's Word of life, the Lord our God, have the name Jesus Christ before He became flesh, but that Jesus Christ, the Son of God the Father, existed before Christ Jesus Emmanuel our Lord was born to be our High Priest—the son of man, God's only begotten son. Romans 8:3 tell us, "For what the law could not do, in that it was weak through the flesh. God sending his own Son—the Word—in the likeness of sinful flesh—King David's—and for sin, condemned sin in the flesh." Got it? God's Son had to exist first in order for God to be able to send Him in the likeness of sinful flesh. Therefore, as we go through the next eleven chapters we will begin to understand more about the Mother "Wisdom" of God's Word. This will help us to understand the truth about the Lord Jesus Christ our God and Christ Jesus Emmanuel our Lord, the mediator between God and man, the man Christ Jesus: "For there is one God, and one mediator between God and men, the man Christ Jesus"—1 Timothy 2:5. Please keep reading and allow us to introduce you to the Lord Jesus Christ our God!

To God Be The Glory!
John 17:3

106

And this is life eternal, that they might know thee the only true God, and Jesus Christ, whom thou hast sent.

CHAPTER 10

The Word God's Word of Wisdom the Christ of God's Redemption

John 1:1-2 & 4 states, "In the beginning was the Word, and the Word was with God, and the Word was God. The same was in the beginning with God. In him was life; and the life was the light of men." This brings us to Genesis Chapter 2, the place where God the Father rested and gave all authority to His Word of life, the Lord God: "And God blessed the seventh day, and sanctified it: because that in it he had rested from all his work, which God—the Word—created and made"—Gen 2:3. You see, God the Father rested on the seventh day because everything He created and made, He did so by speaking His Word of life through His Female, His Mind, Wisdom. God's Word made all things, and without him was not any thing made, that was made, just as John 1:3 says: "All things were made by him—the Word—and without him was not any thing made that was made." Therefore, because God's Word through God's Wisdom made everything that was made, He—the Word of life—then became our owner. He made us all, and with His ownership—the state or fact of being an owner—comes authority, control, and power over us, and this makes Him our Lord. Lord is a person—or Spirit in this case—who has control, authority, or power over others as a master or a ruler. His Lordship—the authority, power, or domain of a Lord—as the Word of God gives Him the divinity/holiness of a God and that divinity makes the Father's Word, the Lord God. The Lord our God, the Father's Word of life, with authority, gives us life eternal—that everlasting life: "In him—the Word of life—was life; and the life was the light of men"—

John 1:4. John 5:24 reads, "Verily, verily, I say unto you, He that heareth my word, and believeth on him that sent me, hath everlasting life, and shall not come into condemnation; but is passed from death unto life." Please understand what this eternal life is: "As thou hast given him power over all flesh, that he should give eternal life to as many as thou hast given him. And this is life eternal, that they might know thee the only true God—the Father—and Jesus Christ—the Word—whom thou hast sent"—John 17:2-3. As we have just heard, eternal life is to know whom the only true God the Father is and to know Jesus Christ—God's Word and Wisdom—whom God sent into the likeness of sinful flesh—Jesus Emmanuel. This is the purpose for this work, that the world might know the only true Father and Jesus Christ—God's Me, Myself, and I, which are one—and not this Trinity of three persons being in a Godhead as to a triune God.

Okay, we learned about the Father God's Me in the earlier chapters, and now let's find out about who the Father God's Myself is—the Lord Jesus Christ our God—and who Christ Jesus Emmanuel our Lord is. The Two that were One while on earth, but yet were Two, and They are Two in Heaven, but yet They are One as We are One with Them. First, we will deal with the Lord Jesus Christ our God in the Old Testament, and then we will deal with both of them in the New Testament. So let us go back to Gen 2:4: "These are the generations of the heavens and of the earth when they, were created, in the day that the LORD God—God's Word of Wisdom—made the earth and the heavens." Now, if you notice the name "God" from Gen 1:1 thru Gen 2:3 was used over thirty time and then after God the Father had rested, the name "God" changed to the name "LORD God" because as God the Father rested He placed all things that was created and made under the authority of Him who did the creating and making, "His Word, the Word of Life, "the Lord our God, our Lord God," the Father's Word of Wisdom, "the Lord Jesus Christ our God. Please understand the Word of God the Father, is our Lord and the Lord, the Father's Word, is our God—our Lord God. Acts 10:36 reads, "The word which God sent unto the children of Israel, preaching peace by Jesus Christ—He—the Word—is Lord of all—and the Lord, He is our God." Mark 12:29 likewise reads, "And Jesus answered him, The first of all the commandments is, Hear, O Israel; The Lord our God is one Lord." That Word, the Father's Word of life, was in charge from Gen. 2:4 until the Father told Him to sit back at His right hand in the Psalms of David: the LORD said unto my Lord, Sit thou at my right hand, until I make thine enemies thy footstool"—Ps 110:1. More proof that the Son of God existed in the Old Testament is Daniel 3:25: "He answered and said, Lo, I see four men loose, walking in the midst of the fire, and they have no hurt; and the form of the fourth is like the Son of God."

Now, we know that God's angels—His ministering spirits—are called sons as well. However, in Dan 3:28 the king used the word "angel," and not knowing God, he was right the first time when he said "Son of God. "Then Nebuchadnezzar spake, and said, Blessed be the God of Shadrach, Meshach, and Abed-nego, who hath sent his angel, and delivered his servants that trusted in him, and have changed the king's word, and yielded their bodies, that they might not serve nor worship any god, except their own God"—Dan. 3:28. Remember, God's Word is Spirit, and God divides His Spirit as He pleases, "even when He is spoken."

Now understanding all the above takes us to John 1:14a, "And the Word was made flesh, and dwelt among us," and to know why and how God's Word became flesh is most important. As we learn this, we need to keep in mind that God is the Father of all spirits. Num 16:22a reads, "And they fell upon their faces, and said, O God, the God of the spirits of all flesh." This includes Jesus Emmanuel, and when we are put in deep sleep—dead—that same Spirit goes back to God as Eccl 12:7 states: "Then shall the dust return to the earth as it was: and the Spirit shall return unto God who gave it." See, it is all about the Spirit leading us when it comes to the true God in this battle for our souls—our souls that the

Lord God blew within us. The true God leads us with His Word in this battle for our souls that we may be able to fight against Satan and Babylon. God uses His sword, which is Spirit—the Word, the Spirit of Life, and His Truth—His Spirit of Truth—to war against the flesh—Satan's home—of the soul, so that the soul itself may be saved from death. Satan also uses his sword, which is an evil spirit—his word, evil thoughts, and suggestions—which are fleshly desired ideas, and fleshly desired ideas are pride and fleshly lust. This fleshly lust is at war against the soul 1 Peter 2:11 reads, "Dearly beloved, I beseech you as strangers, and pilgrims, abstain from fleshly lusts, which war against the soul." Fleshly lust wars against the soul by wearing it down with enticement—lustful thoughts, greedy ideas, or both. If we allow lustful enticement to lead us instead of the Word of God—God's Spirit—then our souls lose the battle unto death, according to James 1:14-15: "But every man is tempted, when he is drawn away—drawn away—of his own lust, and enticed—of his own lust, and then are enticed. Then when lust hath conceived, it bringeth forth sin: and sin, when it is finished, bringeth forth death."

Therefore, because the Lord God is the breath of life of the soul, all souls are His, and Satan is trying to take those souls by getting and keeping them in bondage to fear, greed, and sin. Please know now that, according to Ezekiel, all souls are the Lord God's, and it is the soul that sins and it is the soul that dies. Ezek 18:4 reads, "Behold, all souls are mine; as the soul of the father, so also the soul of the son is mine: the soul that sinneth, it shall die." Now the hidden man of our heart—our spiritual male and female—spiritual brain and mind—the Spirit of Truth or our conscience—the Spirit of God within us, will not die because it is not corruptible. 1 Peter 3:4 tells us this: "But let it be the hidden man of the heart, in that which is not corruptible, even the ornament of a meek and quiet spirit, which is in the sight of God of great price."

Oh the battle, the battle, the battle. God is using His Spirit to free the soul from sin unto life, and Satan is using his spirit to keep the soul captive to sin unto death. Sins and the souls are the two common denominators between God and Satan in this battle. In the day of Noah, the Lord God's decree or law was weakened through the flesh, and sin captured many souls, "all but eight perished." All perished because of sin; that fleshly lust weakened God's law so deeply to the point that the Lord God regretted that He made man upon the earth: "And GOD saw that the wickedness of man was great in the earth, and that every imagination—Satan's suggestions—of the thoughts—fleshly ideas—of his heart—the natural mind influencing the soul mind—was only evil continually—fleshly lusts. And it repented the LORD that he had made man on the earth—Hear! He repented not that God the Father has created man in the waters above the firmament, but repented that He, the Lord God, had made man on the earth—and it grieved him at his heart. And the LORD said, I will destroy man whom I have created—and formed—from the face of the earth.

The man He created from the dust when He formed the spirit man within the earthly man body, making the spirit man weak when the earthly man became a part of the living soul; both man—man/woman—and beast, and the creeping thing, and the fowls of the air; for it repenteth me that I have made them"—Gen 6:5-7.

Then there were the days of Sodom and Gomorrah, when God destroyed them and the surrounding cities. Fleshly lust is what had them destroyed, because the Lord could not find ten that were righteous. The Lord continued to destroy His people in the days after Moses had freed the Hebrews because of their sin and rebellion. Now, because the Lord had made a promise to Abraham, He had to use a different approach to sin in His people. So this time, the Lord God repented from the evil He thought to bring upon the Hebrews and gave them a new written law, the Ten Commandments, because the decree the Lord God gave about the tree in the garden no longer had any effect because Adam and Eve had disobeyed and sinned. Therefore, Moses pleaded with the Lord not to destroy this people. Ex 32:13-16 reads,

"Remember Abraham, Isaac, and Israel, thy servants, to whom thou swarest by thine own self, and saidst unto them, I will multiply your seed as the stars of heaven, and all this land that I have spoken of will I give unto your seed, and they shall inherit it for ever. And the LORD repented of the evil, which he thought to do unto his people. And Moses turned, and went down from the mount, and the two tables of the testimony were in his hand; the tables, were written on both their sides; on the one side and on the other were they written. And the tables were the work of God, and the writing was the writing of God, graven upon the tables."

Now, because this law—the Ten Commandments—of the Spirit of Life was weakened through the flesh as well, God said to the Lord God, "sit thou at my right hand until I make your enemies your footstool." Ps 110:1-2 reads, "The LORD—the Father—said unto my Lord—the Lord God—Sit thou at my right hand, until I make thine enemies thy footstool. The LORD—Father—shall send the rod—Jesus Emmanuel—of thy—Lord God, the Word, the Word's strength—strength out of Zion: rule thou—Lord God—in the midst of thine enemies." The Lord's enemies were sin and death; therefore, God had to come up with a way to destroy sin and death in His people without destroying His people. Therefore, God decided to battle the enemies now using the Lord God, His Word of Life Himself, directly, because the battle—for the soul He breathed within us—is in our heads—the battle of the two minds—our spiritual and natural minds—for the control of the third mind—our soul's mind. He is doing this by washing and purging of His people with the Word of Life—the Lord God Himself—using the Spirit of judgment and the Spirit of burning. Isa 4:3-4 says, "And it shall come to pass, that he that is left in Zion, and he that remaineth in Jerusalem, shall be called holy, even every one that is written among the living in Jerusalem. When the Lord shall have washed away the filth of the daughters of Zion, and shall have purged the blood of Jerusalem from the midst thereof by the Spirit of judgment, and by the Spirit of burning." Paul tells us in Romans 2:12-16, "For as many as have sinned without law shall also perish without law: and as many as have sinned in the law shall be judged by the law; For not the hearers of the law are just before God, but the doers of the law shall be justified. For when the Gentiles, which have not the law, do by nature the things contained in the law, these, having not the law, are a law unto themselves. Which shew the work of the law written in their hearts, their conscience—the Spirit of Truth—also bearing witness, and their thoughts the mean while accusing—the spiritual mind—or else excusing—the natural mind—one another. In the day when God shall judge the secrets of men by Jesus Christ—His Word—according to my Gospel—meaning we are to be doers of the word, and be transformed, into the likeness or image of His Word, His Spirit produced Son." Now the Spirit of judgment and the Spirit of burning—God's Word—are in Revelation chapter 20. John tells us who will be rewarded and who will be judged in John 5:28-29: "Marvel not at this: for the hour is coming, in the which, all that are in the graves shall hear his voice. And shall come forth; they that have done good, unto the resurrection of life; and they that have done evil, unto the resurrection of damnation." That damnation is the result of the Spirit of judgment, which bringeth forth the Spirit of burning. Rev 20:11-15 reads, "And I saw a great white throne, and him that sat on it, from whose face the earth and the heaven fled away; and there was found no place for them. And I saw the dead, small and great, stand before God; and the books were opened: and another book was opened, which is the book of life: and the dead were judged out of those things which were written in the books, according to their works. And the sea gave up the dead which were in it; and death and hell delivered up the dead which were in them: and they were judged every man according to their works. And death and hell were cast into the lake of fire. This is the second death. And whosoever was not found written in the book of life was cast into the lake of fire."

Therefore, the method God chose to implement against His Spirit of judgment and burning—to save the souls

115

the Lord God created—is the washing and purging. This method was done firstly by the washing of the Word of God:

Eph 5:26 – "that he might sanctify and cleanse it—the church, us, our souls—with the washing of water by the word. Purging is by the Truth of God and His Mercy"

Prov 16:6 – "by mercy and truth iniquity is purged: and by the fear—the Understanding—of the LORD men depart from evil. That truth, which purges—sanctifies—us, is God's Word.

John 17:17 – "sanctify them through thy truth: thy word is truth."

For God to do this effectively, He put His Word, Wisdom, Understanding, Power, and Truth—His Son and Female, His Spirit of Life—into the sinful flesh as an example for us. He demonstrates to us that if Jesus Emmanuel can live without sin by being led by Them—God's Word/Wisdom of truth, the Spirit of Life—then so can we. Rom 8:2-3 states, "For the law—God the Father—of the Spirit of Life—God's Word and Wisdom—in Christ Jesus—Emmanuel—hath made me free from the law of sin and death. For what the law—the Ten Commandments—could not do, in that it was weak through the flesh, God sending his own Son—His Word, His Spirit-produced Son—in the likeness of sinful flesh—Jesus Emmanuel—and for sin, condemned sin in the flesh."

You see, once it was by the law that man should live: "For Moses describeth the righteousness—God's Word, Wisdom, Understanding, Power, and Truth—His Son and Female, His Spirit of Life—which is of the law, That the man which doeth those things shall live by them"—Rom 10:5. But because the law—the Ten Commandments—was weakened through the flesh, God's people were perishing. Thereby, God gave us His Truth, Word, Wisdom, Understanding, and Power—His spiritual Son. He put Him in us that we should live by Him. So now, the law for man is not to live by, but it serves as a reminder that when we do not do these Commandments, we are in sin or sinning. Therefore, since

Jesus Emmanuel was born with God's Spirit-produced Son in Him and because He was redeemed, the same is true of us. If we live by God's Word of life—which is Spirit—we too have the Spirit of Life in us, which redeems us and sets us free. Rom 3:20-24 reads, "Therefore by the deeds of the law—doing by nature the things contained in the law—there shall no flesh be justified in his sight: for by the law—the Commandments—is the knowledge of sin. But now the righteousness of God—His truth, His Word, Wisdom, Understanding, and Power—His spiritual Son—without the law is manifested, being witnessed by the law and the prophets. Even the righteousness of God, which is by faith of Jesus Christ—God's Word and Wisdom of Truth—His Spirit of Life—unto all and upon all them that believe: for there is no difference. For all have sinned, and come short of the glory of God; Being justified freely by his grace through the redemption—God's Word and Wisdom of Truth—that is in Christ Jesus—Emmanuel." Moreover, being redeemed through "Them" is the hearing and doing of God's Word—His Spirit-produced Son—which makes us free from sin. John 8:34-38 states, "Jesus answered them, Verily, verily, I say unto you, Whosoever committeth sin is the servant of sin. And the servant abideth not in the house for ever: but the Son—the Spirit-produced Son—abideth ever. If the Son—God's Word, His Spirit-produced Son—therefore shall make you free, ye shall be free indeed. I know that ye are Abraham's seed; but ye seek to kill me, because my word hath no place in you. I—Jesus Emmanuel—speak that which I have seen with my Father—and the Word was with God—and ye do that which ye have seen with your father.

Starting in Isaiah, God tells us how He is going to approach this battle to win the war for the soul. He tells us who in Christ Jesus Emmanuel would be doing it—the work: "For every battle of the warrior is with confused noise and garments rolled in blood; but this—battle—shall be with burning and fuel of fire. For unto us a child—Jesus Emmanuel—is born, unto us a son—the Spirit-produced Son—is given: and the government shall be upon his—the

Son that is given, the Spirit-produced Son—shoulder: and his—the Spirit-produced Son—name shall be called Wonderful, Counseller, The mighty God, The everlasting Father, The Prince of Peace. Of the increase of his government—developed government through faith—and peace there shall be no end, upon the throne of David, and upon his kingdom, to order it, and to establish it with judgment and with justice from henceforth even for ever." The zeal—God's Word and Wisdom of Truth, His Spirit of Life—of the LORD of hosts—the Father—will perform this—Isa 9:5-7. HEAR! THE ZEAL OF THE FATHER WILL PERFORM ALL THAT CHRIST JESUS EMMANUEL DO ON EARTH. The zeal of the LORD is the passionate ardor in the pursuit of anything; eagerness in favor of a person or cause; ardent and active interest; engagedness; enthusiasm; fervor. This passionate ardor in the pursuit of anything—our salvation—eagerness in favor of a person— Jesus Emmanuel—or cause—the fight for our souls—ardent and active interest—God's Truth—engagedness; enthusiasm; fervor is God's Word and Wisdom of Truth—His Spirit of Life within Jesus Emmanuel—for God's Word and Wisdom of Truth, His Spirit of Life is eager and takes active interest in accomplishing God Will. Indeed, according to Is 55:11, the Word of God shall not return unto God void, but shall accomplished that which pleases God: "So shall my word be that goeth forth out of my mouth: it shall not return unto me void, but it shall accomplish that which I please, and it shall prosper *in the thing* whereto I sent it. But, with Isaiah 9:6 many have misunderstood, and now we shall re-read it with God's Spirit of Understanding. For unto us a child is born— Jesus Emmanuel, the begotten son—unto us a son—God's Word, His Spirit-produced Son—is given: and the government—developed in God's Word through faith—shall be upon his—the Son that is given—shoulder: and his name shall be called Wonderful, Counseller, the Mighty God, the Everlasting Father, the Prince of Peace."

The names—Wonderful, Counseller, the Mighty God, the Everlasting Father, the Prince of Peace—are where we get confusion and misunderstanding, because we're being taught that Jesus Emmanuel—the son of David, the begotten son—are those names. Isaiah said that he shall be called these names, and he was called those names, but Jesus Emmanuel himself lets us know that, although he was called those names, it was not him who is the everlasting Father or Mighty God but God the Father Himself. Matt 23:8-10 reads, "But be not ye called Rabbi: for one is your Master, even Christ—Gods Wisdom, Understanding, and Power, which is in His Word—and all ye are brethren. And call no man— Including Jesus Emmanuel—your father upon the earth: for one is your Father—one God—which is in heaven. Neither be ye called masters: for one is your Master, even Christ— Gods Wisdom, Understanding, and Power, which is in His Word."

Jesus Emmanuel, the child that was born, was called these names because the Son that was given within him—the Spirit-produced Son, the Word—is God Himself, our Counselor, the Mighty God, and the Everlasting Father. Hab 1:12 reads, "Art thou not from everlasting, O LORD my God, mine Holy one? we shall not die. O LORD, thou hast ordained them for judgment; and, O mighty God, thou hast established them for correction." God's Word is our Counselor because God's Word is His spoken Wisdom, and His Wisdom is Counsel, Knowledge, and Understanding, which gives Her Might or strength. Likewise, Prov 8:12-14 states, "I Wisdom dwell with prudence, and find out knowledge of witty inventions. The fear of the LORD is to hate evil: pride, and arrogancy, and the evil way, and the froward mouth, do I hate. Counsel is mine, and sound Wisdom: I am understanding; I have strength." God's Word within the child—Jesus Emmanuel—makes His the zeal of God the Father who will perform the work through Jesus Emmanuel. This work being done through him and the suffering of the cross makes him "Christ Jesus Emmanuel our Master." Although he is greater than we are, he served us by giving his life for us. Now He has been exalted by God and we in return must serve Him as our risen Christ Lord.

Therefore, the way we are to serve him in Heaven starts on earth this day, at this time, the here and now. The way we are to serve him on earth is to live the Word of God daily. Rom 12:1 reads, "I beseech you therefore, brethren, by the mercies of God, that ye present your bodies a living sacrifice, holy, acceptable unto God, which is your reasonable service." This service gives our souls a spiritual identity as the sons/daughters of God. We—our souls—must have this spiritual identity in order for us to be a part of the Lord and Saviour Jesus Christ our God's body in which we are members through Christ Jesus Emmanuel, because he is the soul and body of the Father's Word—the Lord and Saviour Jesus Christ our God. His soul being the identity of the Father's Word—the Lord our God—means that the Lord Jesus Christ our God was put within Christ Jesus Emmanuel our Lord—the author and finisher of our faith—as an example or identity for him/us to live by. Read the following scriptures concerning this:

1 Peter 2:19-25 – "For this is thankworthy, if a man for conscience toward God endure grief, suffering wrongfully. For what glory is it, if, when ye be buffeted for your faults, ye shall take it patiently? but if, when ye do well, and suffer for it, ye take it patiently, this is acceptable with God. For even hereunto were ye called: because Christ also suffered for us, leaving us an example, that ye should follow his steps. Who did no sin, neither was guile found in his mouth. Who, when he was reviled, reviled not again; when he suffered, he threatened not; but committed himself to him—the Word of life within himself—that judgeth righteously. Who his own self bare our sins in his own body on the tree, that we, being dead to sins, should live unto righteousness: by whose stripes ye were healed. For ye were as sheep, going astray; but are now returned, unto the Shepherd—the Word—and Bishop—Jesus Emmanuel—of your souls."

Heb 12:1-4 – "Wherefore seeing we also are compassed about with so great a cloud of witnesses, let us lay aside every weight, and the sin which doth so easily beset us, and let us run with patience the race that is set before us. Looking unto Jesus the author and finisher of our faith; who for the joy that was set before him endured the cross, despising the shame, and is set down at the right hand of the throne of God. For consider him that endured such contradiction of sinners against himself, lest ye be wearied and faint in your minds. Ye have not yet resisted unto blood, striving against sin.

Matt 23:11-12 – "But he that is greatest among you shall be your servant. And whosoever shall exalt himself shall be abased—the lower in rank or degraded—and he that shall humble himself shall be exalted." Therefore, Jesus Emmanuel humbled himself every time with words like "not I but the Father," and God exalted him to be Wonderful, Counselor, and Prince of Peace, thereby making Him our mediator, that one man Jesus Emmanuel.

1 Tim 2:1-6 – "I exhort therefore, that, first of all, supplications, prayers, intercessions, and giving of thanks, be made for all men. For kings, and for all that are in authority; that we may lead a quiet and peaceable life, in all godliness and honesty; For this is good and acceptable in the sight of God our Saviour. Who will have all men to be saved, and to come unto the knowledge of the truth. For there is one God, and one mediator between God and men, the man Christ Jesus—Emmanuel—Who gave himself a ransom for all, to be testified in due time."

Therefore, understanding this lets us know that Jesus Emmanuel is not the Mighty God or Everlasting Father, which is also true because he is flesh. Please listen closely to what Jesus Emmanuel said in John 8:38-42: "I speak that which I have seen with my Father—the Word was with God—and ye do that which ye have seen with your father. They answered and said unto him, Abraham is our father. Jesus saith unto them, 'If ye were Abraham's children, ye would do the works of Abraham. But now ye seek to kill me, a man that hath told you the truth—the Word of God—which

121

I have heard of God: this did not Abraham. Ye do the deeds of your father. Then said they to him, We be not born of fornication; we have one Father, even God.' Jesus—The Spirit-produced Son—remember although they were One while on earth, They were Two—Spirit and flesh—said unto them, 'If God were your Father, ye would love me: for I—the Word—proceeded forth and came from God; neither came I of myself, but he sent me.'" Matt 4:4 states, "But he answered and said, 'It is written, Man shall not live by bread alone, but by every word that proceedeth out of the mouth of God.' Also, see Deuteronomy 8:3.

See, it is God's Word, His Spirit-produced Son—the Lord our God—that is in God's begotten son, Jesus Emmanuel our Lord, that taught him what God wanted him to say. John 8:26-32 confirms this: "I have many things to say and to judge of you: but he that sent me is true; and I speak to the world those things which I have heard of him. They understood not that he spake to them of the Father. Then said Jesus unto them, When ye have lifted up the Son of man—Jesus Emmanuel—then shall ye know that I am he— the begotten son—and that I do nothing of myself; but as my Father hath taught me—using His Spirit-produced Son—I, speak these things—the Word of God. And he that sent me is with me: the Father hath not left me alone; for I do always those things that please him. As he spake these words, many believed on him. Then said Jesus to those Jews which believed on him, If ye continue in my word—God's Spirit-produced Son—then are ye my disciples indeed; And ye shall know the truth—God's Word of Wisdom—and the truth— God's Word of Wisdom—shall make you free."

That truth, that freedom, comes from God's Word, which is Truth, the Word of Truth. James 1:17-18 reads, "Every good gift and every perfect gift is from above, and cometh down from the Father of lights, with whom is no variableness, neither shadow of turning. Of his own will begat he us with the word of truth, that we should be a kind of firstfruits of his creatures."

Now to eat of this bread, we need to understand the

spiritual body and the natural body. The spiritual body is the Lord God, the Father's Word of life, the Lord Jesus Christ our God, and the Word, Truth, Wisdom, Understanding, Knowledge, and Power—the Spirit of Life. The natural body is Christ Jesus Emmanuel our Lord, the body and soul of the Spirit of Life, which is the Father's Word of life. Being the body and soul of God's Spirit of Life—the Word of Life— means that He is our risen Lord and Christ. Acts 2:36 tells us this: "Therefore let all the house of Israel know assuredly, that God hath made that same Jesus, whom ye have crucified, both Lord and Christ. Moreover, us—all believers—we are members of that body, which is how we are in Christ Jesus Emmanuel through our faith in God's Word. He—the man— is our risen Lord and Christ, the mediator between God and man, because He is the soul of God the Father's spiritual Son, His Word, the Spirit of Life and we are the body. We also will serve him, because the body always serves the soul—or head—in God's sight. Moreover, the same is true of us; our bodies serve our souls—or head—and it is the soul that lives or dies. We know that the body—the flesh—returns to the earth from which it came and the spirit goes back to God from whom it came, but the living soul—that the Spirit of Life—breathed in between the two. He is what the battle is for; we either live an eternal, holy life or an eternal, damned life.

Now, the importance of the soul is this: the spirit of man—the spirit-filled creature that the waters brought forth—that was formed within the body—of the dust of the ground—was given an identity when the Lord God—the Spirit of Life—breathed in the breath of life, the soul. Our soul is who we are, because afterward man—the spirit-filled creature—became that living soul: "And the LORD God formed man—the spirit-filled creature—of the dust of the ground—our natural body—and breathed into his nostrils— in between the two—the breath of life—our souls—and man—the spirit-filled creature—became a living soul"—Gen 2:7.

Now, because of Adam and Eve's disobedience, the

123

life lived on earth by that living soul, the person who we become while on earth before we are put into a deep sleep—dead—be it holy or evil, is that soul's identity. That soul, is needed in the eternal life; it is needed for the spirit that went back to God to give us our identity in Heaven that we had on earth as the children of God. That living soul is a part of our new bodies, be it unto eternal life or unto eternal damnation. This is how we are going to know or recognize each other afterward; this is also how we are going to know who in our lives did or did not make to Heaven. We will know because that spirit that went back to God from them—the sinners—when they died will stay with God and their souls will face eternal torment in the lake of fire.

Please understand, the battle to keep the soul free, or to keep it captive, requires our participation. That free will of man is to choose to serve God or Satan. Satan is sending his word, his own son—which are his thoughts and suggestions—to keep us enslaved to sin and then to death. Therefore, God, being more powerful, is sending His Word, His own Son—the Word of Life which comes with His Wisdom, Understanding, and Power—His Spirit of Life—to empower us unto life everlasting. So understanding God's Word—His Spirit-produced Son—that proceeded from Him and His begotten son, born of woman as the body and soul of God's Spirit-produced Son—is a must. It is as 1 Cor 15:44 tells us: "It is sown a natural body; it is raised a spiritual body. There is a natural body, and there is a spiritual body."

Thus, we know that God gave His Spirit-produced Son who came in the flesh from the stem of Jesse, the name Jesus Christ before He came within that flesh.

1 John 4:2-3 – "Hereby know ye the Spirit of God: Every spirit that confesseth that Jesus Christ—God's Spirit-produced Son—is come in the flesh is of God. And every spirit that confesseth not that Jesus Christ is come in the flesh is not of God: and this is that spirit of antichrist, whereof ye have heard that it should come; and even now already is it in the world."

2 John 1:7 – "For many deceivers are entered into the

world, who confess not that Jesus Christ—God's Spirit-produced Son—is come in the flesh. This is a deceiver and an antichrist. And we know God gave His Begotten Son the name Jesus Emmanuel—God is with us and him."

Matt 1:21-23 – "And she shall bring forth a son, and thou shalt call his name JESUS: for he shall save his people from their sins. Now all this was done, that it might be fulfilled which was spoken of the Lord by the prophet, saying. Behold, a virgin shall be with child, and shall bring forth a son, and they shall call his name Emmanuel, which being interpreted is, God with us."

CHAPTER 11

Oh the Names of Him Who Swallow Up Death

Oh the names, the names, the names, One is the Lord Jesus Christ our God and the other Christ Jesus Emmanuel our Risen Christ Lord— The Two that were One while on earth, but yet were Two, and They are Two in Heaven, but yet They are One as We are One with Them. Now, for the meat we are about to eat, we need to chew it slowly so that the digestion of it will be food for our souls in the sight of God. Although there are two names that represent the spiritual and natural bodies of God's Word, Wisdom, Understanding, Power, and Truth, the Two were One while on earth and yet are Two. However, while Jesus Christ was on earth there was only one physical person: Jesus Emmanuel. Jesus Emmanuel, while on earth, was not called "Jesus Christ" or "Christ Jesus." No, he was just called "Jesus," "Jesus of Nazareth," "the Nazarene," "Jesus the carpenter's son," or "Jesus the son of David." See John 1:45; Ch. 18:5 & 7; Ch 19:19; Acts 2:22. Even after Jesus asked Peter "who say ye I am?" and Peter said "the Christ of God"—Luke 9:20—Jesus was still not called "Jesus Christ." In fact, He charged his disciples to tell no one He was the Christ: "Then charged he his disciples that they should tell no man that he was Jesus the Christ"—Matt 16:20.

Therefore, the writers of the New Testament called Jesus Emmanuel "Christ" when they wrote their books because they knew He, having the Word of God within him, was the Christ of God. Matt 1:16 reads, "And Jacob begat Joseph the husband of Mary, of whom was born Jesus, who is called Christ." Jesus Emmanuel while on earth was not the

Christ but had the Christ—God's Word and Wisdom—living within him, and after he—the natural body—had suffered the cross, God made him perfect when He made him both Lord and Christ. See Acts 2:36. Now, this was done after the suffering of the cross: "Saying with a loud voice, Worthy is the Lamb that was slain to receive—that was slain to receive—power, and riches, and Wisdom, and strength, and honour, and glory, and blessing"—Rev 5:12. And that suffering was for him, as the Lamb of God, to taste death for every man Heb 2:9-10 states, "But we see Jesus, who was made a little lower than the angels for the suffering of death, crowned with glory and honour—God's Word and Wisdom—that he by the grace of God should taste death for every man.—Remember, God told the Lord God, His Spirit-produced Son, to sit on his right hand until He made the Lord God's enemies his footstool. Now Jesus Emmanuel was begotten of God for that purpose—to put sin and death under the Lord God. Moreover, the way Jesus Emmanuel did this was with the Spirit of Life, God's Word and Wisdom, within leading him as the Lamb of God for the suffering of death.

Therefore, after Jesus Emmanuel had suffered death sin was condemned in the flesh, and the Lord God, God's Word of Wisdom entered into the lower parts of earth for a second time to quicken or bring back to life Jesus Emmanuel and then after the Lord God had raised death to life He thereby swallowed up death as He became death. For it—death—became him—the Lord God—for whom are all things, and by whom are all things, in bringing many sons unto glory, to make the captain—Jesus Emmanuel—of their salvation perfect through sufferings." Jesus Emmanuel, our example as the author and finisher of our faith, is the captain of our salvation by the suffering we go through while holding on to our faith. He is not our salvation Himself; our Salvation is God the Father: "He that is our God is the God of salvation—God of salvation, not captain of—and unto God the Lord belong the issues from death"—Ps 68:20. The issue from death belongs to the Lord God, because Isaiah 25:8-9 tells us, "He—the Lord God—will swallow up death—

swallow up death—in victory. And the Lord GOD will wipe away tears from off all faces; and the rebuke of his people shall he take away from off all the earth: for the LORD—the Father—hath spoken it." And it shall be said in that day, Lo, this *is* our God; we have waited for him, and he will save us: this *is* the LORD; we have waited for him, we will be glad and rejoice in his salvation. This was done when Jesus Emmanuel went from mortal to immortal—the rising after the suffering of the cross. 1 Cor 15:54-55 reads, "So when this corruptible have put on incorruption, and this mortal shall have put on immortality, then shall be brought to pass the saying that is written, Death is swallowed up in victory. O death, where is thy sting? O grave, where is thy victory?" Most importantly, the victory in Jesus Emmanuel that helped the Lord God swallowed up—or overcome—death was his faith in the Word of God that abided within Him before the cross. We see this in 1 John 5:3-4: "For this is the love of God, that we keep his commandments: and his commandments are not grievous. For whatsoever is born of God, overcometh the world, and this is the victory that overcometh the world, even our faith." It is our faith that overcomes, and our faith that overcomes comes from God's Word according to Rom 10:17: "So then faith cometh by hearing, and hearing by the word of God."

Please understand, having the Word and believing in the Word requires our actions. He—Jesus Emmanuel—and we must be doers of—or live—the Word of God. James 1:22-25 tells us, "But be ye doers of the word, and not hearers only, deceiving your own selves. For if any be a hearer of the word, and not a doer, he is like unto a man beholding his natural face in a glass, For he beholdeth himself, and goeth his way, and straightway forgetteth what manner of man he was. But whoso looketh into the perfect law of liberty—the law of the Spirit of Life—and continueth therein, he being not a forgetful hearer, but a doer of the work, this man shall be blessed in his deed." Being a doer of the Word—living Him—is to be led by the Spirit of God: "For if ye live after the flesh, ye shall die: but if ye through the Spirit do mortify the deeds of the body, ye shall live. For as many as are led by the Spirit of God, they are the sons of God"—Rom 8:13-14. The same is true of Jesus Emmanuel, who was led by the Spirit of God unto death, that he might have life everlasting. Luke 22:42-44 reads, "Saying, Father, if thou be willing, remove this cup from me: nevertheless not my will, but thine, be done. And there appeared an angel unto him from heaven, strengthening him—or leading him, or encouraging him. And being in an agony he prayed more earnestly: and his sweat was as it were great drops of blood falling down to the ground."

Question, if Jesus Emmanuel was God or in a Godhead with God, why did he need God's angels to strengthen him or lead him, or encourage him to face the cross? Also, if he was God or in a Godhead with God, why did he ask God to remove his cup? Didn't he know, if he was the Word, supposedly in a Godhead with God, that God the Father had already given the Word—supposedly him—power to lay down his life and power to pick it up again? If he was the Word, he would have never doubted or questioned God's Word by asking God to remove his cup from him after God had already told him he would die and be raised again in three days, right?

These scriptures also proves that Jesus Emmanuel is not God nor in a Godhead with God, because he has his own will separate from God's will as he stated: "Father, if thou be willing, remove this cup from me: nevertheless not my will, but thine—or thy will—be done." Think, two different wills means two different thinking heads, Right?

Therefore, Jesus Emmanuel's willingness to die through faith as the Word of God led him, made death to become now the Word of God's, our Lord God's. Heb 2:10 says, "For it—death—became—not it was, but became, like 'the Word became flesh—him—the Lord God—for whom are all things, and by whom are all things, in bringing many sons unto glory, to make the captain—Jesus Emmanuel—of their salvation perfect through sufferings." Some one, please tell me, how do you get "for it was fitting that he" from "for it became Him"? You cannot! This is as simple as it gets! However, as I told you earlier, there is a conspiracy against God's Word, Wisdom, Understanding, and Knowledge to hide the truth and ultimate truth about the Trinity. Here is what God the Father says about His Spirit-produced Son's becoming death in Hebrews 2:9-10: "But we see Jesus—Emmanuel, with God's Word within him—who was made a little lower than the angels for the suffering of death, crowned with glory and honour; that he by the grace of God should taste death for every man. For it—death—became him—the Word within Jesus Emmanuel who made all things—for whom—are—all things, and by whom [are] all things, in bringing many sons unto glory—faith come by hearing and hearing by the Word—to make the captain—Jesus Emmanuel—of their—our—salvation perfect through sufferings—through sufferings." Now, look at how these so-called Bibles have changed God's Word in Hebrews 2:10:

Take a Look!

New International Version (©1984)
In bringing many sons to glory, it was fitting that God, for whom and through whom everything exists, should make the author of their salvation perfect through suffering.

Revised Standard Version
For it was fitting that he, for whom and by whom all things exist, in bringing many sons to glory, should make the pioneer of their salvation perfect through suffering.

New Living Translation (©2007)
God, for whom and through whom everything was made, chose to bring many children into glory. And it was only right that he should make Jesus, through his suffering, a perfect leader, fit to bring them into their salvation.

The Living Bible
And it was right and proper that God, who made everything for his own glory, should allow Jesus to suffer, for in doing this he was bringing vast multitudes of God's people to heaven; for his suffering made Jesus a perfect Leader, one fit to bring them into their salvation.

English Standard Version (©2001)
God, for whom and by whom all things exist, in bringing many sons to glory, should make the founder of their salvation perfect through suffering.

New American Standard Bible (©1995)
For it was fitting for Him, for whom are all things, and through whom are all things, in bringing many sons to glory, to perfect the author of their salvation through sufferings.

International Standard Version (©2008)
It was fitting that God, for whom and through whom everything exists, should make the pioneer of their salvation perfect through suffering as part of his plan to glorify many children,

GOD'S WORD® Translation (©1995)
God is the one for whom and through whom everything exists. Therefore, while God was bringing many sons and daughters to glory, it was the right time to bring Jesus, the source of their salvation, to the end of his work through suffering.

King James Bible
For it became him, for whom [are] all things, and by whom [are] all things, in bringing many sons unto glory, to make the captain of their salvation perfect through sufferings.

American King James Version
For it became him, for whom are all things, and by whom are

all things, in bringing many sons to glory, to make the captain of their salvation perfect through sufferings.

Bible in Basic English
Because it was right for him, for whom and through whom all things have being, in guiding his sons to glory, to make the captain of their salvation complete through pain.

Douay-Rheims Bible
For it became him, for whom are all things, and by whom are all things, who had brought many children into glory, to perfect the author of their salvation, by his passion.

Weymouth New Testament
For it was fitting that He for whom, and through whom, all things exist, after He had brought many sons to glory, should perfect by suffering the Prince Leader who had saved them.

Young's Literal Translation
For it was becoming to Him, because of whom are the all things, and through whom are the all things, many sons to glory bringing, the author of their salvation through sufferings to make perfect.

Jubilee Bible 2000
For it was expedient that he, for whom are all things and by whom are all things, preparing to bring forth many sons in his glory, should perfect the author of their saving health through sufferings.

New American Standard 1977
For it was fitting for Him, for whom are all things, and through whom are all things, in bringing many sons to glory, to perfect the author of their salvation through sufferings.

Aramaic Bible in Plain English
For it was fitting for him by whom are all things and for whom are all things, and bringing many children into the

glory, that The Prince of their life would perfect himself by his suffering.

NET Bible
For it was fitting for him, for whom and through whom all things exist, in bringing many sons to glory, to make the pioneer of their salvation perfect through sufferings.

Holman Christian Standard Bible
For in bringing many sons to glory, it was entirely appropriate that God--all things exist for Him and through Him--should make the source of their salvation perfect through sufferings.

New American Standard Bible
For it was fitting for Him, for whom are all things, and through whom are all things, in bringing many sons to glory, to perfect the author of their salvation through sufferings.

Berean Study Bible
In bringing many sons to glory, it was fitting for God, for whom and through whom all things exist, to make the pioneer of their salvation perfect through suffering.

Berean Literal Bible
For it was fitting to Him, for whom *are* all things and by whom *are* all things, having brought many sons to glory, to make perfect the author of their salvation through sufferings.

Notice that not one of these Bibles in black says anything about death becoming Him, "God's Spirit-produced Son—the Word—him who made all things. Therefore, because Jesus Emmanuel allowed the Lord God, the Word of life within him, to lead him to suffer death, he then afterward received his own power and riches, and Wisdom, and strength, and honour, and glory, and blessing. Rev 5:12 tells us this: "Saying with a loud voice, Worthy is the Lamb that was slain to receive power, and riches, and Wisdom, and strength, and honour, and glory, and blessing." Therefore, for this cause He was called Christ when his disciples wrote their books: "And Jacob begat Joseph the husband of Mary, of whom was born Jesus, who is called—not was called but is called—Christ"—Matt 1:16. God's Male—Brain—and Female—His Wisdom/Mind—and their Word is the Us, the Father God Himself, within Jesus Emmanuel and ourselves. Question: Is there a conspiracy or just some honest mistakes made by these other Bibles?

CHAPTER 12

The Us – God Himself is With Us

Here is food for your thought. Please chew this and the rest of this meat slowly! Because God sent his Son, the Lord Jesus Christ our God and Christ Jesus Emmanuel our Lord, into Mary to save us from sin and death, we are to show gratitude and awe every time we say "Lord Jesus Christ our God." How you ask? Well, the Lord is God's Word, Jesus is "gee, us," and Christ is the Wisdom and power of God, and our God is a form of God the Father Himself—the Word—which means when we say "Lord Jesus Christ our God," we are saying Lord Jesus Christ, God's Word, Gee, us, the Wisdom of God and power of God, Our God, a form of God the Father Himself sent to save us. Chew Slowly! For these Spirits are divided Spirits sent from God, the Holy Spirit, God the Father Himself. In addition, because Emmanuel is interpreted as "God with us," when we say "Christ Jesus Emmanuel our Lord," we are saying. Christ Jesus Emmanuel, the Wisdom and power of God, gee, Us, God, with us, our Lord, God's Word within a form of God the Father himself sent to save us.

Now to say this all together is to say, God's Word, gee, us, the Wisdom and power of God, is a form of God the Father Himself sent to save us from sin and death. The Wisdom and power of God, gee, "Us, God," with us, God's Word within, is a form of God the Father himself sent to save us. For these Spirits are divided Spirits sent from God, the Holy Spirit, God the Father Himself. God's Word within us is a form of God the Father himself sent to save us. The Wisdom and Power of God, gee us, God with us, Us, God Himself is with us. Remember The "Us" in Genesis 1:26:

"And God said, Let us make man in our image, after our likeness" Also see Genesis 3:22, ch 11:7; Isaiah 6:8. The "Us" is God the Father Himself. Genesis 1:27 reads, "So God created man in his own image, in the image of God created he—God—him—Man—male and female created he—God—them—the spiritual male, brain and female, mind, the man.

Here! In all these scriptures it's God—His Male and Female—using their Son, the Lord God—His Word of life—thinking aloud or God allowing Moses to see His thought process or to hear Him think. In each of these scriptures, when God uses "our image, after our likeness or Us," He always has to make a decision. God, in the same way we function, made those decisions with His Brain—His Male—and His Mind—His Female/Wisdom—using His Word—His Spirit-produced Son—the Lord God, to go back and forth between the two in the process of that decision making. This is the Us, who is all Spirit, the Holy Spirit. Even though God's Word is divided from Himself, He is still with His Word, and the same is true of His Wisdom. God's Wisdom is always with His Word, which is with Him, God Himself, the Us, the Holy Spirit, that one Spirit. In this thought process, God shows us how He—and how we should too—respect the Power of His/our Word and Wisdom. God's Word and ours is His/our Power, and that Power comes from the Wisdom of God, and the Wisdom of God comes from God's/our spiritual Mind—the Female. This Word, Wisdom, and Power of God's is released or put into action by God's/our Brain—the Male—through His own dividing Spirit—His Holy Spirit, His body.

You see, our word is our power within us, because if we have no words, we have no thoughts. If we have no thoughts, we have no actions. If we have no actions, we have no life. Moreover, if we have no life, we have no power. Therefore, our words within us are what we live by, be it spiritual or carnal. So what word do you live by? So a man thinketh so is He! Prov 23:6-8 tells us, "Eat thou not the bread of him that hath an evil eye, neither desire thou his dainty meats: For as he thinketh in his heart, so is he: Eat and

138

drink, saith he to thee; but his heart is not with thee. The morsel which thou hast eaten shalt thou vomit up, and lose thy sweet words." Therefore, we should respect our Word and the Wisdom given to our Word. Prov 15:1-33 reads, "A soft answer turneth away wrath: but grievous words stir up anger. The tongue of the wise useth knowledge aright: but the mouth of fools poureth out foolishness. The eyes of the LORD are in every place, beholding the evil and the good. A wholesome tongue is a tree of life: but perverseness therein is a breach in the spirit. A fool despiseth his father's instruction: but he that regardeth reproof is prudent. In the house of the righteous is much treasure: but in the revenues of the wicked is trouble. The lips of the wise disperse knowledge: but the heart of the foolish doeth not so. The sacrifice of the wicked is an abomination to the LORD: but the prayer of the upright is his delight. The way of the wicked is an abomination unto the LORD: but he loveth him that followeth after righteousness—faith in God's Word and Wisdom. Correction is grievous unto him that forsaketh the way: and he that hateth reproof shall die. Hell and destruction are before the LORD: how much more then the hearts of the children of men? A scorner loveth not one that reproveth him: neither will he go unto the wise. A merry heart maketh a cheerful countenance: but by sorrow of the heart the spirit is broken. The heart of him that hath understanding seeketh knowledge: but the mouth of fools feedeth on foolishness. All the days of the afflicted are evil: but he that is of a merry heart hath a continual feast. Better is little with the fear of the LORD than great treasure and trouble therewith. Better is a dinner of herbs where love is, than a stalled ox and hatred therewith. A wrathful man stirreth up strife: but he that is slow to anger appeaseth strife. The way of the slothful man is as an hedge of thorns: but the way of the righteous is made plain. A wise son maketh a glad father: but a foolish man despiseth his mother. Folly is joy to him that is destitute of Wisdom: but a man of understanding walketh uprightly. Without counsel purposes are disappointed: but in the multitude of counsellers they are established. A man hath joy by the answer of his mouth: and a word spoken in due season, how good is it! The way of life is above to the wise, that he may depart from hell beneath. The LORD will destroy the house of the proud: but he will establish the border of the widow. The thoughts of the wicked are an abomination to the LORD: but the words of the pure are pleasant words. He that is greedy of gain troubleth his own house; but he that hateth gifts shall live. The heart of the righteous studieth to answer: but the mouth of the wicked poureth out evil things. The LORD is far from the wicked: but he heareth the prayer of the righteous. The light of the eyes rejoiceth the heart: and a good report maketh the bones fat. The ear that heareth the reproof of life abideth among the wise. He that refuseth instruction despiseth his own soul: but he that heareth reproof getteth understanding. The fear of the LORD is the instruction of Wisdom; and before honour is humility."

Understand now how important it is for us to respect our Word and Wisdom when we put them into action by using our brain. Our thought processor, just like God's, gives us the power to speak life or death—within ourselves—as well as others—our children, for example—according to Prov 18:21: "Death and life are in the power of the tongue: and they that love it shall eat the fruit thereof." Here, look at how powerful God's Word—His Son—is and why He respects Him: "For the word of God is quick, and powerful, and sharper than any twoedged sword, piercing even to the dividing asunder of soul and spirit, and of the joints and marrow, and is a discerner of the thoughts and intents of the heart. Neither is there any creature that is not manifest in his sight: but all things are naked and opened unto the eyes of him with whom we have to do"—Heb 4:12-13. Also look at the power of and the respect God has for His Wisdom—His Female: "All the words of my mouth are in righteousness; there is nothing froward or perverse in them. They are all plain to him that understandeth, and right to them that find knowledge. Receive my instruction, and not silver; and knowledge rather than choice gold. For Wisdom is better than rubies; and all the things that may be desired are not to be compared to it. I Wisdom dwell with prudence, and find out knowledge of witty inventions—just like a mind—God's Mind. The fear of the LORD is to hate evil: pride, and arrogancy, and the evil way, and the froward mouth, do I hate. Counsel is mine, and sound Wisdom—Please know there is sound Wisdom, God's Word, and there is foolish Wisdom, Satan's word—I—Wisdom—am understanding; I have strength—just like a mind—God's Mind. By me kings reign, and princes decree justice. By me princes rule, and nobles, even all the judges of the earth. I love them that love me—It's important to understand that Wisdom loves us just like God and their Son loves us, which means God's Female, Wisdom, is not God's character but helps develop or make up God's character of Love, etc—and those that seek me— Wisdom—early shall find me. Riches and honour are with me; yea, durable riches and righteousness. My fruit is better than gold, yea, than fine gold; and my revenue than choice silver. I lead in the way of righteousness, in the midst of the paths of judgment: That I may cause those that love me to inherit substance; and I will fill their treasures. — Please get this, if we love God's Wisdom and seek Her, She will cause us to inherit substance, and She will fill our treasures. — The LORD possessed me—Wisdom—in the beginning of his way, before his works of old. I—Wisdom—was set up from everlasting, from the beginning, or ever the earth was"—Prov 8:8-23.

Understand now the power of God's Wisdom— Female—and their Word—Son—and the respect God has for them? Both Spirits—God's Word, His Spirit-produced Son, and God's Wisdom, which is His Understanding, Knowledge, and Power, His Female—come from God, and God divided them with us through who He is, the Holy Spirit—that one Spirit who is the Father of all spirits that gives us life. All of these Spirits are God Himself—the one God and Father of all spirits. Heb 12:9b says, "shall we not much rather be in subjection unto the Father of spirits, and live?" You see, there is "one God and Father of all, who is above all, and through all, and in you all"—Eph 4:6.

Therefore, it is Almighty God the Holy Spirit, the Father of all, God, the Us Himself, which is within us all—Christ Jesus Emmanuel included! Acts 10:38 reads, "How God anointed Jesus of Nazareth with the Holy Ghost and with power: who went about doing good, and healing all that were oppressed of the devil; for God was with him."

Question: If God was within Jesus Emmanuel as He is within us, how then could Jesus Emmanuel be in the Godhead with God without us if God is within us all? Also, if Jesus of Nazareth was God or in a Godhead with God, why did God need to anoint him with the Holy Ghost/Spirit and with power? In other words, if Jesus is God, why did God need to anoint Himself with Himself?

Now, some are using these four scriptures—Gen. 1:26a-27, Ch. 3:22, Ch. 11:7; Isa. 6:8—about the Us—or "in Our image—in their teachings to say that God did not create the world alone. We have been taught that the Godhead of three persons—the Father, Son, and Holy Spirit—without Wisdom as a part of them—the Godhead—created the world. Well, again, as we learned in the earlier chapters, that is not true. My people, so that we can all understand from this day forward, the truth and ultimate truth about the Trinity from these scriptures—as for God's real head—we need to look a little closer at each one of these scriptures.

We will start first with Gen 1:26a and then go through the others. Gen 1:26a reads, "And God said, Let us make MAN in our image, after our likeness: and let THEM." Notice that here God said MAN—one—and let THEM— more than one, the MALE and FEMALE. Now, when God said "let Us" in Our image" and "after Our likeness," He was making a decision as to how He should create man. It was His Brain—the Male—deciding by discussing it over with His Mind—the Female—and the way they discussed it was by using His Word—their Spirit-produced Son—who communicated back and forth between the two as to what each thought would be the best for man. This is God using— or putting into action—these three—His Male, Female, and Son—through the fourth—His Holy Spirit or body—which is

142

who He is—the Holy Spirit, Himself—to develop or bring into existence the decisions made by the three—the Brain—Male—the Mind—the Female—and the Word—the Spirit-produced Son. This means that these three within God's head are God—that God's head is being put into action by God, the Father of spirits—one God—using His body and His Spirits within Himself. When Moses wrote Genesis 1:27, he made it clear that the Us—the four who made the decision—are one God. Gen 1:27 states, "So God created—God, one God, the Us created—man in his own—His own, and not their own, as to the Trinity—image, in the image of God—in the image of God—single—created he—God—single—him—Adam—single—male and female created he—God—single—them—the male and female—plural.

Question, if God's image is male and female, as He has just stated, how then can He be a triune God?

Okay, so God created man in His own image. Understand, your image to God is not what you look like, because that is the external—the formed body from the dust, that which when we die goes back to the ground from which it came. The spiritual image of God that we are made in is the male and female. Together they have the ability to produce Word, and by their Word this image of God was formed within us as a spirit man. Zech 12:1 reads, "The burden of the word of the LORD for Israel, saith the LORD, which stretcheth forth the heavens, and layeth the foundation of the earth, and formeth the spirit of man within him." In addition, our brain, word, and spiritual mind, are spirit. We know this because of Eph 4:22-24: "That ye put off concerning the former conversation the old man, which is corrupt according to the deceitful lusts; And be renewed in the spirit of your mind; And that ye put on the new man, which after God is created in righteousness—God's Word and Wisdom—God's and our Spiritual Mind—and true holiness—the Spirit of Truth—our conscience."

You see, we are what we speak and live, and if we are what we speak and live, then what we speak and live is our image to God and too human. Therefore, who we are on the

143

inside is how God sees us, and that spiritual image of God within us is what God is looking for. Again, the image of God in us is not the color of our skin or hair, the shade of our eyes, or our weight and height. The image of God in us was created before our physical bodies were formed—when He—God—created him—man—male and female created he—God—them—the Spirit-filled man—the Spiritual Male, Brain—and Female—Mind—so that they could produce a Son, the Word. Again, Gen 1:27 reads, "So God created man in his own image, in the image of God created he him; male and female created he them." See, when God was thinking about who to give dominion over the things He made this time, so He said "I will make man in my own image—like Me, with a spiritual male—brain—and a female—mind—and by connecting the two they will have the ability to produced word. And I will bless them to be fruitful with their Son--word—and multiply them—the spiritual male, the brain and a female, the mind—in words with understanding and knowledge, and they shall replenish the earth with My understanding and knowledge that I will give from My Wisdom, that they may subdue the earth with the strength in My Word, the power that comes from My Wisdom, "that man—with My Power within him as my people—shall be able to communicate with Me and Me with them, that I may be worshiped in the understanding of My Spirit and in the knowledge of My Truth.

Understand, this is not the male and female, Adam and Eve; no, it is just Adam with a spiritual brain and a mind that can produce a word, the likeness of God and the image of God himself. Here is our proof again that God is male and female and Adam is made in God's image, male and female: "This is the book of the generations of Adam. In the day that God created man, in the likeness of God made he—God—him—Adam—Male and female created he—God—them—Adam—and blessed them—Adam's male, son, and female—and called their—the male and female—name Adam, in the day when they—Adam's brain, word, and mind—were created"—Gen 5:1-2.

Therefore, if the Trinity is three persons in a Godhead—Father, Son, and Holy Spirit—then where is God's Female, Wisdom, because Gen 1:27 says, "God created man in his own image," which is Male and Female that produced a Son, meaning that these three—God's Brain—Male—Word—Son—and Mind—Female, Wisdom—are in God's head and that God's head is in the fourth—Himself, His body, His Holy Spirit, the "Us."

CHAPTER 13

The Us, the Difference Between Caveman & Ourselves

We will soon get back to the remaining four scriptures about the Us, God Himself. First, I need to give you more substantial meat about how important the Us is within us. In doing so we will learn that God did create a world before he created this present world. Now, I am not talking about the world before the flood of Noah. No, I am talking about the prehistoric world—the world in which there were dinosaurs and cavemen, the world that most scientists use to say that man evolved. Moreover, that is because the Bible (KJV) does not say anything about God's creation of dinosaurs or prehistoric man. Thus, scientists say we were not created, and to some that means there is no God. However, yes, God created more than one world, and God does exist. Heb 1:2 reads, "Hath in these last days spoken unto us by his Son, whom he hath appointed heir of all things, by whom also he made the worlds." Notice, it did not say "world, but worlds." In addition, more can be found in Heb 11:3: "Through faith we understand that the worlds—worlds and not third world countries—were framed by the word of God, so that things which are seen were not made of things which do appear."

Hear! Many so-called Bibles have changed the word "worlds" to "world" or "universe" in these two scriptures. Now, don't let anyone try and tell you that the word "worlds" here is talking about this world and the new world to come, because in Heb. 1:2, it says, "He made the worlds"—past tense. This is the case with Heb. 11:3—"worlds were framed," again past tense. Nor let them tell you that these two scriptures are talking about other countries—i.e. third world countries—because there are many different nations and countries but only one present world or earth. The bible tells us this present world or earth is at this time only one. Please, for one world look at these scriptures: Jer. 10:12; John 1:9-10; ch. 17:5, 16-18, 24-25; Rom. 1:20; ch. 4:13; Eph. 3:9; Heb. 11:38; and 2 peter 3:5-7. For one earth look at Gen. 1:1; Ps. 33:6; Isa. 45:12 & 18; and Acts 14:15; ch. 17:24.

Well, please chew this meat slowly! Hear! Notice in Gen. 1:28 that the verse after God had already created man, male and female, in His own image, God said unto them—Adam—be fruitful and multiply, and replenish the earth and subdue it." Chew slowly! If there was only Adam, the male and female, how can he alone be fruitful and multiply and replenish the earth—have children? The first proof that the woman was not yet made and that he was alone at this point is found in Gen 2:18: "And the LORD God said, It is not good that the man should be alone; I will make him an help meet for him." Well, being the only live soul, we know he could not. He could not, because the Lord God did not create woman until long after He had formed all the other creatures from the dust of the ground and after He had warned Adam of the trees in the garden. Gen 2:21-23 reads, "And the LORD God caused a deep sleep to fall upon Adam and he slept: and he took one of his ribs, and closed up the flesh instead thereof. And the rib, which the LORD God had taken from man, made he a woman—made, not created, but made from Adam's rib bone, long after Adam was created. Yes, when you make something you also create it, but you make it from something that had already been created—and brought her unto the man. And Adam said, This is now bone of my bones, and flesh of my flesh: She shall be called Woman, because she was taken out of Man."

Question: If Eve, the woman was the female created in Adam when God created him in His image male and female, "why did Adam say, "this is now bone of my bones, and flesh of my flesh: She shall be called Woman, because

148

she was taken out of Man?" Instead of saying—this is the female of my body that was created when God created me male and female?

Here, I will tell you why, "because woman—Eve—was not created in the image and glory of God," but in the glory—image—of the man, Adam. For a man indeed ought not to cover *his* head, forasmuch as he is the image and glory of God: but the woman is the glory of the man. For the man is not of the woman; but the woman of the man. Neither was the man created for the woman; but the woman for the man.—1 Corinthians 11:7-9 Got it? God created Eve the woman after He had created Adam's male and female—or brain and spiritual mind—within him. It was only Adam created male and female, and the female as we can now clearly see was not Eve the woman.

Therefore—if the woman was not yet made—what was God saying to Adam, being male and female—one—if not to be fruitful, multiply, and replenish with woman? Well, it was with His ability to think, by using the thought process in His head—the Male—His Brain—and the Female—His Mind—that they together produced Adam's son—his word. And this is the thought process: to be fruitful with his Word, his produced Son, and multiply in words with God's Understanding and Knowledge and replenish the earth with God's Understanding and Knowledge, which He will give from His Wisdom, and subdue it with the strength in His Word—the power that comes from God's Wisdom that God will give him—Adam—through His Word, "Adam's Spiritual Mind." Now, understanding this will help us to understand the importance of our Us within ourselves. The Us within ourselves is important because without it, we would not be able to make words, and if we can't make words, we can't speak words, and thus, no fruitfulness, no multiplication, and no replenishing of God's Spiritual Mind through His Word that walked in the garden and talked with Adam. Please notice that the Lord God did not tell Adam to be fruitful and multiply, and replenish the earth until after He joined his spiritual mind to his natural mind by blowing in a soul's mind when man became a living soul.

Please get this, deaf people who can't hear or speak still hear their own words within their heads, and our proof of this is that fact they are able to think, which is the process of producing words—their fruitfulness, multiplication, and replenishing.

The Bible tells us we are a chosen people in 1 Peter 2:9-10: "But ye are a chosen generation, a royal priesthood, an holy nation, a peculiar people; that ye should shew forth the praises of him who hath called you out of darkness into his marvelous light. Which in time past were not a people, but are now the people of God: which had not obtained mercy, but now have obtained mercy." We are special because when God created us in His image—male and female. He equipped man will a connected spiritual brain and mind when the Us made man—Adam—in their image, and that gave man the ability to be created in God's likeness and produce word. Man ability to produce word with his spiritual brain, and mind, gave way to our natural mind to be able to produce word when the Lord God formed this spiritual brain, mind, word—the man, the spirit filled creature—within the natural man—our sinful natural mind—from the dust of the ground and connected the two with the blown in soul's mind, our soul, that man became a living soul. Moreover, this gave man—Adam—and us the ability to think and speak that which we have thought, be it good or be it evil. To be able to build upon thought after thought after thought gives us knowledge after knowledge after knowledge. He also blessed us to be fruitful with His Word and Wisdom and to multiply in our understanding from the Word and Wisdom within Him—to replenish the earth with the Knowledge that comes from His Word, Wisdom, and Understanding and to subdue the earth with the Power that comes from the Knowledge of His Word, Wisdom, and Understanding.

This world is ruled by knowledge, and we were

created in God's image so that we could grow in the Knowledge of God's Word and live. Acts 6:7 says, "And the word of God increased; and the number of the disciples multiplied in Jerusalem greatly; and a great company of the priests were obedient to the faith." Moreover, similar is Acts 19:20-"So mightily grew the word of God and prevailed" and Acts 12:24-"But the word of God grew and multiplied".

Hear! This is it in a nutshell in Col 1:5-11: "For the hope which is laid up for you in heaven, whereof ye heard before in the word of the truth of the Gospel—the Word of the Truth of the Gospel. Which is come unto you, as it—the Word of the Truth of the Gospel—is in all the world; and bringeth forth fruit, as it doth also in you, since the day ye heard of it—the Word of the Truth of the Gospel—and knew the grace of God in truth. As ye also learned of Epaphras our dear fellow servant, who is for you a faithful minister of Christ. Who also declared unto us your love in the spirit. For this cause we also, since the day we heard it the word of the truth of the gospel, do not cease to pray for you, and to desire that ye might be filled with the knowledge of his will in all wisdom and spiritual understanding. That ye might walk worthy of the Lord unto all pleasing, being fruitful in every good work, and increasing in the knowledge of God—the Word of the Truth of the Gospel. Strengthened with all might, according to his glorious power, unto all patience and longsuffering with joyfulness."

The Bible tells us men perish for lack of knowledge. Think, there are scientific facts, which were discovered in the DNA from the bones of Neanderthals, that prove that prehistoric caveman/Neanderthals died by the age of thirty years old. We were created to obtain and grow in knowledge and to use that knowledge and grow in the knowledge of God so that we could live abundantly, holy and forever with God. Our ability to obtain and grow in the Knowledge of God is so important to God. Hos 4:1 reads, "Hear the word of the LORD, ye children of Israel: for the LORD hath a controversy with the inhabitants of the land, because there is no truth, nor mercy, nor knowledge of God in the land." The result of no Word of Truth is no Knowledge of God, and that is the destruction of humanity. See the following scriptures:

Hos 4:6 – "My people are destroyed for lack of knowledge: because thou hast rejected knowledge, I will also reject thee, that thou shalt be no priest to me: seeing thou hast forgotten the law of thy God, I will also forget thy children."

Hos 6:5-6 – "Therefore have I hewed them by the prophets; I have slain them by the words of my mouth: and thy judgments are as the light that goeth forth. For I desired mercy, and not sacrifice; and the knowledge of God more than burnt offerings."

Prov 2:5-6 – "Then shalt thou understand the fear of the LORD, and find the knowledge of God—find the knowledge of God. For the LORD giveth Wisdom: out of his mouth cometh knowledge and understanding.—For the LORD's Knowledge and Understanding is His Wisdom that He gives us out of His mouth, and His Wisdom that cometh out of His mouth is His Word, and together they all are the Us within us."

Hear! God's Word gives us His Wisdom, and the Wisdom of His Word is to us, His Understanding that give us His Knowledge for us to live by that we may have eternal life with the Us within us. Therefore, we are not to depend on our own understanding or Wisdom but upon God's Wisdom in His Word—His Knowledge and His Understanding that give us His Counsel, His Might, His Power, which is His Fear. Prov 3:5-6 tells us, "Trust in the LORD with all thine heart; and lean not unto thine own understanding. In all thy ways acknowledge him, and he shall direct thy paths." Again, this is how, and the reason why, we were created in the image of God—male and female with the ability to produce son. Moreover, it is the same with Jesus Emmanuel; all that he accomplished he did by God's Word—Son—Wisdom—Female—Understanding, and Knowledge within him, who, all together within him are the Power of God—the Us, God Himself, within him and us too.

Now, proof that Jesus Emmanuel—the branch that grew from the root of the rod—David—that came out of the stem of Jesse—accomplished all that he accomplished with God's Word, Wisdom, Understanding, Knowledge, Counsel, Might, and Fear is this: "And there shall come forth a rod out of the stem of Jesse, and a Branch shall grow out of his roots. And the spirit of the LORD—the Word, the Spirit-produced Son—shall rest upon him—Jesus Emmanuel—the spirit of wisdom and understanding, the spirit of counsel and might, the spirit of knowledge and of the fear of the LORD. And shall make him—Jesus Emmanuel—of quick understanding in the fear of the LORD: and he—Jesus Emmanuel—shall not judge after the sight of his eyes, neither reprove after the hearing of his ears"—Isa 11:1-3. Okay, do we understand now that we were created like God—male and female with the ability to produce word—to grow in the Knowledge of God that comes from His Word, which accomplishes in us what God sent it to do—to give us eternal life through faith in that Word? We can, indeed, know this is true because God's Word always accomplishes that which He sends it to do. Isa 55:11 confirms this: "So shall my word be that goeth forth out of my mouth: it shall not return unto me void, but it shall accomplish that which I please, and it shall prosper in the thing whereto I sent it." Our spiritual us within ourselves is just as powerful, and important, within us, as it is within Jesus Emmanuel.

The importance of our us—the blessed male—our brain—the female—our spiritual minds that produce our son, our word—within ourselves and reason why we are a special chosen people is also proof that God created another world with dinosaurs and cavemen before He created this present world. It is proof because God did not create prehistoric man in his image. Yes, they had a male and female—brain and mind—but they wasn't connected and could not be fruitful in the likeness or image of God's because God has a connected spiritual blessed male and female that is fruitful, able to multiply and replenish itself and subdue everything by the power that came from that fruitfulness—His Word, His Spirit-produced Son, and this Power comes from God through God's Commanding Word. Nevertheless, when He

153

created caveman, He created him with a natural male—brain—and female—mind, their earthy wisdom—one that was not connected or blessed to be fruitful—produce word. And if not fruitful, it could not multiply; and if it could not multiply, it could not replenish; and because it could not replenish, it had no power to subdue anything except another weaker cavemen/woman. Therefore, God created man this second time—Adam—with a spiritual male and female—which took place in the waters above the heavens. Then God blessed them—Adam, the male and female—and said unto them, "Be fruitful—produce word—and multiply—in the Word of God's Knowledge—replenish the earth—with the Understanding from that Knowledge—and subdue it—with the Wisdom that comes from God's Word of Knowledge that you understand within the spirit of your mind. Listen, God said be fruitful—"be" meaning God had already equipped this man—Adam—with what he needed to be fruitful. However, caveman, on the other hand, had natural thoughts only—not thoughts in words but thoughts in pictures formed from what they had seen, thoughts that came by watching the violence in the land, which was evil continuously—to kill or be killed. He was not given common sense—a good sense and sound judgment in practical matters—all his way was natural, which meant the strongest, ate and conquered other weaker ones. So they had an evil world—kill or be killed—perpetuated both by other cavemen and all of the meat-eating dinosaurs, because God didn't give prehistoric man dominion. No, God gave dominion in that world to the animals.

Think of all the animals that God created then. They were huge—the size of three or four cavemen up to the size of an eighteen-wheeler truck. These huge animals made cave dwellers/cavemen their prey, and if they were prey themselves, how could they have dominion or subdue these huge giants? They could not; therefore, God gave dominion in that world to His huge animals. Additional proof that God created prehistoric man but did not create them in His own image is the known fact that they were unable to produce words or speak words. In addition, even more proof that God created them before this present world is the answer to this question "why did God plant the Tree of the Knowledge of Good and Evil?" Why did God plant a tree of good and evil, and, being that He is only good, where/when did God get to know evil? Well, I believe God got to know evil by watching and observing His first creations—caveman/prehistoric man's world—and after He had gotten to know evil, I believe He planted the Tree of the Knowledge of Good and Evil as a reminder of the evil of natural man.

You see, the Tree of the Knowledge of Good and Evil was a symbol to God of the two creations or worlds He had created: one naturally evil and the other which was supposed to be spiritually good only. However, evil was advanced within the natural man when Eve, who was manipulated by the serpent, ate of the tree of the Knowledge of Good and Evil, which brought upon us the battle that would take place within us. Rom 8:6-7 reads, "For to be carnally—naturally—minded is death; but to be spiritually minded is life and peace. Because the carnal—natural—mind is enmity against God—the spirit mind/man—for it is not subject to the law of God—God's Word, Wisdom, Understanding, Knowledge, and Power—neither indeed can be."

In addition, the Tree of Life was a symbol also to God that, for those of us who chose good over evil, good would be our reward which is the Tree of Life—or eternal life. Understand, when God created us, He did not create us to live forever in this present world. Proof of that is what the Lord God said in Gen. 3:22b, "and now, lest he put forth his hand, and take also of the tree of life, and eat, and live forever." Therefore, the first man—prehistoric/caveman—lived to be about thirty years or so, and the second man—Adam/us—was likewise not created to live forever but was created to produce between the two—male and female—unto God a holy people, which shall live forever with God. However, because the serpent, which lived in both worlds, advanced evil—the natural man—Adam and Eve realized they were naked and that sin from Adam to the coming of

Jesus weakened the law of the Spirit of Life, which was to do only good.

Read the following scriptures:

Rom 8:3 – "For what the law—the Ten Commandments—could not do, in that, it was weak through the flesh—the natural man—God sending his own Son—His Spirit-produced Son, His Word—in the likeness of sinful flesh—Jesus Emmanuel—and for sin, condemned sin in the flesh—Jesus Emmanuel/us."

John 1:14 – "And the Word—God's Spirit-produced Son—was made flesh—Jesus Emmanuel—and dwelt among us, (and we beheld his glory, the glory as of the only begotten of the Father,) full of grace and truth."

Please understand this: the Word was made flesh, but the flesh itself was not the Word. No, it is the reflection of the Word, the identity or image of the invisible God—our Lord God, the Father's Word! Hear! The flesh—Jesus Emmanuel—himself only spoke the Word that he saw with God: "I speak that which I have seen with my Father: and ye do that which ye have seen with your father." John 8:38 - And the Word was that which he—Jesus Emmanuel—saw with the Father.

Let us return to John 1:1: "In the beginning was the Word, and the Word was with God, and the Word was God." So, if that which Jesus Emmanuel—the flesh—saw with God was the Word, the flesh—Jesus Emmanuel—could not be God or His Word who is a Spirit. In addition, John 4:24 tells us, "God is a spirit: and they that worship him must worship him in spirit and in truth." Please keep in mind that most scholars agree that Jesus is both, "fully God—one Spirit—and fully man—one man who is not Spirit—one full plus another full makes two that are full and two that are full are two whole beings that are totally different from each other. Therefore, the Word was sent into sinful flesh for us to show us that if we abide in the Word as Jesus Emmanuel did, the Word then will abide in us. Moreover, because the Word abides in us, like in Jesus Emmanuel, we too, like Jesus Emmanuel, will have God's Power to overcome and subdue this present world. To receive this Power, to produce word, is why we were created in the likeness or image of God. God's Word is Knowledge, and that Knowledge is our Power. No Word, no Knowledge; no Knowledge, no Power!

Well, I hope you can see now that prehistoric man was created by God but was not created in the likeness or image of God to produce words or speak words. The spiritual male—brain—and female—mind, wisdom—blessed with the ability to produce son—word—is the image or likeness of God, and this is why the us within ourselves is so very important for us and for God. If God had not created us in His own image, we would have been like the prehistoric man, unable to produce Word, and without Word, we could not have the Knowledge of God or fellowship with God.

An article in the Telgraph UK titled, "Cavemen 'may have used language" by Science Correspondent Richard Gary states that *some scientists are saying that the FOXP2 gene is a language gene—a gene which governs the fine control of muscles and that with it prehistoric man was able to form words with the larynx, lips, and tongue. Scientists also say that this language gene they found in Neanderthals is also found in modern humans as well.*

Now, just because this gene is in us also does not mean that prehistoric man was able to speak as we do. To me what this means is that God created them with this gene because He knew it would be discovered and it would be our proof, using this work and this truth about our Us, that He created both them and ourselves.

Evolutionary anthropology said in The Telegraph article *that by looking at Neanderthals' DNA they found that from the point of view of this gene there is no reason Neanderthals would not have spoken like us. But other scientists have dismissed the idea, and the research that is published in the Journal Current Biology cautions us that it is not possible to draw a conclusion about Neanderthals' ability to speak from this research,* and they are right. This gene is not a language gene, and, as they said, this gene controls the fine muscles of the larynx, lips, and tongue.

I will tell you why this gene is not a language gene shortly, but first I want you to read what a blogger from *Red Bird Nation Blogspot* had to say after leaving the introduction seminar of this gene.

She writes, *"After leaving the intro seminar today, I realized that I was one of those thousands of people who looked at these cavemen article and failed to recognize the many flaws of these journalist arguments. First, what is a language gene? There are so many factors (both internal and external) that impact the complicated act of thinking. Thus, how can they call one single isolated gene a language gene?"*

She goes on to say, *"Also, this gene may show that cavemen had the ability to make specific sounds. However, there is a big difference between having the ability to make sound and actually having the ability to make sense of it and communicating."*

Hear! I agree with her. She is right; the muscles that this gene controls have nothing to do with forming or producing words. It only controls the muscles, and these muscles needed for the larynx, lips, and tongue does not form or produce words; they are needed only to make sounds. This is why we should respect our Us, and its importance, and it is why our us is created in the likeness of God and was blessed to be fruitful in Word, to multiply in Word, to replenish with Word, and to subdue with Word. The Word of God is the Word of Wisdom, the Word of Understanding, the Word of Knowledge, and the Word of Power. Therefore, the reason why this gene is not a language gene is because words are not formed or produced with muscles but with the Us. Proof is this: I am going to ask you a question, and when I ask you please do not open your mouth. Do not use your larynx, lips, or tongue to answer. Question: What is two plus two? Now when you answered this question, the answer you heard came from the us within you—your brain and mind/wisdom, which formed or produced your word/answer within your head. This word/answer did not require the use of your muscles that controls your larynx, lips, or tongue. You were able to produce the word/answer in your head without using the gene that controls the fine muscles in the larynx, lips, or tongue.

Understand now that muscles or language gene that controls the larynx, lips, or tongue do not form or produce word; only the us can form or produce word. The blessed male and female created after the likeness of God can produce word, and this, blessed us. Cavemen did not receive this blessing, though. Therefore, my people, starting this day, please respect your us within as God respects His and use it the way God intended for you to use it!

CHAPTER 14

The Conclusion of the Us, God the Father Himself

Now that we clearly understand the Us within ourselves and how important it is to God and ourselves, we can now understand THE US—GOD THE FATHER HIMSELF—within HIMSELF, THE HOLY SPIRIT. Okay, there are three scriptures left that we need to look closely at in which THE US is named or used: Gen 3:22, ch.11:7 and Isa.6:8. Therefore, the next scripture we will be looking at is Gen 3:22 and it is the Lord God in this scripture—the Father's Spirit-produced Son, the Word of life—who is speaking about the need to make a decision. So He said to the Male—Brain—and Female—Mind, His Wisdom—that He had a decision to make as to what to do with man. Gen 3:22 reads, "And the LORD God—the Word—said, 'Behold, the man is become as one of us, to know good and evil: and now, lest he put forth his hand, and take also of the tree of life, and eat, and live for ever.'" Now, the one in the Us that man has become like is Wisdom: "For the LORD giveth wisdom: out of his mouth cometh knowledge and understanding"—Prov 2:6. It is Wisdom because they ate from the Tree of the Knowledge of Good and Evil, and that Knowledge of good and evil is God's Wisdom and Understanding of good and evil. Of this, Gen. 2:17 says, "But of the tree of the knowledge of good and evil, thou shalt not eat of it: for in the day that thou eatest thereof thou shalt surely die." See, the Us of God—God's real Godhead—had to make a decision because the serpent was so subtle and crafty and manipulated Eve. Gen 3:3-6 reads, "But of the fruit of the tree which is in the midst of the garden, God hath said, Ye shall not eat of it, neither shall ye touch it, lest ye die. And the serpent said unto the woman, Ye shall not surely die: For God doth know that in the day ye eat thereof, then your eyes shall be opened, and ye shall be as gods—becoming like one in the Us—knowing good and evil—or knowing God's Wisdom and Understanding of good and evil. And when the woman saw that the tree was good for food—lust of the flesh—and that it was pleasant to the eyes—lust of the eyes—and a tree to be desired—the pride of life—to make one wise—or give her Wisdom—she took of the fruit thereof, and did eat, and gave also unto her husband with her; and he did eat." Therefore, in their hearts, by disobedience, they believed God to be a liar, which is evil. This is the beginning of the lust of the flesh, lust of the eyes, and pride of life, Satan's first three kings.

See, it is Wisdom in the Us that man is become like. In addition, Wisdom, God's Mind, is the Female in the Us, and the Father's Brain is the Male of the Us, and together they produced the Word of the Us, which is the Son of the Us. Prov 3:13-20 tells us, "Happy is the man that findeth Wisdom, and the man that getteth understanding. For the merchandise of it is better than the merchandise of silver, and the gain thereof than fine gold. She is more precious than rubies: and all the things thou canst desire are not to be compared unto her. Length of days is in her right hand; and in her left hand riches and honour. Her ways are ways of pleasantness, and all her paths are peace. She is a tree of life to them that lay hold upon her: and happy is every one that retaineth her. The LORD by Wisdom hath founded the earth; by understanding hath he established the heavens. By his knowledge, the depths are broken up, and the clouds drop down the dew." Therefore, the Word out of Wisdom's mouth is the Spirit-produced Son, God's Word. Prov 8:4-11 demonstrates this: "Unto you, O men, I—Wisdom—call; and my voice—the Word of God—is to the sons of man. O ye simple, understand Wisdom: and, ye fools, be ye of an understanding heart. Hear; for I—Wisdom—will speak of excellent things—the Word of God—and the opening of my lips shall be right things—the Word of God. For my mouth shall speak truth—God's Word is Truth – John 17:17: 'Sanctify them through thy truth: thy word is truth—and wickedness is an abomination to my lips. All the words— their Spirit-produced Son—of my—Wisdom—mouth are in righteousness; there is nothing froward or perverse in them. They are all plain to him that understandeth, and right to them that find knowledge. Receive my instruction, and not silver; and knowledge rather than choice gold. For Wisdom is better than rubies; and all the things that may be desired are not to be compared to it.   "

Got it? This Female is the Wisdom of Jehovah— LORD—and the Father possessed Her ever before the earth was. Prov 8:12-23 confirms this: "I Wisdom dwell with prudence, and find out knowledge of witty inventions. The fear of the LORD is to hate evil: pride, and arrogancy, and the evil way, and the froward mouth, do I—Wisdom—hate. – In other words, Wisdom's hate is the Fear of God .— Counsel is mine, and sound wisdom: I am understanding; I have strength—In other words, when God's Wisdom speaks, She is God's Word, God's Counsel, God's Knowledge, God's Understanding, and God's Might, which is God's Mind that develops God's Fear to hate evil: pride, arrogance, the evil way, and the froward mouth.—By me—Wisdom— kings reign, and princes decree justice. By me—Wisdom— princes rule, and nobles, even all the judges of the earth. I— Wisdom—love them that love me; and those that seek me early shall find me. Riches and honour are with me— Wisdom—yea, durable riches and righteousness. My— Wisdom—Fruit—God's Word—is better than gold, yea, than fine gold; and my revenue than choice silver. I—Wisdom— lead in the way of righteousness, in the midst of the paths of judgment: That I—Wisdom—may cause those that love me to inherit substance; and I will fill their treasures. The LORD—Jehovah—possessed me—Wisdom—in the beginning of his way, before his works of old. I—Wisdom— was set up from everlasting, from the beginning, or ever the earth was." Therefore, the reason man became like Wisdom when he ate of the tree of the knowledge of good and evil because God's Wisdom is His Knowledge—see Prov 8:10-15.

Again, this is the Us in God's real head—God's Brain—His Male—God's Mind—His Female—Wisdom, Understanding, and Knowledge—and God's Word—is Spirit-produced Son—and these three are in the fourth, the Holy Spirit—the Father Himself, "Jehovah." This is the Us within itself, and the one within the Us that man has become like is Wisdom, to know, or have the Knowledge of good and evil.

Remember, every time God has a decision to make, He always, always uses His Man-Child; His Spirit produced Son, His Word to communicate with His Wisdom, His Mind as to what they should do about that situation they are deciding on.

Okay, now that we see how important Wisdom's role is in the Us, I ask you again, who is closer to the truth about the Trinity? Theophilus of Antioch—the first recorded using this Greek word Τριάς, meaning "a set of three" or Trinity [Τριάδος] of God, His Word, and His Wisdom. And the fourth is the type of man who needs light, so that there may be God, the Word, Wisdom, and man—or Tertullian—the first to use the Latin words "Trinity," "person," and "substance" to explain that the Father, Son, and Holy Spirit are "one in essence—not one in Person?"

Our next scripture of the Us in Jehovah is when He came down to see the city and the tower, which the children of men built. Again, God has a decision to make, so, thinking to himself, He said with His Word and to Wisdom in Gen. 11:7, "Go to, let us go down—to carry out the decision that we have made to confound their language—and there confound their language, that they may not understand one another's speech." Again, this is Jehovah thinking out aloud or He is allowing Moses to hear His thoughts at that time as he—Moses—wrote, and it is the same with Isa 6:8 when the Lord God had to decide whom He will send to speak for the Us: Also I heard the voice of the Lord—the Word—saying, 'Whom shall I—single—send, and who will go for us—

single, Male, Female and Child, or Brain, Mind and Word?' Then said I, 'Here am I; send me—Isa 6:8. Again, the Us is the Father—His Wisdom and His Word; the Male, Female, and Son; His Brain, Mind, and Word. Jehovah—the Male and Female—is always with the Son—His Word of life, the Lord God our God—and all that the Us does is done through the Spirit—God the Father Himself, the Holy Spirit. God the Father Himself is His Us within Himself—the Holy Spirit, "Jehovah"—and we are our us within ourselves as well, which is also why we should respect the Us within our us. Got it? If we do not respect the Us within us, we don't respect ourselves or Jehovah. Here is an example for you to try so that you can use your us within you. Think of a decision you need to make. Now, the spirits you are using as you are thinking of what to do are your brain—the male— your mind—the female, Wisdom—and the Word—your son, your spirit-produced word/son. Now, listen to yourself thinking. What your brain—male—is using to communicate with your mind—female—is your word—son—and that word—son—is produced between the two—male and female or brain and mind—within. Now, the decision that is being made is being made by the Wisdom of the word that you— your soul's mind—understand of that particle thing—that which you—your soul's mind—are deciding upon. In addition, that word of Wisdom that gives you—your soul's mind—understanding of that thing is the knowledge you- your soul's mind—earned or learned of that thing that gave you—your soul's mind—the decision you—your soul's mind—made about that thing. Then the brain, after the decision is made by your soul's mind, sends the correct signal to itself to make the body act upon that decision.

This thought process—in our soul's mind—that puts our body—and God's body—His Holy Spirit—into action is the us within our head and the Us within God's real head. The Us—God's/our Brain, Mind—Wisdom—and Word—is the Male and Female of God's image that produced their Son, the Word. Gen 5:1-2 reads, "This is the book of the generations of Adam. In the day that God created man, in the likeness of God made he—God—him—Adam—Male and female created he—God—them—Adam's spiritual brain and mind, which produced Adam's word—and blessed them--Adam's spiritual brain, mind, and word—and called their—Adam's spiritual brain, mind, and word—name Adam, in the day when they—the male and female—were created."

This is the Us, God Himself in these four scriptures—Gen. 1:26a-27; ch. 3:22; ch. 11:7, and Isa. 6:8—and the reason why we should respect the Us within ourselves. This same Us of God is the Word of God's Wisdom that grew unto Jesus Emmanuel—see Isa 11:1-2. Therefore as you can see The Us, "let Us create, in our image, and after our likeness, "is God using His Brain, His Male, His Mind, Wisdom, His Female and Their Word, their Spirit produced Son in His thought process as to what they think is best for any particular situation.

Please understand that because of Telltullian invention of the Trinity and the teaching of it, our Christian world has did what Satan wanted us to do and that is to take God's Wisdom out of His Word. Satan in Revelation 12 could not kill the man-child of Wisdom's so he went after God's Wisdom in the Word. Therefore, by us believing and teaching the Trinity we take the Female, Wisdom out of God. Every scholar believes God is only Male and not Male and Female.

Telltullian's invention of the Trinity draws us away from God's Truth of Himself being Male and Female. Hear. We have been taught by our Trinitarian's scholars that when we read Genesis 1:26 that the words, "Let Us make, in Our image, after Our likeness, " is our proof that the Trinity is true, but again that's not correct. By the Trinity denying the role God's Wisdom plays in God's Own Head and teaching us to do the same, we are being deceived by Telltullian's invention of the Trinity; this is false and incorrect teaching, which is a form of Heresy that will reveal the wrath of God upon men who suppress the truth of God by their wickedness.

Romans 1:18—The wrath of God is being revealed from heaven against all the godlessness and wickedness of men who suppress the truth by their wickedness.

Ephesians 2:2—In which you used to walk when you conformed to the ways of this world and of the ruler of the power of the air, the spirit who is now at work in the sons of disobedience.

Ephesians 5:6—Let no man deceive you with vain words: for because of these things cometh the wrath of God upon the children of disobedience.

Colossians 2:8—See to it that no one takes you captive through philosophy and empty deception, which are based on human tradition and the spiritual forces of the world rather than on Christ.

Colossians 3:6—Because of these, the wrath of God is coming on the sons of disobedience.

2 Thessalonians 2:3—Let no one deceive you in any way, for it will not come until the rebellion occurs and the man of lawlessness (the son of destruction) is revealed.

Hebrews 13:9—Do not be carried away by all kinds of strange teachings, for it is good for the heart to be strengthened by grace and not by ceremonial foods, which are of no value to those devoted to them.

This deception of us being taught by our Trinitarian's scholars that when we read Genesis 1:26 that the words, "Let Us make, in Our image, after Our likeness, "proves the Trinity is true, but we know now by God's Wisdom, His Female being added to the Godhead shows that God is not a Triune God but that He is One God, Male and Female with the ability to produced word. To understand how easily we were deceived will upset your spirit and soul. The easy deception they used was the words Us and Our to say ok this must means the Trinity, but these two word are going to show us how easily we were deceived. Hear, let us reads Gen 1:26-27 again, it reads, "And God said, Let us make man in our image, after our likeness: and let them have dominion over the fish of the sea, and over the fowl of the air, and over the cattle, and over all the earth, and over every creeping thing that creepeth upon the earth. So God created man in his *own* image, in the image of God created he him; male and female created he them. Now lets take out the dominion part and see what we get; Gen 1:26-27 And God said, Let us make man in our image, after our likeness: So God created man in his *own* image, in the image of God created he him; male and female created he them. Now think, God said let Us, in Our, after Our, then God created Man—on the sixth day—Male and Female and according to God that is His Own Image, in the image of God created he—God—him—Adam—male and female created he—God—them—Adam, the male and female. Understand now that God's Us are the male and female who is using their Son to speak this to Moses as he wrote. I mean, "Hello "is any one home? God said, Let us make man in our image, after our likeness and God then said His Likeness; His Image is male and female, "in the image of God created he—God—him—Adam—male and female. If we don't get this we need to ask ourselves where we stand in the sight of God when it comes to John 17:3, which states, "And this is life eternal, that they might know thee the only true God, and Jesus Christ, whom thou hast sent?"

CHAPTER 15

The Two That Were One While on Earth

Okay, now that we know who the Us is, God's and ours, let us see who the Lord Jesus Christ our God is and who Christ Jesus Emmanuel our Lord is altogether. The Lord Jesus Christ our God means Jehovah's Word, gee us, the Wisdom and Power of God the Father, a form of the Father Himself that was sent into sinful flesh to save us. Chew slowly! For these Spirits divided from God the Father are the Spirits of Jehovah—the Holy Spirit Himself. Also, Christ Jesus Emmanuel our Lord means "the Wisdom and power of God," gee—The—US, God is with us, God's Word, a form of the Father Himself that is within Christ Jesus Emmanuel our Lord—our mediator, our high priest after the order of Melchisedek—sent to save us from sin and death. Now this is Melchisedec status with Jehovah according to Heb 7:1-4 : "For this Melchisedec, king of Salem, priest of the most high God, who met Abraham returning from the slaughter of the kings, and blessed him. To whom also Abraham gave a tenth part of all; first being by interpretation King of righteousness, and after that also King of Salem, which is, King of peace. Without father, without mother, without descent, having neither beginning of days, nor end of life; but made like unto the Son of God; abideth a priest continually. Now consider how great this man was, unto whom even the patriarch Abraham gave the tenth of the spoils."

Understanding now that Jesus Emmanuel was made a high priest after the order of Melchisedec, he being made like unto the Son of God is the King of Peace and Jesus Emmanuel being made like unto the Son of God is the Prince of Peace. Please keep this in mind, because it will help understand Hebrews 5:5-12. Now Jesus Emmanuel, unlike the world's high priest, was made a better testament: "By so much was Jesus made a surety of a better testament—Heb 7:22. Jesus Emmanuel was made a better testament because of God's Word—the Lord Jesus Christ our God—God's Word of oath within him. Heb 7:28 goes on to say, "For the law maketh men high priests which have infirmity; but the word of the oath, which was since the law, maketh the Son, who is consecrated for evermore."

See, it's the Word of God—a form of God Himself—within Jesus Emmanuel that maketh him a better testament, and that Word of life sometimes spoke of Himself while being within Jesus Emmanuel, such as in John 8:58: "Jesus said unto them, Verily, verily, I say unto you, Before Abraham was, I am." This is God's Word, God Himself within Jesus Emmanuel, who is speaking and who is before Abraham. Isa 41:4 reads, "Who hath wrought and done it, calling the generations from the beginning? I the LORD, the first, and with—with—the last—the begotten, Jesus Emmanuel—I—the LORD—am he—the Lord God, the Word." The last, the begotten "Jesus Emmanuel," would sit on the throne of his father David, whose throne is over the house of Israel, and God would be his Father and he would be God's Son. Chronicles 22:10 reads, "He is the one who will build a house for my Name. He will be my son, and I will be his father. And I will establish the throne of his kingdom over Israel forever." Question: If God had a Son before the world was, and Jesus Emmanuel is that Son, why then did God say, "He will be—future—my son and I will be—future—his father," instead of saying, "he is my Son and I am his father?"

On the other hand, the Lord Jesus Christ our God's throne is a throne of righteousness: "Thy throne, O God, *is* for ever and ever: the sceptre of thy kingdom *is* a right scepter"—Psalm 45:6. And when God said "Son" in Hebrews 1:8—But unto the Son *he saith*, 'Thy throne, O God, *is* for ever and ever: a sceptre of righteousness *is* the sceptre of thy kingdom—he was not talking about Jesus Emmanuel, He was talking about His Spirit-produced Son because He is the Lord God our righteousness. Jer 23:6 establishes this: "In his days Judah shall be saved, and Israel shall dwell safely: and this *is* his name whereby he shall be called, THE LORD OUR RIGHTEOUSNESS." Unlike Christ Jesus Emmanuel our Lord, whose throne is of his father David, the Lord God our righteousness's thone—the throne of the Lord Jesus Christ our God—is within the Father because He is now glorified back within the Father as the Word, as He was before the world began. John 17:1-5 reads, "These words spake Jesus, and lifted up his eyes to heaven, and said, Father, the hour is come; glorify thy Son, that thy Son also may glorify thee. As thou hast given him power over all flesh—remember Jesus Emmanuel was flesh—that he—the Father's Word—should give eternal life to as many as thou hast given him. And this is life eternal, that they might know thee the only true God— Jehovah—and Jesus Christ—Me, Your Word—whom thou hast sent. I have glorified thee on the earth: I have finished the work which thou gavest me to do. And now, O Father, glorify thou me—Your Word—with thine own self—notice He said 'with thine own self' and not 'set me at your right hand' or 'on my father David's throne—with the glory which I had with thee before the world was. Now we know the glory He had with God the Father before the world was, were His Word." In light of this scripture, recall John 1:1: "In the beginning was the Word, and the Word was with God, and the Word was God."

Therefore, while on earth, Christ Jesus Emmanuel our Lord had God's Word, which is Truth and life, within him as the Word that he spoke. That Truth and life of God's Word came with God's Wisdom, Understanding, Knowledge, and Power, a form of God the Father Himself. The Lord Jesus Christ our God—God's Spirit-produced Son, the Spirit of Life, that Word of life, the Father's Word—is that Spirit, Truth, and Life within Jesus Emmanuel. John 6:63 tells us, "It is the spirit that quickeneth; the flesh profiteth nothing: the words—God's Word—that I—Jesus Emmanuel—speak unto you, they are spirit, and they are life." This means that if

171

we allow the Word of God to live within us by leading our lives and believe Christ Jesus Emmanuel our Lord is the begotten son of Jehovah who died for our sins that we may be save, we too have God within us, and this is our life eternal.

Oh, the names, the names, the names. Christ Jesus Emmanuel himself had to learn to obey God's Word and Wisdom just like us. This obedience—to suffer death or die for God or to deny one's carnal/natural mind daily—is what makes him and us prefect in the sight of God that we should attain eternal life. Heb 5:5-12 reads, "So also Christ glorified not himself to be made an high priest; but he that said unto him, Thou art my Son, to day have I begotten thee. As he saith also in another place, Thou art a priest for ever after the order of Melchisedec. Who in the days of his—Christ Jesus Emmanuel—flesh, when he had offered up prayers and supplications with strong crying and tears unto him that was able to save him from death, and was heard in that he feared. Though he were a Son, yet learned he obedience by the things which he suffered. And being made perfect, he became the author of eternal salvation unto all them that obey him; Called of God an high priest after the order of Melchisedec. Of whom we have many things to say, and hard to be uttered, seeing ye are dull of hearing.—Of whom we have many things to say, and hard to be uttered, seeing ye are dull of hearing.—For when for the time ye ought to be teachers, ye have need that one teach you again which be the first principles of the oracles of God; and are become such as have need of milk, and not of strong meat."

Notice that verse 8 reads "a Son—and not 'the Son—learned he obedience by the things he suffered." Now, this learning of obedience by suffering is different from the obedience and suffering of the cross. This obedience and suffering is what led him to the obedience and suffering of the cross. This suffering is his dying daily, denying himself of his fleshly wants—the wants of pleasure and pride such as sex and getting even with those whom did him wrong. See, when his flesh craved sex or whatever else, he suffered in the decision of not to do them or to give in. This in turn chastened or inflicted suffering upon his soul and flesh, and by the chastening or inflicting of suffering upon his soul and flesh, he humbled them to the obedience of Jehovah Word within him. The same is the case with us. If we—through our blessed mind—humble our souls—which already knows right from wrong—and flesh to the obedience of the Word within us, our souls then learn that those craving are against the Word of Jehovah, and, in time, with the Spirit of Jehovah's leading it, it will stop the body—our flesh—from craving those sinful pleasures. This is the mind transforming itself according to Jehovah's Word to stop sending those influences of fleshly pleasures to the brain, which sends signals to the body to act out or give in to that fleshly pleasure which is lust.

Therefore, learning to obey Jehovah's Word by that suffering of not giving in to the flesh teaches the mind that the body—flesh—did not need that which it was craving, and that knowledge gives us the mind power to continue to transform. If we live according to Jehovah's Word—by the suffering of denying ourselves earthly sinful pleasures—whatever they might be—because they are against Jehovah's Word—then we have learned obedience. This learned obedience is what led Jesus to the obedience of the suffering of the cross, and it will lead us too, through the suffering of our crosses—whatever they may be—and this is what makes us prefect in the sight of Jehovah.

Therefore, the perfection or benefit of that suffering is that we will be able to do as Romans 12:1-3 states: I beseech you therefore, brethren, by the mercies of God, that ye present your bodies a living sacrifice, holy, acceptable unto God, which is your reasonable service. And be not conformed to this world: but be ye transformed by the renewing of your mind, that ye may prove what is that good, and acceptable, and perfect, will of God. For I say, through the grace given unto me, to every man that is among you, not to think of himself more highly than he ought to think; but to think soberly, according as God hath dealt to every man the measure of faith—in His Word."

Please chew thoroughly, for the meat gets more substantial with the Spirit-produced Son and the begotten son. We learned earlier in this work that God sent his Spirit-produced Son in the likeness of sinful flesh to manifest Himself and quicken the begotten son, and we learned that Jehovah's Spirit-produced Son—His Word—were produced from His Male—Jehovah's Brain—and His Female—Jehovah's Mind, Wisdom. We also learned that the Female of Jehovah is His Wisdom, Understanding, and Knowledge, which is Power, the Christ of Jehovah.

Note: This is why I call the Father God's name "Jehovah"—yes, His real name, the name that we should call Him. Ex 6:2-3 is where we find this: "And God spake unto Moses, and said unto him, 'I am the LORD: And I appeared unto Abraham, unto Isaac, and unto Jacob, by the name of God Almighty, but by my name, JEHOVAH was I not known to them.'" Oh, the names, the names, the names. What is it with the names?" The Lord Jesus Christ our God—God's Spirit-produced Son, the Spirit of Life, that Word of life, the Father's Word—is that Spirit, Truth, and Life within Jesus Emmanuel, and Christ Jesus Emmanuel our Lord—our mediator, our high priest after the order of Melchisedek. The Two that were One while and yet are Two and They are Two in Heaven and yet they are One as we are One with Them. Got it?

CHAPTER **16**

The Birth of the Spiritual Son of the Two that were One

Remembering all that we have learned throughout this work thus far will help us understand about the birth of the two sons. First, we will start with the birth of the Spirit-produced Son—or the dividing of the Word from the Us—how the Female of Jehovah, His Christ within Himself, gave birth. In addition, we will also cover how Satan, "the dragon," tried to kill Him while He was still in Heaven, right before He was caught up unto the Father—the Holy Spirit— and sent into sinful flesh as the Spirit of Life.

To understand this we will need to go through all of Revelation chapter 12, starting with verse 1: "And there appeared a great wonder in heaven; a woman clothed with the sun, and the moon under her feet, and upon her head a crown of twelve stars." This woman clothed in the sun is the Christ of Jehovah, the Female—His Wisdom, Understanding, Knowledge, and Power. She is Wisdom clothed within God, who is the Sun. For the LORD God *is* a sun and shield: the LORD will give grace and glory: no good *thing* will he withhold from them that walk uprightly. Psalms 84:11; See Deut 4:24; Ch 9:3; Ps 27:1; Mal 4:2; Dan 10:6; Matt 17:20; John 8:12; Heb 12:29.

Verse 2: "And she—Wisdom—being with child cried, travailing in birth, and pained to be delivered." Here, Wisdom cried travailing in birth and pain, because the Spirit-produced Son—the Word—had to be divided from the Us and put into the likeness of sinful flesh. In the Old Testament, the Word was not divided from the Us; it was only spoken

175

out of the Us to the prophets who would carry it out to the people. This spoken Word caused Her—Wisdom—no travailing of pain. She was able to bring the spoken Word forth before the travailing of pain came. She, in one day, brought forth the man-child—the Word—unto God's People. Of this, Isa 66:7-8 says, "Before she—Wisdom—travailed, she—Wisdom—brought forth; before her pain came, she—Wisdom—was delivered of a man child—God's spoken Word. Who hath heard such a thing? who hath seen such things? Shall the earth be made to bring forth in one day? or shall a nation be born at once? for as soon as Zion—God's Holy Mountain—travailed, she brought forth her children—the young Israelites."

Verse 3: "And there appeared another wonder in heaven; and behold a great red dragon, having seven heads and ten horns, and seven crowns upon his heads." This red dragon is Satan, the devil himself.

Verse 4: "And his tail drew the third part of the stars of heaven, and did cast them to the earth: and the dragon stood before the woman—Wisdom—which was ready to be delivered, for to devour her—Wisdom—child as soon as it was born." Here, Satan is trying to destroy the Word—the Spirit-produced Son—before He could be sent into the likeness of sinful flesh.

Verse 5: "And she—Wisdom—brought forth a man child—the Word—who was to rule all nations with a rod of iron: and her—Wisdom—child—the Word—was caught up unto God, and to his throne." This man-child is Jehovah's Spirit-produced Son, His Word, which will rule all nations with a rod of iron. Rev 19:13-15 reads, "And he was clothed with a vesture dipped in blood: and his name is called The Word of God. And the armies which were in heaven followed him upon white horses, clothed in fine linen, white and clean. And out of his mouth goeth a sharp sword, that with it he should smite the nations: and he shall rule them with a rod of iron: and he treadeth the winepress of the fierceness and wrath of Almighty God." This man-child—the Spirit-produced Son—was caught up unto Jehovah and to His throne. This is the birth of the Spirit-produced Son, how Jehovah was able to divide His Spirit of Life—the Word of life, His Spirit-produced Son—from His Spirit—the Male and Female, Jehovah Himself.

Verse 6: "And the woman—Wisdom—fled into the wilderness, where she—Wisdom—hath a place prepared of God, that they—Wisdom's children, us, our forefathers—should feed her—Wisdom—there a thousand two hundred and threescore days."

Verse 7: "And there was war in heaven: Michael and his angels fought against the dragon; and the dragon fought and his angels,"

Verse 8: "And prevailed not; neither was their place found any more in heaven." Now, Jehovah had to remove Satan from his place in Heaven before He could send His Spirit-produced Son—His Word of Life—into the lower parts of the earth for the first time to bring to life or quicken the begotten son—His sacrificial offering for His people, the Lamb, Christ Jesus Emmanuel our Lord. Now some are teaching that this war took place before the world began, and that is not true. After Satan had deceived Eve, he was still able to go to and fro between Heaven and earth. This is true because in Job, when the angels—sons—of Jehovah came to present themselves before Him in Heaven, Satan was there as well: "Now there was a day when the sons of God—angels of God—came to present themselves before the LORD, and Satan came also among them. And the LORD said unto Satan, Whence comest thou? Then Satan answered the LORD, and said, from going to and fro in the earth, and from walking up and down in it"—Job 1:6-7.

Verse 9: "And the great dragon was cast out, that old serpent, called the Devil, and Satan, which deceiveth the whole world: he was cast out into the earth, and his angels were cast out with him." See, Satan was cast out of his place in Heaven after he had deceived the whole world of those of the Old Testament and after the war with Michael. With Satan now cast out, Jehovah was able to send His Spirit-produced Son into sinful flesh to make known to us His New Covenant, the New Testament of His Word. That Word within His begotten son would lead him—Jesus Emmanuel—to taste death for every man. Heb 2:9-10 reads, "But we see Jesus—Emmanuel—who was made a little lower than the angels for the suffering of death, crowned with glory and honour—God's Word of Wisdom—that he by the grace of God—God's Word of Wisdom—should taste death for every man. For it—death—became him—the Word—for whom are all things, and by whom are all things, in bringing many sons unto glory, to make the captain—Jesus Emmanuel—of their salvation perfect through sufferings."

Hear! Jehovah's Word—the Lord Jesus Christ our God—within Jesus Emmanuel will make known to us the Knowledge of Jehovah. Eph 3:8-10 states, "Unto me, who am less than the least of all saints, is this grace given, that I should preach among the Gentiles the unsearchable riches of Christ—and the riches of Christ is Jehovah's Wisdom, Understanding, and Knowledge, which is in His Word. And to make all men see what is the fellowship of the mystery, which from the beginning of the world hath been hid in God—Jehovah—who created all things by Jesus Christ—His Word, Wisdom, Understanding, Knowledge, and Power—our God. To the intent that now unto the principalities and powers in heavenly places might be known by the church—us—the manifold Wisdom of God." And that understanding Knowledge of Jehovah's Wisdom gives us strength to overcome Satan through faith in the blood of the Lamb that tasted death for our sins.

Verse 10: "And I heard a loud voice saying in heaven, Now is come salvation, and strength—Jehovah's Word—and the kingdom of our God—truth and righteousness—and the power of his Christ—His Wisdom, Understanding, and Knowledge. For the accuser of our brethren is cast down, which accused them before our God day and night." Satan accusing us before God is his blinding of the mind Please keep in mind that, if your soul's mind is not blinded by

178

Satan's lies, thoughts and suggestions, he cannot accuse you before God.

Verse 11: "And they—Wisdom children, us of the New Testament—overcame him by the blood of the Lamb, and by the word of their testimony; and they loved not their lives unto the death."

Verse 12: "Therefore rejoice, ye heavens, and ye that dwell in them. Woe to the inhabiters of the earth and of the sea! for the devil is come down unto you, having great wrath, because he knoweth that he hath but a short time—see he was cast down right before the Word was to be sent into the likeness of sinful flesh and has but a short time left, for these are the last days."

Verse 13: "And when the dragon saw that he was cast unto the earth, he persecuted—annoyed or disturbed in a way that displeases—the woman—Jehovah's Wisdom—which brought forth the man-child—Jehovah's Word. Therefore, now that Satan could not destroy the Word of Jehovah, he then goes after the woman, Jehovah's Female—His Wisdom, Understanding, and Knowledge in the Word. This is why we see so many different beliefs in the churches today, and this is the dividing of Christ's body, Jehovah's Wisdom in the Word, being wrongfully divided—or disturbed—from the Truth of the Word. In addition, this is why we are warned to study the Word in truth for ourselves with Jehovah's Spirit teaching us how to rightly divide the Word of Truth. 2 Tim 2:15 tells us, "Study to shew thyself approved unto God, a workman that needeth not to be ashamed, rightly dividing the word of truth." Please get this, Satan in these days are going after God's Wisdom in God's Word, because he could not kill the Word that will destroy him, he now goes after us to make war with us—the remnant of her—Wisdom's—seed—children—by trying to confuse us as to what the true Wisdom of God's Word is. All over this present world, if we look around will our spiritual eyes, we will see no longer God's Word challenged anymore, but God's Wisdom in His Word is being challenged everyday.

Therefore, also said the Wisdom of God, "I—Wisdom

of God—will send them prophets and apostles, and *some* of them they shall slay and persecute. Luke 11:49; and all of Luke 11 is necessary read to understand how God's Wisdom in His Word is being confused.

Verse 14: "And to the woman were given two wings of a great eagle, that she might fly into the wilderness, into her place, where she is nourished for a time, and times, and half a time, from the face of the serpent." O the depth of the riches both of the Wisdom and Knowledge of God! how unsearchable *are* his judgments, and his ways past finding out!—Romans 11:33. In addition, to understand this please read all of 1 Corinthians 1:17 thru 2:16.

Verse 15: "And the serpent cast out of his mouth water as a flood after the woman, that he might cause her to be carried away of the flood." The water that Satan cast out of his mouth was his thoughts, his suggestions, his lies, his deceptions, his distractions, and his distortions, that he might swallow up or alter the original Truth, Understanding, and Knowledge of Jehovah's Wisdom—the woman—in His Word—His Spirit-produced Son.

Verse 16: "And the earth helped the woman, and the earth opened her mouth, and swallowed up the flood which the dragon cast out of his mouth." The "earth" here is the saints, those of us who study to show ourselves approved unto God, we are the workmen that needeth not to be ashamed, rightly dividing the Word of Truth, those of us who really seek Jehovah's kingdom and all of its righteousness—the Understanding of the Wisdom of God by our study of the Word of Truth of God, demonstrated by the life of God we live. Matt 6:33-34 reads, "But seek ye first the kingdom of God, and his righteousness; and all these things shall be added unto you—Meaning not only food and clothing, but all things, including His Word, Wisdom, Understanding, and Knowledge in all Truth.—Take therefore no thought for the morrow: for the morrow shall take thought for the things of itself. Sufficient unto the day is the evil thereof." It is us—the saints—because we desire the Truth of the Word of His Wisdom and allow Jehovah's Spirit to teach us. That Truth is what sets us free from the waters that come out of Satan's mouth: "And ye shall know the truth, and the truth shall make you free—John 8:32. Moreover, that Truth is Jehovah Word, His Spirit-produced Son. John 17:17 reads, "Sanctify them through thy truth: thy word is truth." Moreover, that Word of Truth is Jehovah's Spirit-produced Son within His begotten son that sets us free. John 8:36 – "If the Son—the Spirit-produced Son—therefore shall make you free, ye shall be free indeed. This freedom, by teaching the Truth of the Gospel—Jehovah's Word—to others, is Wisdom's—the Woman's—help. That help—seeking the Truth in the Word, knowing the Truth in the Word, believing the Truth in the Word, teaching the Truth in the Word and living the Truth in the Word—is our hope in the Truth of Jehovah's Wisdom—in His Word. It is as Col 1:5-6 states, "For the hope which is laid up for you in heaven, whereof ye heard before in the word of the truth of the Gospel. Which is come unto you, as it is in all the world; and bringeth forth fruit, as it doth also in you, since the day ye heard of it, and knew the grace of God in truth."

Verse 17: "And the dragon was wroth with the woman, and went to make war with the remnant of her seed, which keep the commandments of God, and have the testimony of Jesus Christ." See now that Satan could not distort the Truth of Jehovah's Wisdom completely with the Word of Truth having come within the flesh Himself to make us free, Satan then goes after the remnant of Wisdom's seed, us, Wisdom's children, the saints. Satan comes after us time and time again, over and over, trying to get us weary in our minds, that we should faint—to lose faith or hope in spirit. Paul sums it all up this way in Gal 6:6-9: "Let him that is taught in the word communicate unto him that teacheth in all good things. Be not deceived; God is not mocked: for whatsoever a man soweth, that shall he also reap. For he that soweth to his flesh—fleshly lusts, speaking lies, deceptions, distractions, and distortions—shall of the flesh reap corruption. But he that soweth to the Spirit—seeking the Truth of the Word, knowing the Truth of the Word, believing the Truth of the Word, teaching the Truth of the Word, and living the Truth in the Word—shall of the Spirit reap life everlasting. And let us not be weary in well doing: for in due season we shall reap, if we faint not—or lose not faith in the Spirit." Now, therefore, without controversy, this is the birth of Jehovah's Spirit-produced Son—His Word, our Word of life, the Lord Jesus Christ our God, Jehovah's Spirit of Life divided from the Us into those of us who believe and Jesus Emmanuel.

CHAPTER 17

The Birth of the Reincarnation of Life

Now, before we get to the birth of the begotten son or the reincarnation of King David, I would like to explain first the reincarnation of Elijah or Elias—John the Baptist. Okay, so that we can understand this reincarnation, we need to get some background about Elijah—Elias—and God's Power within him, starting with 2 Kings 2:7-15: "And fifty men of the sons of the prophets went, and stood to view afar off: and they two stood by Jordan. And Elijah took his mantle, and wrapped it together, and smote the waters, and they were divided hither and thither, so that they two went over on dry ground.—Now this is also what happened with Moses and the Red Sea when he raised up his arms.—and it came to pass, when they were gone over, that Elijah said unto Elisha, Ask what I shall do for thee, before I be taken away from thee. And Elisha said, I pray thee, let a double portion of thy Spirit be upon me. And he said, Thou hast asked a hard thing: nevertheless, if thou see me when I am taken from thee, it shall be so unto thee; but if not, it shall not be so.— Listen, Elijah said, 'ask what *I* shall do for thee,' and what Elisha asked was granted to him by Elijah through God— And it came to pass, as they still went on, and talked, that, behold, there appeared a chariot of fire, and horses of fire, and parted them both asunder; and Elijah went up by a whirlwind into heaven.—Hear! Elijah did not die; God took him to Heaven alive.—And Elisha saw it, and he cried, My father, my father, the chariot of Israel, and the horsemen thereof. And he saw him no more: and he took hold of his own clothes, and rent them in two pieces. He took up also the mantle of Elijah that fell from him, and went back, and stood by the bank of Jordan; And he took the mantle of Elijah that fell from him, and smote the waters, and said, Where is the LORD God of Elijah? and when he also had smitten the waters, they parted hither and thither: and Elisha went over.—Notice here what Elisha had to say after he smote the waters that Elijah didn't have say.—And when the sons of the prophets which were to view at Jericho saw him, they said, The spirit of Elijah doth rest on Elisha. And they came to meet him, and bowed themselves to the ground before him." Also see 1 Kings 17:13-24 and all of chapter 18 of 1 Kings—a must read.

So, understanding the Power of God that was with this man of God takes us to Isa 40:3, which states, "The voice of him that crieth in the wilderness, Prepare ye the way of the LORD—Jehovah—make straight in the desert a highway for our God—the Word, our Lord God." Now this messenger— the voice of him that crieth in the wilderness, Prepare ye the way of the LORD—Is Elijah/Elias. We read this in Mal 3:1-3: "Behold, I will send my messenger—Elijah/Elias—and he shall prepare the way before me—Jehovah, His Word, the message. And the Lord—the Word, my message—whom ye seek, shall suddenly come to his temple—Jesus Emmanuel— even the messenger of the covenant, whom ye delight in: behold, he—the Spirit-produced Son—shall come, saith the LORD of hosts—Jehovah. But who may abide the day of his—the Word, my messenger—coming? and who shall stand when he—the Word—appeareth? for he—the Word— is like a refiner's fire, and like fullers' soap: And he—the Word—shall sit as a refiner and purifer of silver: and he—the Word—shall purify the sons of Levi, and purge them as gold and silver, that they may offer unto the LORD an offering in righteousness—God's Word and Wisdom." As I said, this messenger who prepared the way for the Message is Elijah/Elias. Mal 4:4-6 reads, "Remember ye the law of Moses my servant, which I commanded unto him in Horeb for all Israel, with the statutes and judgments. Behold, I will send you Elijah the prophet before the coming of the great and dreadful day of the LORD. And he shall turn the heart of

184

the fathers to the children, and the heart of the children to their fathers, lest I come and smite the earth with a curse." He, Elijah/Elias. is the voice of him that crieth in the wilderness—that hairy man clothed in camel's hair with a girdle of leather about his loins. 2 Kings 1:8 – "And they answered him, He was an hairy man, and girt with a girdle of leather about his loins. And he said, It is Elijah the Tishbite."

In addition, this Elijah, the messenger, is John the Baptist. Matt 3:1-4 states, "In those days came John the Baptist preaching in the wilderness of Judaea. And saying, Repent ye: for the kingdom of heaven is at hand. For this is he that was spoken of by the prophet Esaias, saying, The voice of one crying in the wilderness, Prepare ye the way of the Lord, make his paths straight. And the same John—Elijah—had his raiment of camel's hair, and a leathern girdle about his loins; and his meat was locusts and wild honey."

See, it is John the Baptist reincarnated from Elijah/Elias who did not die, but was taken up into Heaven alive. He being a man of God and taken to Heaven alive, means that he—as an angel of God was full of God, the Holy Ghost. This is why John was full of the Holy Ghost/Spirit before he was born. Luke 1:13-17 reads, "But the angel said unto him, Fear not, Zacharias: for thy prayer is heard; and thy wife Elisabeth shall bear thee a son, and thou shalt call his name John. And thou shalt have joy and gladness; and many shall rejoice at his birth. For he shall be great in the sight of the Lord, and shall drink neither wine nor strong drink; and he shall be filled with the Holy Ghost, even from his mother's womb. And many of the children of Israel shall he turn to the Lord their God. And he—John—shall go before him—the Word—in the spirit and power of Elias—Elijah—to turn the hearts of the fathers to the children and the disobedient to the Wisdom of the just; to make ready a people prepared for the Lord." Again, this John the Baptist who is full of the Holy Ghost/Spirit, "in the spirit and power of Elias—Elijah—who will "turn the hearts of the fathers to the children," is Elijah. Mal 4:5-6 likewise says, "Behold, I will send you Elijah the prophet before the coming of the great and dreadful day of the LORD. And he shall turn the heart of the fathers to the children, and the heart of the children to their fathers, lest I come and smite the earth with a curse."

Understand, John the Baptist was born filled with the Holy Ghost/Spirit. Unlike Jesus Emmanuel who was born of the Holy Ghost/Spirit and had the Holy Ghost/Spirit descend upon him in Luke 3:22: "And the Holy Ghost descended in a bodily shape like a dove upon him, and a voice came from heaven, which said, Thou art my beloved Son; in thee I am well pleased." This is our proof that john the Baptist was Elijah/Elias and why God considered John greater than all who were born of woman, except Jesus Emmanuel, who was also born of woman. This is found in Matt 11:10-11: "For this is he, of whom it is written, Behold, I send my messenger before thy face, which shall prepare thy way before thee. Verily I say unto you, Among them that are born of women there hath not risen a greater than John the Baptist. Notwithstanding—or 'although—he—the Lamb—that is least in the kingdom of heaven is greater than he."

The Lamb is the least in the Kingdom of Heaven because he is the body and soul of the Word of the Kingdom. Moreover, the Word is the least in the kingdom of heaven because the Kingdom of Heaven is the Father's Brain and Mind—the Male and Female—that produced the third—the Word, the Spirit-produced Son—within the fourth—the Holy Spirit/Ghost, Jehovah Himself—and Jesus Emmanuel, the fifth, is at the right hand of this Kingdom. Matt 6:13 reads, "And lead us not into temptation, but deliver us from evil: For thine—the possessive case of 'thou—is the kingdom, and the power, and the glory, for ever. Amen." Matt 11:12-15 goes on to state, "And from the days of John the Baptist until now the kingdom of heaven suffereth violence, and the violent take it by force. For all the prophets and the law prophesied until John. And if ye will receive it, this is Elias—Elijah—which was for to come. He that hath ears to hear, let him hear." Note: Elijah/Elias was called the man of God with power, and Jesus Emmanuel was called the Son of Man/God

186

with God's Word as his power. Got it?

This is the reincarnation of Elijah/Elias to John the Baptist. Moreover, our final proof of this comes from Jesus Emmanuel himself in Matt 17:10-13: "And his disciples asked him, saying, Why then say the scribes that Elias must first come? And Jesus answered and said unto them, Elias truly shall first come, and restore all things. But I say unto you, That Elias—John the Baptist/Elijah—is come already, and they knew him not, but have done unto him whatsoever they listed. Likewise shall also the Son of man suffer of them. Then the disciples understood that he spake unto them of John the Baptist."

Therefore, understanding all thus far helps us to see that it is the Word of Jehovah in all three of these prophets: Elijah/Elias or John, Moses, and Jesus Emmanuel. And that is what Jehovah was trying to show Peter, James, and James' brother John—not John the Baptist—in Matthew. He also wanted them to know that it was the Word that led the three prophets when the Word in Jesus Emmanuel transformed himself into who He really were—the Spirit-produced Son our God.—In this vision that Jehovah allowed them to see in Matt 17:1-9: "And after six days Jesus taketh Peter, James, and John his brother, and bringeth them up into an high mountain apart. And was transfigured—or transformed— before them: and his face did shine as the sun, and his raiment was white as the light. And, behold, there appeared unto them Moses and Elias talking with him. Then answered Peter, and said unto Jesus, Lord, it is good for us to be here: if thou wilt, let us make here three tabernacles; one for thee, and one for Moses, and one for Elias. While he yet spake, behold, a bright cloud overshadowed them: and behold a voice out of the cloud, which said, This is my beloved Son— the Word, the Spirit-produced Son—in whom I am well pleased; hear ye him—the Word.—And when the disciples heard it, they fell on their face, and were sore afraid. And Jesus came and touched them, and said, Arise, and be not afraid. And when they had lifted up their eyes, they saw no

187

man, save Jesus—Emmanuel—only. And as they came down from the mountain, Jesus charged them, saying, Tell the vision to no man, until the Son of man be risen again from the dead."

Now, with the understanding of this reincarnation of Elijah/Elias and John the Baptist, we can move on to the birth of the begotten son or the reincarnation of King David.

CHAPTER 18

The Lived Birth of the Begotten Son of the Two that were One

The birth of the begotten son—the lamb—with the Word—the Spirit-produced Son, the Lord God, God Himself—within him helps us to understand Isa 41:4, which states, "Who hath wrought and done it, calling the generations from the beginning? I the LORD—Jehovah—the first—Son, My Word, My Spirit-produced Son—and with the last—the begotten son—I am he." In this scripture, He is saying, "I am He because My Word is Myself; I am the Spirit that will lead the last, and the Word that the last shall speak. I am He." His being the Word and the Spirit that would lead Jesus Emmanuel means that sometimes the Lord God spoke of Himself through the begotten son. For example, at the birth of the begotten son in Luke 1:32, the Lord God—the spiritual Son—gives Jesus Emmanuel—the begotten son— his father's David throne: "He—Jesus Emmanuel—shall be great, and shall be called the Son of the Highest—Jehovah— and the Lord God—the Word, the Spirit-produced Son— shall give unto him—the Begotten Son—the throne of his father David." Now we can be sure of the fact that the angel of God said Lord God—the Father's Spirit produced Son— shall give unto him—the Begotten Son—Jesus Emmanuel— the throne of his father David. Understanding Jesus Emmanuel is the son of his father David, helps us to see the Word—the Spirit produced Son, the Lord Jesus Christ our God—is not Jesus Emmanuel who is David son. It helps us as we see the Lord God in Luke who also spoke of Himself and said He is not David's son. And he—the Lord God—said unto them, How say they that Christ—God's Word of

Wisdom—is David's son? And David himself saith in the book of Psalms, The LORD—Jehovah—said unto my Lord—the Spirit-Produced Son—Sit thou on my right hand, Till I make thine enemies thy footstool. David calleth him Lord, how is he then his son?—Luke 20:41-44. Please understand that the bible does not contradict itself with these two scriptural passages, but explains the Two that were One while on earth, but yet are Two, and they are Two in heaven. See, Jehovah told the Lord God, His Spirit-produced Son, "sit thou on my right hand til I make thine—the Word— enemies—Satan's thoughts, his suggestions, his lies, his deceptions, his distractions, and his distortions—thy footstool. In addition, the Lord God, who is within Jesus Emmanuel, gave him—Jesus Emmanuel—his father David's throne.

Luke 1:32 and Luke 20:41-44 are not contradictory one to the other but are here to make sure there is no doubt about the first Spirit-produced Son—the Lord Jesus Christ our God—being within the last begotten son—the son of David—and show us that sometimes the Word—the Spirit produced Son—speaks of Himself through the begotten son. These two are the spiritual body and natural body of the one reincarnated body, Jesus Emmanuel—the soul and body of Jehovah's Word.

Now, as for the birth of the begotten son, Matt 1:18-23 records, "Now the birth of Jesus Christ—the spiritual and natural—was on this wise: When as his mother Mary was espoused to Joseph, before they came together, she was found with child of the Holy Ghost—Jehovah. Then Joseph her husband, being a just man, and not willing to make her a publick example, was minded to put her away privily. But while he thought on these things, behold, the angel of the Lord—the Spirit-produced Son—appeared unto him in a dream, saying, Joseph, thou son of David, fear not to take unto thee Mary thy wife: for that which is conceived in her is of the Holy Ghost—Jehovah. And she shall bring forth a son—the begotten son—and thou shalt call his name

190

JESUS—the Word's name—for he shall save his people—his people—from their sins. Now all this was done, that it might be fulfilled which was spoken of the Lord—the Lord God— by the prophet, saying, Behold, a virgin shall be with child, and shall bring forth a son, and they shall call his name Emmanuel, which being interpreted is, God with us—the Word our God, a form of Jehovah Himself, is with Jesus Emmanuel and Us." Even though the begotten son was led by the Lord God—the Word—within him, he still at a young age had to learn and grow in the Wisdom of the Word just like us. Luke 2:40 & 49-52 reads, "And the child grew—Got older, He was twelve years old at this time—and waxed— grew or became—strong in spirit—the Word of Wisdom within him—ffilled with Wisdom: and the grace of God was upon him. And he said unto them, How is it that ye sought me? wist ye not that I must be about my Father's business?— Again, this is the Spirit-produced Son speaking of Himself here, through Jesus Emmanuel.—And they understood not the saying which he spake unto them. And he went down with them, and came to Nazareth, and was subject unto them: but his mother kept all these sayings in her heart. And Jesus—the begotten son—increased—became greater or grew—in Wisdom and stature, and in favour with God and man."

This growth in Wisdom and stature is Jesus Emmanuel getting older, denying self, and allowing the Spirit—the Word—to lead him into all obedience. In other words, he—Jesus Emmanuel—is living the Lord Jesus Christ our God—the Word, Truth, Understanding, Knowledge, and Power within him—and all of these Spirits are divided from Jehovah's Wisdom—the Father Himself, the Male and Female—see Gen. 5:1-2.

Therefore, after Jesus Emmanuel had grown in Wisdom, stature, and favor with the Father, now thirty years old, it was time for God to use him. But first—although symbolic for the Word—he—Jesus Emmanuel—had to be born again—born again just like us by water and by Spirit, the baptism and the receiving of the Holy Ghost.

This process in the scriptures of his being born again is very important for us to understand, because some are using the three names in these scriptures to try to explain Tertullian's invention of the Trinity as three persons in a Godhead—the Father, the Son—Jesus Emmanuel, the begotten son instead of the Word, the Spirit-produced Son—and the Holy Ghost—which is heresy, because Jehovah is not, I repeat IS NOT, a Godhead of three persons. No, the Father is not a triune God; He is more than that if you want to count spirits as persons. The baptism of the begotten son in Luke 3:21-23 demonstrates this: "Now when all the people were baptized, it came to pass, that Jesus also being baptized, and praying, the heaven was opened. And the Holy Ghost descended in a bodily shape like a dove upon him, and a voice came from heaven, which said, Thou art my beloved Son; in thee I am well pleased. And Jesus himself began to be about thirty years of age, being—as was supposed—the son of Joseph, which was the son of Heli."

Now some, not knowing the truth about the Trinity, err in their teachings of these scriptures. Therefore, knowing the truth about the Trinity helps to make these scriptures clear. It clarifies that Jesus Emmanuel, according to the flesh, having been baptized and having received the Holy Spirit, then become the Son of God just as we become sons and daughters of God by following his example. You see, Jesus Emmanuel didn't receive earthly glory and honor, nor public acknowledgement as God's Son, until after the baptism. 2 Peter 1:17 confirms this: "For he received from God the Father honour and glory, when there came such a voice to him from the excellent glory, This is my beloved Son, in whom I am well pleased." This beloved Son in whom God is well pleased is the son of David, God's begotten son. Heb 5:5 states, "So also Christ glorified not himself to be made an high priest; but he that said unto him, Thou art my Son, to day have I begotten thee." The day on which God said to Jesus Emmanuel, "thou art my Son; to day have I begotten thee," He was showing us that He was talking about King David being His begotten son because, in the book of Psalms, He said the same words to King David in Ps 2:7, which states, "I will declare the decree: the LORD hath said unto me, Thou art my Son; this day have I begotten thee." Tell me, if Jesus Emmanuel is the son of David or David himself—a Son of God's as we are too—how then can he be our God in a Godhead with God if we aren't as well? In addition, if he is in a Godhead, how can he be set down at the right hand of the Father, outside of the Father? Moreover, if he is in a Godhead outside of the Father, how then can the Father and he be one inside of a Godhead when outside is different than inside? In addition, if outside is different than inside and he is in an Godhead with the Father, doesn't that mean they are two different Gods? This cannot be, because God is a Spirit and Jesus Emmanuel is the flesh born of that Spirit. Rom 1:3-4 reads, "Concerning his Son Jesus Christ our Lord, which was made of the seed of David according to the flesh, And declared to be the Son of God with power, according to the spirit of holiness, by the resurrection from the dead."

Therefore, he is not a third of a Godhead; he is only the Begotten Son, the body and soul of the Spirit-produced Son, the Word. Moreover, because he is the body and soul of the Word, he became our Lord and Christ, not our God, but our brother. Here, maybe we can understand it all this way by looking at Rom 8:14-18: "For as many as are led by the Spirit of God, they are the sons of God. For ye have not received the spirit of bondage again to fear; but ye have received the spirit of adoption, whereby we cry, Abba, Father. The Spirit itself beareth witness with our spirit, that we are the children of God: And if children, then heirs; heirs of God, and joint-heirs with Christ—joint-heirs—if so be that we suffer with him, that we may be also glorified together. For I reckon that the sufferings of this present time are not worthy to be compared with the glory which shall be revealed in us." There you have it; we are joint heirs with Jesus Emmanuel our brother through the Spirit of adoption—God's Word,

Wisdom, Understanding, Knowledge, and Power—as members of the body—the body of the Word."

More proof that when God said, "this art my beloved Son, whom I am well please with; to day have I begotten thee," He was speaking of Jesus Emmanuel and not the Word is this: Jesus Emmanuel had within him the Spirit of God's Word, Truth, Wisdom, Understanding, and Knowledge and the Power that came from God, and after the baptism, he was full of the Holy Ghost—God's body, God's Spirit in action, God Himself. Now although Jesus had these Spirits within himself, he still had to live as a man, just like us and unlike the Spirit-produced Son—the Word who is attached to these Spirits. Mark 1:11-13 is our picture of this: "And there came a voice from heaven, saying, Thou art my beloved Son, in whom I am well pleased. And immediately the Spirit—God's Word, Wisdom, and Holy Spirit—driveth him into the wilderness. And he was there in the wilderness forty days, tempted of Satan; and was with the wild beasts; and the angels ministered unto." Just like us, Jesus Emmanuel had to learn to live God's Word, Wisdom, and Truth, and he, just like us as God's progressing holy people, needed to be ministered to before—as he learned and grew in the Wisdom of the Word—during—while being tempted—and after—after Satan left—him/us. Matt 4:11 records this: "Then the devil leaveth him, and, behold, angels came and ministered unto him." Understand, Jesus Emmanuel was led by Jehovah's Spirit to be tempted of the devil. In addition, when he said in Matt 4:10, "Get thee hence, Satan: for it is written, Thou shalt worship the Lord thy God, and him only shalt thou serve," he gave us proof that he is not the Lord God but that he was a man full of Jehovah—His Wisdom and His Word, the head of the Spirit, the Father Himself—whom he used all while being tempted of the devil. This was his final test before Jehovah could use him. Just like Jesus, we are tempted of Satan in the areas of our lives that we struggle with, and we are to overcome them so that God can use us too. This is the washing and purging that makes us perfect in the sight of God, which in turn gives us eternal life.

Therefore, although Jesus Emmanuel came by water and by blood—Spirit and flesh—he was still a man who had to go through life challenges as we do. The difference is that he was born of direct Spirit from God with God's Word, Truth, and Christ within him as a child to lead and teach him as he learned obedience through the things he suffered not to do when tempted by Satan and by flesh. Heb 5:8-9 tells us, "Though he were a Son, yet learned he obedience by the things which he suffered; And being made perfect, he became the author of eternal salvation unto all them that obey him." He was a man who overcame as we should overcome—one who was made from a woman under the law of a carnal commandment, but not after—in agreement or conformity with—the law, rather after—in agreement or conformity with—the power of an endless life—the Word. Heb 7:14-16 reads, "For it is evident that our Lord sprang out of Juda; of which tribe Moses spake nothing concerning priesthood. And it is yet far more evident: for that after the similitude—Order, Likeness; resemblance or a person that is like another, the counterpart of another—of Melchisedec there ariseth another priest—another priest like Melchisedec. Who is made, not after—in agreement or conformity with—the law of a carnal commandment, but after—in agreement or conformity with—the power of an endless life—God's Word, Wisdom, etc." Jesus Emmanuel was made to walk in agreement with the Spirit and not with the flesh. We, on the other hand, were made to walk after or in agreement with the flesh and then learn how to walk after or in agreement with the Spirit—"them who had no condemnation because they walk not after—in agreement or conformity with—the flesh, but after—in agreement or conformity with—the Spirit— Jehovah." Once we learn and live this, then there is no condemnation upon our souls, because the law—Jehovah—of the Spirit of Life—the Word, Truth, and Christ—in Jesus Emmanuel that led him to overcome has made us free from the law—Satan—of sin and death—Satan's Word, his thoughts, his suggestions, his lies, his deceptions, his distractions, and his distortions—as well. Rom 8:1-3 states,

195

"There is therefore now—the word "now" here is used to strengthen a command—which is Jehovah's Word, Truth, and Christ within Jesus Emmanuel—no condemnation to them—the Word, Truth, and God's Christ, Wisdom—which are in Christ Jesus—Emmanuel—who walk not after—in agreement or conformity with—the flesh, but after—in agreement or conformity with—the Spirit—Jehovah. For the law—Jehovah—of the Spirit of Life—the Word, Truth, and Jehovah's Christ—in Christ Jesus hath made me—Jesus Emmanuel and us—free from the law—Satan—of sin and death—Satan's Word, his thoughts, his suggestions, his lies, his deceptions, his distractions, and his distortions. For what the law—the Ten Commandments—could not do, in that it was weak through the flesh. God sending his own Son—the Word—in the likeness of sinful flesh—Jesus Emmanuel who had the likeness of sinful flesh, King David, but didn't sin in the flesh—and for sin, condemned sin in the flesh." Must read Romans chapters 6 and 7 and then 1 Peter chapter 4 to understand "condemned sin in the flesh.

I pointed out earlier that because the Spirit-produced Son was within the begotten son leading him, He sometimes spoke of himself and the things pertaining to the son of man, and I also pointed out that the begotten son, when he spoke, he spoke the Spirit-produced Son. Look at the following scriptures:

John 3:34 – "For he—Jesus Emmanuel—whom God hath sent speaketh the words of God—the Spirit-produced Son—for God giveth not the Spirit—His Word, Wisdom, Knowledge, etc—by measure unto him."

John 8:38 – "I—Jesus Emmanuel—speak that—God's Word of Wisdom—which I have seen with my Father—and the Word was with God and the Word was God—and ye do that which ye have seen with your father."

John 12:48-49 – "He that rejecteth me—Jesus Emmanuel—and receiveth not my words—the Spirit-produced Son—hath one that judgeth him: the word—the Lord God—that I have spoken, the same shall judge him in the last day.—Please understand, it is God's Word of

Wisdom within Jesus Emmanuel that will judge us, because it is the Word that we should believe in and the only way to believe in the Word is to live the Word.—For I—Jesus Emmanuel—have not spoken of myself; but the Father which sent me, he gave me a commandment, what I should say, and what I should speak."

See, it is the Word within Jesus Emmanuel that lives and speaks; they are two lives that are one. Now listen to The Word explain John 14:8-24, we reads, "Philip saith unto him, Lord, shew us the Father, and it sufficeth us. Jesus—the Word—saith unto him, Have I—God's Myself—been so long time with you, and yet hast thou not known me—the Word, and the Word was with God, and the Word was God—Philip? he that hath seen me—the Word within Jesus Emmanuel—hath seen the Father; and how sayest thou then, Shew us the Father? Believest thou not that I am in the Father—as the Father's Word and Jesus Emmanuel as My soul—and the Father in me—as the Word He speaks and Jesus Emmanuel as the Word he lives? the words—God's Word of Wisdom—that I—Jesus Emmanuel—speak unto you I speak not of myself: but the Father that dwelleth in me—Jesus Emmanuel—he—the Word—doeth the works. Believe me that I—Jesus Emmanuel—am in the Father—as His Word's, soul—and the Father in me—as the Word I live—or else believe me for the very works'—of the Word's—sake. Verily, verily, I—the Word—say unto you, He that believeth on me, the works that I do—as the Word within Jesus Emmanuel—shall he do also; and greater works than these shall he do; because I—the Word—go unto my Father. And whatsoever ye shall ask in my name, that will I—the Word—do, that the Father may be glorified in the Son—His Word—if ye shall ask any thing in my name, I—the Word—will do it. If ye love me, keep my—the Word—commandments. And I—the Word—will pray the Father, and he shall give you another Comforter, that he may abide with you for ever; Even the Spirit of Truth; whom the world cannot receive, because it seeth him not, neither knoweth him: but ye know him—the Spirit of Truth—for he dwelleth with you, and shall be in you. —Please remember that the other comforter—the Spirit of Truth—while Jesus was still on earth, dwelled with the disciples within Him as the Truth of Jehovah—the Word of Truth—and when Jesus left earth, he—the comforter, the Truth of Jehovah's Word within the Word, the Spirit of Truth—shall be in us.—I will not leave you comfortless: I will come to you. – Hear! The Word said 'I will not leave you comfortless, I will come to you. I, the Truth of Jehovah's Word within the Word, will come to you.' Wait a minute, is not he already here with them? Yes, But remember, the Word is the way, the life, and the truth according to John 14:6. – Yet a little while, and the world seeth me no more; but ye see me: because I live, ye shall live also. At that day ye shall know that I—the Word—am in my Father, and ye in me, and I in you. – See the Word is in the Father and us, the Saints who believe the Truth in the Word, are in the Word, and because we believe the Truth in the Word, the Word then is in us as the Truth of the Word—the Spirit of Truth that we live each day! – He that hath my commandments, and keepeth them, he it is that loveth me: and he that loveth me shall be loved of my Father, and I will love him, and will manifest—make clear—myself—as the Word—to him. Judas saith unto him, not Iscariot, Lord, how is it that thou wilt manifest thyself unto us, and not unto the world? Jesus—Emmanuel—answered—by God's spoken Word within him—and said unto him If a man love me he will keep my words—God's Word he speaks—and my Father will love him, and we—the Father, His Wisdom, Word, and Holy Ghost—will come unto him, and make our—the Father, His Wisdom, Word, and Holy Ghost— abode with him. He that loveth me—Jesus Emmanuel—not keepeth not my sayings: and the word—God's Word that I speak—which ye hear is not mine, but the Father's which sent me."

Understand now that Jesus Emmanuel spoke and lived the Lord Jesus Christ our God, the Father's Word within him. See, the Spirit-produced Son—the Word—was sent directly into King David's bowels to quicken him from the dead first and raise him up to heaven. This made Jehovah an embryo—Jesus Emmanuel, the son of man with the Word within him, or the Lord Jesus Christ, the Word, the Spirit-produced Son that is of a man—David's flesh—the one who came by water—Spirit—and blood—flesh—the beloved Son. Then God took that embryo, the son of man with the Spirit of Life within him, and sent him into the world as He put him into a woman. John 3:11-13 states, "Verily, verily, I say unto thee, We—the Spirit produced Son, God's Word of Wisdom within Jesus Emmanuel—speak that we do know—We here are not the disciples. Remember, the disciples are learning, they are not yet ready to speak or testify.— And testify that we—God's Word of Wisdom within Jesus Emmanuel—have seen—again, the disciples have not yet seen what is going on in Heaven—and ye receive not our witness—the Spirits within Jesus Emmanuel. If I—as the Spirits within Jesus Emmanuel—have told you earthly things, and ye believe not, how shall ye believe, if I tell you of heavenly things? And no man hath ascended up to heaven, but he that came down from heaven, even the Son of man which is in heaven. Here ask yourself, "If Jesus Emmanuel and King David—the son of man—aren't the same, "How then could Jesus Emmanuel—the son of man—be here on earth with the Lord Jesus Christ our God as He talks to Nicodemus and be in heaven at the same time— And no man hath ascended up to heaven, but he that came down from heaven, even the Son of man—King David—which is in heaven.? Got it? The Word descended down first to the lower parts of the earth to quicken or begat King David God's begotten son, thereby making God an embryo made of Water—Spirit—and Blood then He—the Word, the Lord Jesus Christ our God—ascended back to Heaven with the son of man—King David's flesh—so that God, the Holy Spirit Himself could send that embryo down from Heaven into that certain woman called Mary. Then, after the resurrection, the son of man who first ascended up to Heaven with the Word became that same Son of Man who descended down from Heaven with the Word as God's embryo.

Now that certain woman—Mary—brought him—the spirit produced Son and begotten son—forth, and God, the Spirit in the son of man sent him into the world, that through them—the Sons—the Word that is within the son of man, and the Son of man, King David's flesh, Jesus Emmanuel, the begotten Son—the Soul—or image—and Body—with us as members—of that invisible God, the Word—and their blood the world might be saved. If we believe on/in the name of the Spirit-produced Son, Jesus Christ, we will have everlasting life, all because of faith in the Word that liveth. John 3:16-18 tells us this: "For God so loved the world, that he gave his only begotten son—Jesus Emmanuel—that whosoever believeth in him should not perish, but have everlasting life. For God sent not his Son—the Word—into the world to condemn the world; but that the world through him—the Word—might be saved. He that believeth on him—the Word—is not condemned: but he that believeth not is condemned already, because he hath not believed in the name—the name of the begotten is the name of the Word, meaning when we believe in the name of the Word, we believe in the Word—of the only begotten Son of God." Again, the name of the begotten son is the name of Jehovah's Word, meaning he that believes in the Word, with the same faith as Jesus Emmanuel, has eternal life. Heb 12:1-3 reads," Wherefore seeing we also are compassed about with so great a cloud of witnesses, let us lay aside every weight, and the sin which doth so easily beset us, and let us run with patience the race that is set before us. Looking unto Jesus— Emmanuel—the author and finisher of our faith; who for the joy—being chosen by God—that was set before him endured the cross, despising the shame, and is set down at the right hand of the throne of God. For consider him that endured such contradiction of sinners against himself, lest ye be wearied and faint in your minds."

This is the Lived Birth of the Begotten Son of the

Two that were One as he is led by the Spirit of Life—the Soul's Mind—within him.

CHAPTER 19

The Mind of the Soul of the Birth Begotten Son

See, we must use the soul's mind within to believe in, obey, and live the Word of the Us. It is the Mind of the Us—the Mind—the Female—that creates God's/our Word—God's and our Spirit-produced Son—which communicates with God's/our Brain—the Male—as to what She thinks the Spirit and soul needs. Then the soul's mind, after listening to the Word that came from the communication of the spiritual Mind and Brain, carries out the decision made among the three by sending a signal to the Brain to act. It is all about the Us within Jehovah and us, which is why the truth and ultimate truth about the Trinity is so very important for us to completely understand. Therefore, understand that the soul's mind only knows what he/she is fed, and the only two things that he/she can be fed is Jehovah's Word or Satan's word. So tell me, what are you feeding your soul's mind?

The spiritual soul's mind within us—Jehovah's Us and our us—are so very important, which is why Paul said in Romans that the law is spiritual and that we serve the law of God with the—soul's—mind. The mind within Jesus Emmanuel/us—the saints—contains the Spirit of Life—Jehovah's Word, Truth, Wisdom, Understanding, and Knowledge—which is his/our Power to overcome Satan's power. Eph 4:23 states, "And be renewed in the spirit of your—soul's—mind." Therefore, the Spirit of God is in our spiritual soul's mind—His Word, Truth, and Christ/Wisdom—and the spirit of Satan is in our evil carnal mind—his word, lies, and antichrist.

Look at the following scriptures:

Rom 8:6 – "For to be carnally minded is death; but to be spiritually minded—in the soul's mind—is life and peace."

Rom 7:14-16 – "For we know that the law is spiritual but I am carnal, sold under sin. For that which I do I allow not: for what I would, that do I not; but what I hate, that do I. If then I do that which I would not, I consent unto the law that it is good.

Let us pause here for a moment. It is good because now he—his soul's mind—with the Spirit of God's mind guiding him, is able to recognize Satan or sin within himself. This is good because once you are able to recognize the sin within you, you are then able to understand the sin, and once you have the understanding of the sin, you can be truthful with yourself about the sin. Then, once you are truthful with yourself about the sin within you, you have the power to overcome that sin, because the Spirit mind the soul's mind listened to was God's Word, Wisdom, Understanding, and Knowledge, which is Power. Power because the soul's mind believed in the Truth of God's Word of Wisdom, and belief is power. Now let us continue to read further into Romans 7:

Romans 7:17-25 – "Now then it is no more I that do it, but sin that dwelleth in me—again, the sin that dwells within us is our carnal mind—Satan's home, the flesh. For I know that in me—that is, in my flesh—dwelleth no good thing: for to will—the soul's mind—is present with me; but how to perform that which is good I find not. For the good that I would I do not: but the evil which I would not, that I do. Now if I do that I would not, it is no more I that do it, but sin that dwelleth in me. I find then a law, that, when I would do good, evil is present with me. For I delight in the law of God after the inward man—the spirit-filled creature—But I see another law in my members, warring against the law of my—soul's—mind, and bringing me—the soul—into

204

captivity to the law of sin which is in my members. O wretched man that I am! who shall deliver me from the body of this death? I thank God through Jesus Christ our Lord. So then with the mind—the soul's mind—I myself—the soul—serve the law of God—the Truth of God's Word of Wisdom—but with the flesh—the carnal mind—the law of sin—the lie of Satan's word of Wisdom—Babylon."

Understand, us, using God's Lord and Christ or His Word and Wisdom to serve Jehovah with the spirit of our minds—our mind, the soul's mind—we must learn to obey and believe in the Word of God—His Word of Truth, His Word of Wisdom, His Word of Understanding, His Word of Knowledge—which gives us His Word of Power, the fullness of the Godhead within Jesus Emmanuel and us. Because He—God's Word of Wisdom—is within him—Jesus Emmanuel/us—through faith in Him—God's Word of Wisdom—we too shall overcome him—Satan—the ruler of this dark world, all because we believed in Him, the Word that liveth. THE WORD LIVETH AND THE WORD WITHIN LIVETH!!!! Isa 55:10-11 tells us, "For as the rain cometh down, and the snow from heaven, and returneth not thither, but watereth the earth, and maketh it bring forth and bud, that it may give seed to the sower, and bread to the eater. So shall my word be that goeth forth out of my mouth: it shall not return unto me void, but it shall accomplish that which I please, and it shall prosper in the thing whereto I sent it." THE WORD LIVETH!!!!! Isa 45:21-23 reads, "Tell ye, and bring them near; yea, let them take counsel together: who hath declared this from ancient time? who hath told it from that time? have not I the LORD—Jehovah? and there is no God else beside me—the Word—a just God and a Saviour; there is none beside me—the just Word of Jehovah that saves lives. Look unto me, and be ye saved, all the ends of the earth: for I am God, and there is none else. I have sworn by myself, the word—My Spirit-produced Son, His Myself—is gone out of my mouth in righteousness—God's Wisdom, Understanding, Knowledge, and Power—and shall not return, That unto me every knee shall bow, every tongue shall swear." THE WORD LIVETH!!!!! THE WORD LIVETH!!!!! Heb 4:12 additionally states, "For the word of God—the Lord Jesus Christ our God—is quick, and powerful, and sharper than any twoedged sword, piercing even to the dividing asunder of soul and spirit, and of the joints and marrow, and is a discerner of the thoughts and intents of the heart—the soul's mind."

The Word liveth and the Word within liveth! The Word of Wisdom—Jesus Christ—liveth, and because the Word lived within Jesus Emmanuel, He sometime spoke of Himself while within Jesus Emmanuel, and he—Jesus Emmanuel—by faith in the Word, was led by the Word to live the Word, making the two one. The Two that were One while on earth had that wonderful name of the Word: the Lord Jesus Christ our God. This wonderful name was giving to Christ Jesus Emmanuel our Lord that we/he should believe on/in. Yes, we are to believe on/in the Word with the same faith Jesus Emmanuel had in the Spirit-produced Son, whose name is the Lord Jesus Christ our God, Him who is within the begotten son, making the two one! Read Isa 41:4: "Who hath wrought and done it, calling the generations from the beginning? I—Jehovah—the LORD—My Word—the first—Spirit-produced Son—and with the last—begotten son—I—Jehovah—am he—Spirit-produced Son." This scripture helps us understand in a so very important way that although they are two—Spirit and soul—they are also one fleshly body and all of this helps give us an understanding of Colossians 1:5-6 and 9-22, which is the two in the one.

Col 1:5-6 – "For the hope—the Truth of God's Word of Wisdom—which is laid up for you in heaven, whereof—the hope—ye heard before, in the word of the truth, of the Gospel. Which is come unto you, as it—the Word of the Truth, the Spirit of Truth—is in all the world; and bringeth forth fruit, as it—the Word of the Truth—doth also in you—as He did in Jesus Emmanuel—since the day ye heard of it—God's Word of Wisdom—and knew the grace of God in truth—the Spirit of Truth."

Col 1:9-17 – "For this cause we also, since the day we heard it, do not cease to pray for you, and to desire that ye—the soul's mind—might be filled with the Knowledge of his—Jehovah—will in all Wisdom and spiritual understanding—His Female, the Mind. That ye might walk worthy of the Lord unto all pleasing—in agreement or conformity with—being fruitful in every good work, and increasing—in the soul's mind—in the Knowledge of God. Strengthened with all might—Wisdom—according to his glorious power—the Word—unto all patience and longsuffering with joyfulness—with joyfulness—Also see James 1:2-5. Giving thanks unto the Father, which hath made us meet to be partakers of the inheritance of the saints in light: Who hath delivered us from the power of darkness—Satan—and hath translated—transformed—moved from one condition to another—us into the kingdom of his dear Son—the son of David, Jesus Emmanuel—In whom we have redemption through his blood—which is the Word's blood, even the forgiveness of sins. Who is the image—soul or identity—of the invisible God—the Word—the firstborn of every creature. – He is the image of the invisible God because he is the identity of God's Word—the soul of the Spirit-produced Son, the Word, the Invisible God—making him, Jesus Emmanuel, the risen firstborn of every creature—the soul and body of the Word, God's Word of Life. – For by him—the Word, the invisible God—were all things created, that are in heaven, and that are in earth, visible and invisible, whether they be thrones, or dominions, or principalities, or powers: all things were created by him—the Word the invisible God—and for him—Jehovah. And he—Jehovah's Word—is before all things, and by him—Jehovah's Word—all things consist—made or cause to stand."

Hear! Isaiah 41:4 makes verses 15-17 easier to understand, because although the Spirit-produced Son—the Word—is within the last begotten son, He is still the Word of Jehovah, and that divided Word of God's within the begotten son is He that created all things—see John 1:1-4. That Word is He who is the head of the body—us, the church—because

Christ—Emmanuel—is the soul and body of the Word and we are members of that body, making the body of Christ our head because, as members of that body, that body cannot live without the soul, making the soul the head of the body, and the soul cannot live forever without the Word of God, making the Word the head of all. 1 Cor 11:3 reads, "But I would have you know, that the head of every man is Christ—the soul and body—and the head of the woman is the man—the members of that body—and the head of Christ is God—the Word." Now, let us break down more of Colossians 1, beginning at verse 18:

Verses 18 & 19: "And he—the Word—is the head—or Spirit—of the body—and Jesus Emmanuel the soul and body of], the church—us, the saints who believed in the Word through the soul are members of that body—that body—who is the beginning—of the New World—the firstborn from the dead—Jesus Emmanuel—that in all things he—Jesus Emmanuel—might have the preeminence—over all of us as our risen Lord and Christ. For it pleased the Father that in him—Jesus Emmanuel—should all fullness—Jehovah's Word, Truth, and Christ—dwell."

This same fullness in Jesus Emmanuel is also in us, according to John 1:16: "And of his fullness—God's Word of Wisdom—have all we received, and grace for grace—growth in the Wisdom of God's Word." Therefore, God's Me, Myself, and I, dwell in us through faith, which is demonstrated in us by us living the Word daily. This fullness of God's head—His Word, Truth, and Christ—makes him—Jesus Emmanuel—and us full of the Godhead—the Lord Jesus Christ our God, the Father's Word, Truth, and Christ—within the body. It is as Col 2:9 states: "For in him—Jesus Emmanuel—dwelleth all the fullness—the Truth of God's Word of Wisdom—of the Godhead bodily."

Verse 20: "And, having made peace through the blood of his—Jesus Emmanuel—cross, by him—the Word—to reconcile all things unto himself—the Word—by him—Jehovah—I say, whether they be things in earth, or things in heaven."

Verse 21: "And you, that were sometime alienated—in the soul's mind—and enemies in your—soul and natural—mind, by wicked works, yet now hath he—the Word—reconciled."

See, we are enemies of God's in our natural minds when we alienate ourselves from, turn away from, or become indifferent or hostile toward the Word of God in our soul's mind. To be enemies by the lack and distrust of God's Word of Wisdom in our soul's minds means that we—the soul—are serving the carnal mind by living Satan's word through our soul's mind. Thus, our living God's Word of Wisdom through our soul's mind is His reconciling us back unto Himself.

Verse 22: "In the body—Jesus Emmanuel—of his—the Word—flesh—King David—through death—of the two that were One while on earth—to present you holy and unblameable and unreproveable in his—Jehovah's—sight."

So then, it is with the soul's mind, I myself serve the law of God—Jehovah's Word, Truth, and Christ—but with the flesh—the natural mind—I serve the law of sin—Satan's word, lie, and antichrist. Therefore, this same soul mind that we uses to serve God with is the same mind of the soul of the begotten son that he used to overcome Satan within his natural mind, that he may serve God with his Soul's Mind.

CHAPTER 20

The Spiritual Mind Speaking of Himself Through the Soul's Mind

I want to take us through this journey of the two that is one so that we can see the Spirit-produced Son speaking of Himself while within the begotten son. That we may be able to understand that, although they were One while on earth, they are Two and they are two in Heaven— the Word—the Lord Jesus Christ our God—and the reincarnated King David—Jesus Emmanuel our Lord. Please chew this meat slowly so that the digestion of it will be eased, because there is more of the Spirit-produced Son speaking of Himself while within Jesus Emmanuel. John 14:6-10 reads, "Jesus—the Word—saith unto him, I am the way, the truth, and the life: no man cometh unto the Father, but by me. If ye had known me—God's Word of Wisdom— ye should have known my Father also: and from henceforth ye know him, and have seen him. — If you see me, God's Word of Wisdom within Jesus Emmanuel.— Philip saith unto him, Lord, shew us the Father, and it sufficeth us. Jesus—the Word—saith unto him, Have I been so long time with you, and yet hast thou not known me—the Word, and the Word was with God, and the Word was God—Philip? he that hath seen me—the Word within Jesus Emmanuel—hath seen the Father; and how sayest thou then, Shew us the Father? Believest thou not that I am in the Father—I am in the Father, as The Father's Word—and the Father in me—the Father is in me because I am the Father's Word of Wisdom? the words—the Spirit-produced Son—that I—Jesus Emmanuel whom you see—speak unto you I—Jesus Emmanuel—speak not of myself: but the Father—and the

Word was God—that dwelleth in me—Jesus Emmanuel—he—His Word of Wisdom—doeth the works." Here, the Word, God's Spirit-produced Son, is speaking of Himself through the begotten son, and He, God's Word of Wisdom, is the head of Jesus Emmanuel that leads him to speak this truth that it is not him who does the work we see but the Father, God's Word of Wisdom, within him that doeth the work he does. Heb 11:3 states, "Through faith we understand that the worlds were framed by the word of God, so that things which are seen were not made of things which do appear." Take a look at the Holy Spirit of the Word and Christ of God's Power who anointed Jesus Emmanuel with God, the Holy Spirit in Acts 10:38: "How God—His Word of Wisdom—anointed Jesus—Emmanuel—of Nazareth with the Holy Ghost and with power: who went about doing good, and healing all that were oppressed of the devil; for God was with him—For God was with him—Jesus Emmanuel—the Word was with God and the Word was God. Understand now that the anointing of God with the Holy Ghost and with power on Jesus Emmanuel was God the Father Himself. "For God was with him. Please help me on this, "If God—the whole 100% of God, who is not man—for God is one and there's none else—is with Jesus Emmanuel, the 100% man who is not God, "How then can Jesus Emmanuel— the 100% man—be that God—the whole 100% God—that is within himself? God is with His Word because His Word is Him, but God is Jesus Emmanuel because He anointed Jesus Emmanuel with Himself when He anointed Jesus—Emmanuel—of Nazareth with the Holy Ghost and with power: who went about doing good, and healing all that were oppressed of the devil; for—or because—God was with him. Again we know God was with Jesus Emmanuel as His Word of Life, "For the Word became flesh which is God manifested in the flesh or being made clear in the flesh." For God was with him—Jesus Emmanuel—the Word was with God and the Word was God. See, it is this Word, the Lord Jesus Christ our God within Jesus Emmanuel our Lord, making the Lord Jesus Christ our God—the Word, the way, the truth, and the life. Hear, the

Word within said "I am the way, truth, and life in John 14:6: "Jesus—the Word—saith unto him, I am the way, the truth, and the life: no man cometh unto the Father, but by me." This is the Word within Jesus Emmanuel who is speaking here, because Jesus Emmanuel himself said no man can come to Him except that the Father—through His Word of Wisdom—draws them to him in John 6:44: "No man can come to me, except the Father which hath sent me draw him: and I will raise him up at the last day." With this understanding, we can clearly see that it is the Word who is the way, the truth, and the life within Jesus Emmanuel.

The Word is the way because the Father draws us—the members of the body—to Jesus Emmanuel—the soul and body of His Spirit-produced Son—with His Word, through faith in the Word, because faith, our victory, is the only way to the Father. 1 John 5:4 speaks of this: "For whatsoever is born of God overcometh the world: and this is the victory that overcometh the world, even our faith." The only way faith comes is by way of the Word of faith. Rom 10:8 reads, "But what saith it? The word is nigh thee, even in thy mouth, and in thy heart: that is, the word of faith, which we preach." It is the Word of faith that is the way because faith cometh by hearing and hearing by the Word, according to Rom 10:17: "So then faith cometh by hearing, and hearing by the word of God." This Word of God's is the only way that leads us to be incorruptible, which is the way to eternal life. 1 Peter 1:23 tells us this: "Being born again, not of corruptible seed, but of incorruptible, by the word of God, which liveth and abideth for ever."

The Word is also the Truth—the Truth of God's Word that leads us to the Father. James 1:17-18 reads, "Every good gift and every perfect gift is from above, and cometh down from the Father of lights, with whom is no variableness, neither shadow of turning. Of his own will begat—through the Spirit of adoption—he us with the word of truth, that we should be a kind of firstfruits of his creatures." Understand, it is the Word of God, which is the way and truth, that leads us to sanctification, and sanctification through the truth of God's Word of faith is the only truth way to the Father. John 17:17 – "Sanctify them through thy truth: thy word is truth.— We are told in scripture that we are sanctified by the Truth of God's Word of Wisdom within Jesus Emmanuel — That he—Jesus Emmanuel—might sanctify and cleanse it—the church, us—with the washing of water by the word—Eph 5:26.

The Word is the life as well. Hear, listen to what Jesus Emmanuel says about the Lord Jesus Christ our God—the Word—in John 6:63-65: "It is the spirit that quickeneth; the flesh profiteth nothing: the words—God's Word of Wisdom—that I—Jesus Emmanuel—speak unto you, they are spirit, and they are life. But there are some of you that believe not. For Jesus knew from the beginning who they were that believed not, and who should betray him. And he said, Therefore said I unto you, that no man can come unto me—Jesus Emmanuel—except it were given unto him of my Father—by His Word of Wisdom." The Word is the life also because of the words of Hebrews 4:12 For the word of God *is* quick, and powerful, and sharper than any twoedged sword, piercing even to the dividing asunder of soul and spirit, and of the joints and marrow, and *is* a discerner of the thoughts and intents of the heart. Deut 8:3b like wise read: "That he might make thee know that man doth not live by bread only, but by every word that proceedeth out of the mouth of the LORD doth man live." This is the same life as in John 1:1 In the beginning was the Word, and the Word was with God, and the Word was God. The same was in the beginning with God. All things were made by him; and without him was not any thing made that was made. In him was life; and the life was the light of men.

See, God's Word of Wisdom is the life in the bread that draws us to the bread, and the begotten son is the bread of that life. John 6:47-48 reads, "Verily, verily, I—Jesus Emmanuel—say unto you, He that believeth on me—as God's Word of life within doing all the work—hath everlasting life. I am that bread of life—his flesh." This means that Jesus Emmanuel is the bread—flesh or body—the messenger—soul—of the covenant, and that the Lord Jesus Christ our God is the nutrition—Word of Life—in that bread—the message, the covenant Himself, the Word of the covenant. Therefore, No Word no truth. No Truth no way, No Way no sanctification. No Sanctification no life. And No life through faith in the Truth of God's Word of Wisdom is no Eternal Life, which means the Way, Truth, and Life is the Father's Word of Wisdom within Jesus Emmanuel—the Eternal Life.

Now, because God's Word of Wisdom was within Jesus Emmanuel, Jesus Emmanuel is also the way, truth, and life, but only through faith in the Word first. He is the way, truth, and life in a very different way. Col 3:3-4 states, "For ye are dead, and your life is hid with Christ in God—the Word, the nutrition. When Christ—the soul and body of the Father's Word—who is our life—the body—us—cannot live without the soul—Jesus Emmanuel—making the soul—Jesus Emmanuel—of God's Word our Life—shall appear, then shall ye also appear with him in glory—He being the soul and Us being members of the body.

Jesus Emmanuel is our life, because, he is the soul and body—flesh—of the Word. The Spirit who is our life—that is hidden within himself, and we are just members of that body, and the body cannot live without the soul giving it life, thereby making him—the bread of the Word's life, our living bread—the life of our bodies—us. John 6:51 confirms this: "I am the living bread—the spiritual Son within the begotten son—which came down from heaven. If any man eat of this bread—the Gospel of God's Word of Wisdom preached by Jesus Emmanuel—he—Jesus Emmanuel and us—shall live for ever: and the bread that I will give is my flesh—the body of the Word—which I will give for the life of the world." Please understand, the life and the bread—the living bread—are the Two that were One while on earth, but They are, indeed, Two, and They are Two in Heaven, but They are also One as we are One with Them! See, we are a part of one

215

bread, one body, and we are all—including Jesus Emmanuel—are made to drink from one Spirit. 1 Cor 10:16-17 reads, "The cup of blessing which we bless, is it not the communion of the blood of Christ? The bread which we break, is it not the communion of the body of Christ? For we being many are one bread—flesh—and one body—Christ's—for we are all partakers of that one bread." So because we are partakers of that one bread/body if we believe, we are then made to drink into one Spirit—Jehovah, the Father, the Word, and that one Holy Spirit. 1 Cor 12:12-13 continues on to say, "For as the body is one, and hath many members, and all the members of that one body, being many, are one body: so also is Christ—Jesus Emmanuel. For by one Spirit—the Spirit-produced Son—are we all baptized into one body—the Word's body, which is Jesus Emmanuel—whether we be Jews or Gentiles, whether we be bond or free; and have been all made to drink into one Spirit—one Spirit, Jehovah."

Jesus Emmanuel is the truth because the Truth of the Word is in him as he believed and because he lived the Word through His soul's mind by living the truth and testifying of the truth. Moreover, to those who believe him, he is then to those believers the truth. He is also the truth because he is the soul of the Word of Truth—the image or identity of the Word of God—within the body, making him the truth of the Word's soul within the body—us, the church—all because we believed in the Truth of God's Word within him. Eph 4:21-22 tells us, "If so be that ye have heard him, and have been taught by him, as the Truth is in Jesus—Emmanuel, as the Truth is in Jesus Emmanuel. That ye put off concerning the former conversation the old man, which is corrupt according to the deceitful lust." Hear, if I have the Truth of the Word within me, it does not make me the sole truth; it makes the Word of Truth within me the truth. In addition, because I believe in the Truth of the Word within me, I am then made to be truth to whosoever believes in me or my acts of faith through the Word.

Jesus Emmanuel is the way because he is our example

of the way we should believe in the Word of God, making him the way, in faith, through the Word. 1 Peter 2:21 states, "For even hereunto were ye called: because Christ also suffered for us, leaving us an example, that ye should follow his steps." Our following his steps makes him the way—our author and finisher in faith through the Word, as Heb 12:1-3 says, "Wherefore seeing we also are compassed about with so great a cloud of witnesses, let us lay aside every weight, and the sin which doth so easily beset us, and let us run with patience the race that is set before us. Looking unto Jesus the author and finisher of our faith; who for the joy that was set before him endured the cross, despising the shame, and is set down at the right hand of the throne of God. For consider him that endured such contradiction of sinners against himself, lest ye be wearied and faint in your minds."

Again, the Spirit-produced Son—the Lord Jesus Christ our God—speaks through the begotten son—Christ Jesus Emmanuel our Lord—so that we will hear His Gospel, which draws us back to God the Father. These are the Two that were One while on earth, but yet were Two, and They are Two in Heaven, but yet They are One as We are One with Them. God's Word, Wisdom, and Understanding that speak through Jesus Emmanuel is in his/our head and speaks through our soul's mind. The Spiritual Mind Speaking of Himself through the Soul's Mind.

CHAPTER 21

The Mind the Differences and Misunderstandings of
the Two that's One

The mind, the mind, the mind. Again, for us it all
comes back to the mind. Please hear, our soul's mind in us is
us, and it is responsible for our soul who is us—see 1 John
5:8. Whatever we feed our soul's mind, be it good or evil, we
also feed our soul. That feeding of the soul's mind
determines which of the minds we are serving—or
growing—be it spiritual unto life or carnal unto death.
Moreover, whatsoever we feed our soul, we also feed our
body, and whatsoever we feed the body through our eyes—
lusts and pride—we also feed the soul's mind. Remember,
we have a spiritual mind—God's Words and the six Spirits
that come with Him—and a natural mind—Satan's words
and the evil spirits that comes with him—see Rom 12:2. That
means that our soul's mind and God's mind within us are
spirits. Through God's spiritual mind we are to be renewed in
the spirit of our soul's mind—see Eph. 4:23-24, that we are
to transform or subdue our natural mind—Satan's home—to
the spiritual mind—God's home—by training our natural
mind to obey our soul's mind, whose head is God's spiritual
Mind. God's spiritual Mind—the Truth of His Word of
Wisdom—within our soul's mind is connected to our
conscience, God's Spirit of Truth within us. God's Spirit of
Truth—the conscience or head of our soul's mind, our
Righteous Meter—within our soul is identical to God's
spiritual Mind within our head. Hear, Jesus Emmanuel sums
it all up this way in John 15:1-5: "I am the true vine—the
soul of God's body—and my Father is the husbandman—the
Spirit and spiritual Mind in us. Every branch—us, members

219

of the body—in me that beareth not fruit—those who don't believe—he—the Word, the Spirit of Life, the Father Jehovah Himself—taketh away. And every branch—us, members of the body—that beareth fruit—those of us who believe—he—the Word, the Spirit of Life, the Father Jehovah Himself—purgeth—cleans—it that it—us, the members of the body—may bring forth more fruit. Now ye are clean—purged—through the word—the Spirit-produced Son, the nutrition in the bread—which I have spoken unto you. Abide in me—the soul of God's body—and I in you—the body of God's soul, members of that one body. As the branch—the body of God's soul—cannot bear fruit of itself, except it abide in the vine—the soul of God's body—no more can ye—the body of God's soul—except ye abide in me—the soul of God's body. I am the vine—the soul and body—ye are the branches—members of that one body—us—who believe in the Truth of God's Word of Wisdom—that abideth—remain or dwell—in me—as the soul of God's body—and I in him—as the body of God's soul—the same bringeth forth much fruit: for without me ye can do nothing."

The Body without the soul cannot live! Therefore, Jesus Emmanuel, being the soul and body and us being a member of that body he was an example for us. By his faith in the Truth of God's Word of Wisdom, he shows us that God's Word is true and that he came to bear witness to that Truth that is within himself. John 18:37 states, "Pilate therefore said unto him, Art thou a king then? Jesus answered, Thou sayest that I am a king. To this end was I born, and for this cause came I into the world, that I should bear witness unto the truth—God's Word of Wisdom. Every one that is of the truth—God's Word of Wisdom—heareth my voice." This is what John meant in John 1:17 when he said, "for the law was given by Moses, but grace and truth came by Jesus Christ." That grace and truth came by Jesus Emmanuel, because God's Word of Wisdom within him is that truth that made him full of the truth and not the truth Himself. John 1:14 reads, "And the Word was made flesh, and dwelt among us, (and we beheld his glory, the glory as of the only begotten of the Father)—the Word—full of grace and truth." Understand, when the Word became flesh, He was at the time begotten from God into flesh, making both the Word and King David's flesh begotten—the two in one, the only begotten of the Father. "Begotten"/"beget" means to "produce as an effect; a belief that Power—the Word of Jehovah—begets Power—the Power that Jesus Emmanuel had while on earth." Got it? It is the Word that was made flesh, and it is the Word who is full of grace and truth.

Now I hear some of you saying, "See the Word became flesh, so Jesus Emmanuel is the way, truth, and life." No, what that means is the flesh—Jesus Emmanuel—became the identity or image of the Word—the invisible God— because he was full of God's Word of Wisdom. Col 2:9 tells us, "For in him—Jesus Emmanuel—dwelleth all the fulness of the Godhead—God's Word, Wisdom, Understanding, Knowledge, Counsel, Might, and Fear—bodily." God's Word within His head is the fullness of Jesus Emmanuel/us bodily because He—the Word—has all of the Father with/within Him. God's Word is God's Truth, God's Wisdom, God's Understanding, God's Knowledge, and God's Power, and this is the fullness of the Godhead within Jesus Emmanuel's body, making him full of the Godhead bodily. Therefore, while on earth, Jesus Emmanuel was led by the fullness of the Word, the fullness of God's head, and all of God's Spirits were divided from one Spirit. Now, Jesus Emmanuel's Spirit—the Spirit of Life, the seven Spirits within Him—are one Spirit, and before his soul and body slept for three days, he—Jesus Emmanuel—gave up only one Ghost, one Spirit. Luke 23:46 tells us this: "And when Jesus had cried with a loud voice, he said, Father, into thy hands I commend my spirit: and having said thus, he gave up the ghost." He gave up "the ghost"—one Spirit, the Word of life—which went back to the Father where He had been since the beginning, before the world was. John 17:5 reads, "And now, O Father, glorify thou me—Your Word—with thine own self with the glory which I had with thee before the world was." Even though the Word, Jesus Emmanuel's

Spirit, went back to God, his soul and body was not left in hell. Acts 2:30-31 tells us, "Therefore being a prophet, and knowing that God had sworn with an oath to him, that of the fruit of his loins, according to the flesh, he would raise up Christ—Jesus Emmanuel—to sit on his—David's—throne. He seeing this before spake of the resurrection of Christ, that his soul—Jesus Emmanuel—was not left in hell, neither his flesh—us, the body—did see corruption." Understand, the soul and body of the Father's Word was raised from the dead by God's Word—the Lord Jesus Christ our God—and that soul is set down at the Father's right hand. In addition, because we are the body, when we are raised unto the soul, we too will be like him. Sons of God, according to 1 John 3:2-3: "Beloved, now are we the sons of God, and it doth not yet appear what we shall be: but we know that, when he shall appear, we shall be like him; for we shall see him as he is." And every man that hath this hope in him purifieth himself, even as he is pure.

Tell me, if Jesus Emmanuel is at the right hand of God, on his father David's throne, how then can he be God or in a Godhead with God? Moreover, if he is God, how can we have the same mind as him—Christ—and not the same mind as the Lord—the Word, who is the fullness of God's head? 1 Cor 2:16 reads, "For who hath known the mind of the Lord—the Word, the Lord God—that he may instruct him? But we have the mind of Christ." This mind we both—Christ and we ourselves—have from God is God's Word, Truth, Wisdom, Understanding, and Knowledge—our power through each of our individual faiths in that spiritual mind. It works this way: if we abide in the Word of God, He will give us the Wisdom of God. That Wisdom will give us the Understanding of God, and that Understanding will give us the Knowledge of God. That Knowledge will give us the Power of God, and that Power gives us the strength to overcome Satan through the Spirit of God to obtain eternal life and live like Christ. Think, none of us has the Mind of Jehovah—one Mind—but we do have the mind of Christ Jesus Emmanuel—two minds. two different minds means two different people—or in this case the Spirit Mind of God and the Spirit Mind of a person. In addition, knowing they have two different minds is our proof that Christ Jesus Emmanuel in not in a Godhead with God, but that God is in his/our heads as the fullness of Himself according to our faith.

Remember, these Spirits are all divided Spirits from that one Spirit—Jehovah's Spirit, the Holy Spirit—and His Spirit—His body—is His Power: "through mighty signs and wonders, by the power of the Spirit of God—Rom 15:19a. Moreover, the only way we can get that Power, that Mind, is to abide in the Word. To obtain this Mind that was in Christ Jesus, we have to want Him/Her and their benefits or power. Phil 2:5-11 reads, "Let this mind be in you, which was also in Christ Jesus. Who—the Mind—being in the form of God, thought it not robbery to be equal with God, But made himself of no reputation, and took upon him the form of a servant, and was made in the likeness of men—Jesus Emmanuel. And—the Mind—being found in fashion as a man, he—the Mind—humbled himself—in the man, the body—and became obedient unto death—see John 10:17-18—even the death of the cross. Wherefore God also hath highly exalted him—the man—and given him a name which is above every name. That at the name of Jesus every knee should bow, of things in heaven, and things in earth, and things under the earth. And that every tongue should confess that Jesus Christ is Lord, to the glory of God the Father."

Understand, this Mind that was in Christ Jesus Emmanuel—God's Word of Wisdom, the Spirit of Life—is the form of God within him. God's Spirit-produced Son—the Lord Jesus Christ our God—is this Mind—God's head, his Word, Truth, and Christ, the six Spirits—within Jesus Emmanuel, who made himself of no reputation, and because the Mind is in him and because he is a servant, the Mind then took upon himself the form of a servant, the likeness of a man. And the Mind, being found in fashion as a man, humbled himself—in the man, the body—and the man became obedient to the mind within him, unto death—the death of the cross. This man was given—not obtained, but

223

given, which I will explain later—a name, which is above every name. See, the Mind humbled Himself to the will of God the Father, and the will of God within the Word of God humbled the man—the soul and body or flesh—unto death—see John 10:18.

Again, it is the Two that were One while on earth, but yet were Two, and They are Two in Heaven, but yet They are One as We are One with Them. Indeed, the Spirit-produced Son spoke of Himself while within the begotten son all the way before the death of the cross and while on the cross.

Hear, this is the Spirit-produced Son speaking of Himself as He leads the soul's mind within Christ Jesus Emmanuel that would humble him unto the death of the Cross. John 10:18 reads, "No man taketh it—My life—from me, but I—the Word—lay it—My life—down of myself. I have power to lay it down, and I have power to take it again. This commandment have I received of my Father." See, this is the Word within the son of man who knew God did not forsake Him while on the cross, because He—the Word—had already received the command to lay down His life—humble Himself momentarily by making Himself of effect in the man—and then take it up again. Our proof that this is the Word, the Spirit-produced Son, within that is speaking through Jesus Emmanuel is this: Jesus Emmanuel thought that Jehovah had forgotten him and allowed them to take his life. He momentarily lost faith and thought God had forsaken him and left him to die for ever when he spoke the words of Mark 15:34: "And at the ninth hour Jesus cried with a loud voice, saying, Eloi, Eloi, lama sabachthani? which is, being interpreted, My God, my God, why hast thou forsaken me?" Note: Some are teaching that this is God talking to God, and some scholars are teaching that this is a line from a song in the Psalter hymnbook. That by Jesus saying it, he was reminding the people of the song and by doing that he was showing the people that he himself was suffering those things sang in the song in its entirety, which is not true. Some are also teaching that God did forsake Jesus Emmanuel, but with the meaning of "forsake," we know that God did leave from within him, but did not forsake him.

Forsake means to quit, to stop believing in your plan; to leave entirely, completely; or to give up on, to walk away from, to abandon. Not only do we know this by the definition of the word, but we also know by the Word of God in Heb 13:5-6: "Let your conversation be without covetousness; and be content with such things as ye have: for he—Jehovah—hath said, I will never leave thee, nor forsake thee. So that we may boldly say, The Lord is my helper, and I will not fear what man shall do unto me." Also, see Deut. 31:6; Josh. 1:5; 1 Sam. 12:22; Ps. 37:25 & 28; and Isa. 41:17. Therefore, with this understanding we see that the Word knew what was going on when Jesus Emmanuel did not, because had Jesus Emmanuel known that the Word had been given a command by the Father to lay down and take up their life again, he would not have questioned or doubted Jehovah, saying, "Eloi, Eloi, lama sabachthani? Which is, being interpreted, My God, my God, why hast thou forsaken me." Although Jesus Emmanuel knew God had said that in three days he would be raised again, but when he was on the Cross, he momentarily wavered in his faith, as he thought God was abandoning him when he questioned Jehovah.

Again as we can see the Spirit-produced Son—the Lord Jesus Christ our God—speaking through the begotten son as He said, "No man taketh it—My life—from me, but I—the Word—lay it—My life—down of myself. I have power to lay it down, and I have power to take it again. This commandment have I received of my Father." And we can see Jesus Emmanuel our risen Christ Lord is totally different from Him because he did not know the Word had already received a commandment from the Father that He have the power to lay His life down, and He have the power to take it again. Our proof again is the fact that Jesus Emmanuel said," My God, my God, why hast thou forsaken me." Think, If Jesus Emmanuel knew he had the power to lay his life down, and he have the power to take it again he would have never doubted God as he did when he momentarily lost faith and thought God has forsaken him, "Right? —We will understand entirely about this "Forsakenness" in part two.

Please keep in mind that this happened before Jesus Emmanuel committed his Spirit into God's hand, while the Spirit was still within him. Now, because he/we are humble and faithful unto death and will die after he/we give up the Ghost does not mean that God has left or forsaken him/us, but that God will now give him/us the crown of life eternal. Rev 2:10 tells us, "Fear none of those things which thou shalt suffer: behold, the devil shall cast some of you into prison, that ye may be tried; and ye shall have tribulation ten days: be thou faithful unto death, and I will give thee a crown of life." Again, the Word, the Lord Jesus Christ our God, our Lord God, knew what was going on when Christ Jesus Emmanuel our Lord did not. The Two that were One while on earth but were Two and they are two on the cross even though they are in one physical body. Then, after the cross, Jesus Emmanuel became our risen Lord and Christ. Acts 2:36 teaches, "Therefore let all the house of Israel know assuredly, that God hath made that same Jesus—Emmanuel—whom ye have crucified, both Lord and Christ." God had made that same Jesus Emmanuel whom ye have crucified—or after you crucified him—both Lord and Christ. Got it? See, Jesus Emmanuel did not receive his own honor and power until after he was crucified. Rev 5:12 reads, "Saying with a loud voice, Worthy is the Lamb that was slain—that was slain, crucified—to receive power, and riches, and Wisdom, and strength, and honour, and glory, and blessing." Therefore, while on earth, Jesus Emmanuel had Jehovah's Power through the Father's Word, Truth, Wisdom, Understanding, and Knowledge, which are all one Spirit that we receive when we abide in the Word of God's Wisdom. God's Spirit-produced Son is the invisible, immortal God—the Word of the Father's Wisdom—which no man can see.

Again, I want to take us through this journey of the Spirit-produced Son's speaking of Himself while within the begotten son—the Two that were One while on earth. That we may be able to understand that, although they were One while on earth, they are Two in Heaven: the Word—the Lord Jesus Christ our God—and the reincarnated King David—Jesus Emmanuel our Lord, the Lamb of God.

Please chew this meat slowly so that the digestion of it is eased, because there is more of the two being one while on earth but are two. Therefore, taking all this in with faith helps us to digest 1 Tim 6:14-16, which states: "That thou keep this commandment without spot, unrebukeable, until the appearing of our Lord Jesus Christ: Which in his times he shall shew, who is the blessed and only Potentate, the King of kings, and Lord of lords. Who only hath—'hath' here means 'possessed with or accompany by,' which means 'to cause to be associated with'—immortality—God's Word of Wisdom—dwelling in the light—the Word. 'In him was life; and the life was the light of men' which no man can approach unto; whom no man hath seen: nor can see to whom—the Word—be honour and power everlasting. Amen." Here, Christ Jesus Emmanuel our Lord is the potentate King of kings and the potentate Lord of lords, who had immortally—the immortal Word of God's Wisdom—dwelling in him as the light—the light, the Word.—see John 1:4—which no man can see, nor has seen. Understand please, we have a potentate King—Christ Jesus Emmanuel our Lord—which is a person who possesses great power as a sovereign being: from the KJV lexicon potentate is a ruler, king, or a reigning being. From Dictionary.com, "Possess" here means, "to have as a faculty, quality, or the like," and "faculty" is one of the powers of the mind such as speech—God's Word of Wisdom, the Gospel of God, is Jesus Emmanuel's speech. Jesus Emmanuel speaking God's Word of Wisdom made him, as the Lamb of God, our Potentate King of king and Lord of lords. Rev 17:14 states, "These shall make war with the Lamb, and the Lamb shall overcome them: for he is Lord of lords, and King of kings—notice the upper and lowercase letters—and they that are with him are called, and chosen, and faithful." In addition, we also have an eternal King—Jehovah—which we read of in 1 Tim 1:16-17: "Howbeit for

227

this cause I obtained mercy, that in me first Jesus Christ might shew forth all longsuffering, for a pattern to them which should hereafter believe on him to life everlasting. Now unto the King eternal, immortal, invisible, the only wise God, be honour and glory for ever and ever. Amen." This Eternal King is the God of gods and Lord of lords. Deut 10:17 reads, "For the LORD—Jehovah—your God—His Word—is God of gods, and Lord of lords, a great God, a mighty, and a terrible, which regardeth not persons, nor taketh reward." Jehovah, the eternal King, is King over all the world: "For the LORD most high—Jehovah—is terrible; he—His Word—is a great King over all the earth"—Ps 47:2. Jehovah's Word of Wisdom—the King eternal, the God of gods, and the Power within the potentate King is THE KING OF KINGS AND THE LORD OF LORDS. Rev 19:13-16 tells us, "And he—the Spirit-produced Son—was clothed with a vesture dipped in blood: and his name is called The Word of God. And the armies which were in heaven followed him upon white horses, clothed in fine linen, white and clean. And out of his mouth goeth a sharp sword, that with it he should smite the nations: and he shall rule them with a rod of iron: and he treadeth the winepress of the fierceness and wrath of Almighty God. And he—the Word of God—hath on his vesture and on his thigh a name written, KING OF KINGS, AND LORD OF LORDS—notice all uppercase letters."

All things Jehovah made He made by the Power of His Word of Wisdom, and without His Word of Wisdom—the Spirit-produced Son, the Lord Jesus Christ our God, our Lord God—was not any thing made that was made! FOR GOD'S WORD OF WISDOM, THE KING OF KINGS AND THE LORD OF LORDS, LIVETH FOR EVER MORE!

Now, understanding that there are two different Lord of lords and two different King of kings helps us to understand the three—the Father, His Spirit-produced Son, and His begotten son—plus the other six Spirits that are always before Jehovah in Revelation 1:1-18. Let us break down these verses.

Verse 1: "The Revelation of Jesus Christ—Emmanuel—which God gave unto him—which God gave unto him—to shew unto his—God—servants things which must shortly come to pass; and he—God—sent and signified it by his—God—angel unto his servant John." Question: If Jesus Emmanuel is in a Godhead with God as His Word of Wisdom, why would God then have to give him Revelation?

Verse 2: "Who bare record of the word of God—the Spirit-produced Son—and of the testimony of Jesus Christ—the begotten son—and of all things that he saw." John bore record of the Word of God, and the record of the Word is the testimony of Jesus Emmanuel, God's Word of Wisdom, speaking through Jesus Emmanuel.

Verse 3-4: "Blessed is he that readeth, and they that hear the words of this prophecy, and keep those things which are written therein: for the time is at hand. John to the seven churches which are in Asia: Grace be unto you, and peace, from h—Jehovah—which is—the LORD, the I Am—and which was—the Lord God Almighty—and which is to come—Jehovah, the LORD God Almighty—and from the seven Spirits—God's Word, Wisdom, Knowledge, Understanding, Counsel, Might, and Fear—see Isa 11;1-2—which are before his throne."

First, notice the words from him: "which is"—the Father, the I Am—which is also found in Ex 3:14: "And God—Jehovah—said unto Moses, I AM THAT I AM: and he said, Thus shalt thou say unto the children of Israel, I AM hath sent me unto you." Moreover, Him "which was" was Him who was known by the name of "God Almighty" in Ex 6:3a: "And I appeared unto Abraham, unto Isaac, and unto Jacob, by the name of God Almighty." In addition, Him "which is to come" is Jehovah who is to come, which we read in Ex 6:3b: "but by my name JEHOVAH was I not known to them." He, here, which is, and which was, and which is to come, is Jehovah, the Ancient of days. We read of it in Dan 7:13: "I saw in the night visions, and, behold, one like the Son of man—Jesus Emmanuel—came with the clouds of heaven, and came to the Ancient of days, and they brought him near before him—Jehovah." Notice: The clouds of heaven that the son of man came on brought him—Jesus Emmanuel—to the Ancient of days—Jehovah—and they— the clouds—brought him—Jesus Emmanuel—near before Him—Jehovah. See, Jesus Emmanuel is not in a Godhead with Jehovah. If he was, the clouds would not need to bring him near before Jehovah. Now verses 9 and 10 of Dan. 7 let us know that the Ancient of days is Jehovah, and they also let us know that verses 12-16 of Rev. 1 refer to Jehovah and the Word. Dan 7:9-10 reads, "I beheld till the thrones were cast down, and the Ancient of days did sit, whose garment was white as snow, and the hair of his head like the pure wool: his throne was like the fiery flame, and his wheels as burning fire. A fiery stream issued and came forth from before him: thousand thousands ministered unto him, and ten thousand times ten thousand stood before him: the judgment was set, and the books were opened." Also, notice the clouds brought Jesus Emmanuel near—near Jehovah—proof that the two are separate. Moreover, that means Jesus Emmanuel is not in a Godhead with Jehovah. Think, if Jesus Emmanuel is already in a Godhead with the Father, why then do the clouds need to bring him near Jehovah?

This is the Father in verse 4 of Rev. 1 because in John's greetings, he said "from Him—Jehovah—and from the seven spirits, which are before his throne." Moreover, the seven Spirits that are before God are these in Isa 11:2: "And the spirit—the Word—of the LORD—Jehovah—shall rest upon him—King David's flesh—the spirit of wisdom and— the Spirit of—understanding, the spirit of counsel and—the Spirit of—might, the spirit of knowledge and—the Spirit—of the fear of the LORD." These seven spirits, which are God's/our righteousness, are always before Jehovah, and they are/were before Jesus Emmanuel, and these same spirits are before all the children of God. The word "before" here means "in the face of or jurisdiction of." Remember, Jehovah is the kingdom, the Power, and the glory; Jehovah's Word—His

230

Spirit-produced Son, our God—is our righteousness. Heb 1:6-10 reads, "And again, when he bringeth in the firstbegotten into the world, he saith, And let all the angels of God worship him. And of the angels he saith, Who maketh his angels spirits, and his ministers a flame of fire. But unto the Son—His Spirit-produced Son—he saith, Thy throne, O God, is for ever and ever: a sceptre of righteousness is the sceptre of thy kingdom. Thou hast loved righteousness, and hated iniquity; therefore God, even thy God, hath anointed thee with the oil of gladness above thy fellows. And, Thou, Lord, in the beginning hast laid the foundation of the earth; and the heavens are the works of thine hands." Note: Hebrews 1:1-14 is all about the Spirit-produced Son. I have used verse 6 again to explain "Firstbegotten"—the Word, the Spirit-produced Son—because we have in Rev 1:5 the first begotten—Jesus Emmanuel, the begotten son.

Please notice the ways this word, "Firstbegotten" is spelled in both scriptures. In Hebrews 1:6, the two words are spelled together as one—signifying Jehovah and His Word of Wisdom—but in Rev 1:5, the word is spelled separately as two—signifying the Water—God's Word of Wisdom—and the Blood—the begotten son as it is written in the second Psalms—King David/Jesus Emmanuel—and the two makes the only begotten son of Jehovah. Therefore, when God said, "thou are my Son this day have I begotten thee," He was talking to both of them. Moreover, throughout the whole Bible we cannot find any other scriptures other than these two that say "Firstbegotten" or "first begotten." Now hear! We learned earlier that the Word and Jesus Emmanuel are both begotten, both of God—one from the Spirit of God—the Word—and the other, by the Spirit of God—the Word—from the flesh of King David—Jesus Emmanuel—the Two that were One while on earth and yet are Two.

Hear! The Word is God's Firstbegotten, and the same is true of us. Our Word is our firstbegotten. When we get up in the morning, our word is the first to greet us. When we start to think or make a decision, our word is the first to greet us. When it is time to end the day, our word is the first to greet us. Every time we speak, our word is then begotten from us, and the same is the case with God. His Spoken Word is His Firstbegotten: "In the beginning was the Word" and "God said let there be light and there was light!" You see, it was begotten from Jehovah to bring forth light, and He did so. Prov 18:21 reads, "Death and life are in the power—the Word—of the tongue: and they that love it shall eat the fruit thereof." His Word is His Firstbegotten, and our word is our firstbegotten. And our word is not only our firstbegotten; it is also our lord, our lord god within us, and the same is true of Jehovah. It is our lord god because we live by it; whatever it tells us we will do, be it good or evil. This is why it is so important to understand what word we are feeding our soul's mind: Jehovah's or Satan's. Ask and be honest with yourself, who am I feeding my Soul's mind with?

This Word and the six Spirits within Him are our path to Jehovah, and because the Word is Jehovah, He then becomes the Lord our righteousness. Jer. 23:6-8a states, "In his days Judah shall be saved, and Israel shall dwell safely: and this is his name whereby he—the Word—shall be called, THE LORD OUR RIGHTEOUSNESS. Therefore, behold, the days come, saith the LORD, that they shall no more say, The LORD liveth, which brought up the children of Israel out of the land of Egypt; But, The LORD liveth, which brought up and which led the seed of the house of Israel out of the north country." This Word, this righteousness, is the path of Jehovah that we all are to walk in, and the only way we can access or enter into them is by faith in and obedience to the Truth of God's Word of Wisdom.

Now, our proof that verse 4 of Rev. 1 is not talking about the begotten son—Jesus Emmanuel—the first born, is the next verse, as it uses the words "and from." Meaning more than from the first two, "*And from* Jesus Christ—Emmanuel—who is the faithful witness, and the first begotten of the dead, and the prince of the kings of the earth." Unto him that loved us, and washed us from our sins in his own blood"—Rev 1:5. Now we see here the first begotten the two—the Word and Jesus Emmanuel. As John said in the second verse of Rev. 1, he bore record of the Word of God, and that Word is the testimony of Jesus Emmanuel—the first begotten from the dead. He is the faithful witness who gives testimony that the Truth of God's Word of Wisdom is true. Again, it is the Word speaking through Jesus Emmanuel—the truth of God's Gospel, the two being one.

Verse 6-8: And—Jesus Emmanuel—hath made us kings and priests unto God—God's Word of Wisdom our Lord God—and his Father—Jehovah the Male and Female—to him—Jesus Emmanuel—be glory and dominion for ever and ever. Amen. Behold, he—Jesus Emmanuel—cometh with clouds; and every eye shall see him, and they also which pierced him: and all kindreds of the earth shall wail because of him. Even so, Amen. I am Alpha and Omega, the beginning and the ending, saith the Lord, which is, and which was, and which is to come, the Almighty."

This is the Word—the Lord God Almighty—speaking here through Jesus Emmanuel, He which is the Word, and He which was the Word, and He which is to come the Word within the Father. John 1:1 reads, "In the beginning was the Word, and the Word was with God, and the Word was God." It is the Word who is the Lord God who sits on the throne—the right hand of Jehovah, which extends from the right arm of Jehovah's Wisdom—within the Father. He is the one that liveth always, even before Jesus Emmanuel was begotten—see Psalms 2:7. The Word liveth, and He is the Lord God Almighty, which was the Word, and is the Word, and is to come back within Jehovah as the Word. Rev 4:8-11 reads, "And the four beasts had each of them six wings about him; and they were full of eyes within: and they rest not day and night, saying, Holy, holy, holy, Lord God Almighty, which was—the Word—and is—the Word—and is to come—the Word. And when those beasts give glory and honour and thanks to him that sat on the throne, who liveth for ever and ever. The four and twenty elders fall down before him—Jehovah—that sat on the throne, and worship him—

Jehovah's Word of Wisdom—that liveth for ever and ever, and cast their crowns before the throne, saying. Thou art worthy, O Lord, to receive glory and honour and power: for thou hast created all things—God's Word of Wisdom—see John 1:1-3—and for thy pleasure they are and were created."

Please understand, the Lord God Almighty—the Word of God, our Lord God—is the Lord Jesus Christ our God. The Word of God's Wisdom that is the same yesterday—which was—and today—which is—and forever—which is to come—life eternal! We read this in Heb 13:7-8: "Remember them which have the rule over you, who have spoken unto you the word of God: whose faith follow, considering the end of their conversation. – The Word of God, the Lord—Jesus Christ—our God—the same yesterday, and to day, and for ever." We know this is the Word who is the same; because we know Jesus Emmanuel will change, as he will be given a new body and a new name. The Word, the Lord Jesus Christ our God, is also the beginning and the ending. He is the beginning because He made us all, according to John 1:1-3: "In the beginning was the Word, and the Word was with God, and the Word was God. The same was in the beginning with God. All things were made by him; and without him was not any thing made that was made." In addition, He is the ending because the Word is the one that goes to make war on behalf of Jehovah, the Lamb, and us, He is the one who judges all. We read of this in Rev 19:11-13, which states, "And I saw heaven opened, and behold a white horse; and he that sat upon him was called Faithful and True, and in righteousness he doth judge and make war. His eyes were as a flame of fire, and on his head were many crowns; and he had a name—Jesus Christ—written, that no man knew, but he himself. And he was clothed with a vesture dipped in blood: and his name is called The Word of God." Yes, the Word of God is the ending, because He, not Jesus Emmanuel, is the one that will judge us all. John 12:47-48 reads, "And if any man hear my words, and believe not, I—Jesus Emmanuel—judge him not: for I came not to judge the world, but to save the world. He that rejecteth me, and receiveth not my words, hath one that judgeth him: the word—the Lord Jesus Christ our God—that I—Jesus Emmanuel—have spoken, the same—Word of God—shall judge him in the last day." Understand now, Christ Jesus Emmanuel our Lord came not to judge, but the Word, the Lord Jesus Christ our God, came to judge. And the judgment of this world is the end of this world.

Question: if one came not to judge—Christ Jesus Emmanuel our Lord—and the other came to judge—the Lord Jesus Christ our God—tell me, are they the same or are they the Two that were One while on earth but are Two? In addition, this Word, the Lord Jesus Christ our God, had declared this ending of the world in the beginning of the world. Isa 46:9-10 states, "Remember the former things of old: for I am God, and there is none else; I am God, and there is none like me, Declaring the end from the beginning, and from ancient times the things that are not yet done, saying, My counsel—His Wisdom in the saints—shall stand, and I will do all my pleasure."

Verse 9 – "I, John, who also am your brother, and companion in tribulation, and in the kingdom and patience of Jesus Christ, was in the isle that is called Patmos, for the word of God, and for the testimony of Jesus Christ." Hear! Again, John is letting us know that this is the Word of God speaking through Jesus Emmanuel as he gives his testimony to us that the Gospel of Jehovah is the truth unto salvation.

Verse 10-11 – "I was in the spirit on the Lord's day, and heard behind me a great voice, as of a trumpet. Saying, I am Alpha and Omega, the first and the last: and, What thou seest, write in a book, and send it unto the seven churches which are in Asia; unto Ephesus, and unto Smyrna, and unto Pergamos, and unto Thyatira, and unto Sardis, and unto Philadelphia, and unto Laodicea."

This first and last is Jesus Emmanuel speaking. We can identify him by his voice that is as a trumpet in verse 10. His voice occurs again in Rev 4:1: "After this I looked, and, behold, a door was opened in heaven: and the first voice which I heard was as it were of a trumpet—the first voice, th first voice which I heard was as it were of a trumpet—talking with me; which said, Come up hither, and I will shew thee things which must be hereafter." This voice is the voice of the son of man, Jesus Emmanuel, and not God, who we will also identify by His voice, which is the sound of many waters. Again, the voice of Jesus Emmanuel, the son of man, is the sound of a trumpet. Matt 24:30-31 reads, "And then shall appear the sign of the Son of man in heaven: and then shall all the tribes of the earth mourn, and they shall see the Son of man coming in the clouds of heaven with power and great glory. And he shall send his angels with a great sound of a trumpet, and they shall gather together his elect from the four winds, from one end of heaven to the other."

Jesus Emmanuel is the first and the last as well—the first King David and the last King David. Rev 22:16 is our confirmation of this: "I Jesus have sent mine angel to testify unto you these things in the churches. I am the root—the first David—and the offspring of David—the last David—and the bright and morning star—our risen Lord Christ."

Verse 12: "And I turned to see the voice that spake with me. And being turned, I saw seven golden candlesticks—the seven Spirits of God that are always before God—the seven lamps of fire burning before Jehovah Throne." Please understand the voice John heard and turned to see—the trumpet—is not who he saw, because the voice he heard was Jesus Emmanuel—and who he saw was Jehovah's Word of Wisdom whose voice is as the sound of many waters. Ezek 43:2 tells us, "And, behold, the glory of the God of Israel came from the way of the east: and his voice was like a noise of many waters: and the earth shined with his glory."

Verse 13: "And in the midst of the seven candlesticks—the seven Spirits of God—God's Word, Wisdom, Understanding, Knowledge, Counsel, Might and Fear—that are always before God—one like unto the Son of man, clothed with a garment down to the foot, and girt about the paps with a golden girdle." Again, listen to what John said: "I saw one like unto the Son of Man—Jesus Emmanuel—in the midst of God's Word, Wisdom, Understanding, Knowledge, Counsel, Might and Fear—the seven candlestick or lamps of fire burning." Think. If Jesus Emmanuel—the son of man—is in the midst of God's Spirit-produced Son and God's other six spirits—Wisdom, Understanding, Knowledge, Counsel, Might and Fear— "How then is he God or in a Godhead with God?" If he is in a Godhead with God and the other seven spirit, isn't that eight and if it's eight, how could it be a Trinity or a Triune God? Also, how could a man—the son of man—be in God's Spiritual Head or be a Spiritual God?

Verse 14-15: "His head and his hairs were white like wool, as white as snow; and his eyes were as a flame of fire. And his feet like unto fine brass, as if they burned in a furnace; and his voice as the sound of many waters."

Again, this is Jehovah's Word of Wisdom whom John saw when he turned around, because the voice he first heard—a great voice, as of a trumpet—is not the voice of the one whom he saw. No, the voice of whom he saw had the voice as the sound of many waters, which is Jehovah's Voice. Dan 7:9-10 reads, "I beheld till the thrones were cast down, and the Ancient of days did sit, whose garment was white as snow, and the hair of his head like the pure wool: his throne was like the fiery flame, and his wheels as burning fire. A fiery stream issued and came forth from before him: thousand thousands ministered unto him, and ten thousand times ten thousand stood before him: the judgment was set, and the books were opened." Please know without a doubt that this is Jehovah—the one whose voice sounds as of many waters, which we read of in Ezek 1:24-28: "And when they went, I heard the noise of their wings, like the noise of great waters, as the voice of the Almighty, the voice of speech, as the noise of an host: when they stood, they let down their wings. And there was a voice from the firmament that was over their heads, when they stood, and had let down their wings. And above the firmament that was over their heads was the likeness of a throne, as the appearance of a sapphire stone: and upon the likeness of the throne was the likeness as the appearance of a man above upon it. And I saw as the colour of amber, as the appearance of fire round about within it, from the appearance of his loins even upward, and from the appearance of his loins even downward, I saw as it were the appearance of fire, and it had brightness round about. As the appearance of the bow that is in the cloud in the day of rain, so was the appearance of the brightness round about. This was the appearance of the likeness of the glory of the LORD. And when I saw it, I fell upon my face, and I heard a voice of one that spake." Also, see Dan 10:6. This is Jehovah and His voice of many waters, not Jesus Emmanuel, the Lamb of God. We find Jehovah's voice again in Rev 14:1-2: "And I looked, and, lo, a Lamb stood on the mount Sion, and with him an hundred forty and four thousand, having his Father's name written in their foreheads. And I heard a voice from heaven, as the voice of many waters, and as the voice of a great thunder: and I heard the voice of harpers harping with their harps."

Verse 16: "And he had in his right hand seven stars: and out of his mouth went a sharp twoedged sword: and his count-enance was as the sun shineth in his strength."

This is Jehovah and His Word, and we know this because the Word is the sword of the Spirit—Jehovah—and this sword, the Word of God, is also our helmet of salvation, according to Eph 6:17: "And take the helmet of salvation, and the sword of the spirit, which is the word of God." Again, in verse 16 of Rev. 1, this is Jehovah, and the sharp twoegded sword out of His mouth is His Word. Heb 4:12 also supports this, saying "For the word of God—Jehovah— is quick, and powerful, and sharper than any twoedged sword, piercing even to the dividing asunder of soul and spirit. And of the joints and marrow, and is a discerner of the thoughts and intents of the heart." Please know that the two—Jehovah and His Word—are one, who is also the first and the last.

Verse 17: "And when I saw him, I fell at his feet as dead. And he laid his right hand upon me, saying unto me,

Fear not; I am the first and the last."

Jehovah is the first, The LORD, and He is the last, the Word of God that makes war and does judge—the Lord God, the Lord Jesus Christ our God, the Word, our God. Isa 44:6 tells us this: "Thus saith the LORD—Jehovah—the King of Israel, and his redeemer the LORD of hosts—the Lord God—I—Jehovah—am the first, and I am the last—the Lord God—and beside me there is no God—the Word, Jehovah Spoken Word, His Firstbegotten."

Verse 18 – "I am he that liveth, and was dead; and, behold, I am alive for evermore, Amen; and have the keys of hell and of death.

This is The Word, He that liveth and was dead, and, behold, He is alive for ever more. The Word, the Lord God, is He who liveth and is alive forevermore. Rev 4:8-9 reads, "And the four beasts had each of them six wings about him; and they were full of eyes within: and they rest not day and night, saying, Holy, holy, holy, Lord God Almighty, which was—the Word—and is—the Word—and is to come—the Word, within Jehovah. And when those beasts give glory and honour and thanks to him that sat on the throne, who liveth for ever and ever." Again, the Word is He who also liveth forever, according to 1 Peter 1:23: "Being born again, not of corruptible seed, but of incorruptible, by the word of God, which liveth and abideth for ever." Okay, okay, I hear some of you saying that Jesus Emmanuel is the one that liveth, which is true, but he liveth unto God—Jehovah, the Word— and the same is the case with us; we live by the Power of God. Rom 6:10 tells us, "For in that he died, he died unto sin once: but in that he liveth, he liveth unto God." Moreover, the reason it is this way is so that our High Priest who lives by the Power of God can make intercession to the Father on our behalf. Heb 7:25-26 reads, "Wherefore he is able also to save them to the uttermost that come unto God by him, seeing he ever liveth to make intercession for them. For such an high priest became us, who is holy, harmless, undefiled, separate from sinners, and made higher than the heavens." Again this is done in both Jesus Emmanuel and us, and the life that we shall live, we liveth by the Power of God. We read this in 2 Cor 13:4: "For though he was crucified through weakness, yet he liveth by the power of God. For we also are weak in him, but we shall live with him by the power of God toward you." In addition, it is the Word who was dead; the Word is dead in us all who do not believe in Him and who are sinners, us who live by our own traditions, making the Word of no effect. Mark 7:13 tells us this: "Making the word of God of none effect through your tradition, which ye have delivered: and many such like things do ye." The Word was dead also when He lay down His life as the Father had commanded Him to do. John 10:18 states, "No man taketh it—life—from me, but I lay it down of myself. I have power to lay it down, and I have power to take it again. This commandment have I received of my Father."

John best explains all that we have learned thus far and Rev. 1:1-18 this way in Rev 19:1-13: "And after these things I heard a great voice of much people in heaven, saying, Alleluia; Salvation, and glory, and honour, and power, unto the Lord our God—the Word. For true and righteous are his judgments: for he hath judged the great whore, which did corrupt the earth with her fornication, and hath avenged the blood of his servants at her hand. And again they said, Alleluia. And her smoke rose up for ever and ever. And the four and twenty elders and the four beasts fell down and worshipped God that sat on the throne, saying, Amen; Alleluia. And a voice came out of the throne, saying, Praise our God, all ye his servants, and ye that fear him, both small and great. And I heard as it were the voice of a great multitude, and as the voice of many waters, and as the voice of mighty thunderings, saying, Alleluia: for the Lord God— The Word—omnipotent reigneth. Let us be glad and rejoice, and give honour to him—the Word." Why should we be glad and rejoice? Because He, within the Lamb, reconciled us back unto Jehovah. 2 Cor 5:18-19 tells us clearly: "And all things are of God, who hath reconciled us to himself by Jesus Christ, and hath given to us the ministry of reconciliation. To wit, that God was in Christ, reconciling the world unto himself, not imputing their trespasses unto them; and hath committed unto us the word of reconciliation." This reconciliation of Jehovah's children is needed before the marriage of the Lamb can take place; for the marriage of the Lamb is come, and his wife hath made herself ready.

This reconciliation is not our marriage to the Lamb because (1) we are the body—flesh—of the Lamb. John 6:51-53 reads, "I am the living bread which came down from heaven: if any man eat of this bread, he shall live for ever: and the bread that I will give is my flesh, which I will give for the life of the world. The Jews therefore strove among themselves, saying, How can this man give us his flesh to eat? Then Jesus said unto them, Verily, verily, I say unto you, Except ye eat the flesh of the Son of man, and drink his blood, ye have no life in you."

We also know that this reconciliation is not our marriage to the Lamb because (2) we are not married to the Lamb. The Lamb will be married to Jehovah's tabernacle the New Holy City, "New Jerusalem." Rev 21:2 states, "And I John saw the holy city, new Jerusalem, coming down from God out of heaven, prepared as a bride—the wife—adorned for her husband—the Lamb." Our further proof is Rev 21:9-10 and Rev 19:8:

Rev 21:9-10 – "And there came unto me one of the seven angels which had the seven vials full of the seven last plagues, and talked with me, saying, Come hither, I will shew thee the bride, the Lamb's wife. And he carried me away in the spirit to a great and high mountain, and shewed me that great city, the holy Jerusalem, descending out of heaven from God."

Rev 19:8-13 – "And to her was granted that she should be arrayed in fine linen, clean and white: for the fine linen is the righteousness of saints. And he saith unto me, Write, Blessed are they which are called unto the marriage supper of the Lamb—they which are called unto the marriage supper of the Lamb. –And he saith unto me, These are the true sayings of God. And I fell at his feet to worship him. And he said unto me, See thou do it not: I am thy

241

fellowservant, and of thy brethren that have the testimony of Jesus—God's Word of Wisdom—worship God: for the testimony of Jesus is the spirit of prophecy—the Word, God's Word of Wisdom. And I saw heaven opened, and behold a white horse; and he that sat upon him was called Faithful and True, and in righteousness he doth judge and make war. His eyes were as a flame of fire, and on his head were many crowns; and he had a name written, that no man knew, but he himself. And he was clothed with a vesture dipped in blood: and his name is called The Word of God."

I understand that this is some heavy meat to digest. But Jehovah wanted us to digest this meat first, for there is more of the Two that were One while on earth, but yet were Two, and They are Two in Heaven, but yet They are One as We are One with Them. Please, please chew this meat slowly, for the meat gets even heavier with Hebrews 1:1-10, because, even though the Two while on earth were One, they are Two—the Word our God—the King eternal—and the begotten son—the potentate King our Lord. Hear, we have the Father and His Word—our God, the Spirit-produced Son—which were brought forth from Jehovah by Jehovah's Wisdom—the Female within Him, the three that are one—which is within the potentate Son our Lord, who was born from woman—flesh—through the Father's Spirit—God Himself, the Holy Spirit.

Now, with the knowledge of Rev. 1:1-18, we will start to chew on Hebrews 1:1-10: "God, who at sundry times and in divers manners spake in time past unto the fathers by the prophets, Hath in these last days spoken unto us by his Son, whom he hath appointed heir of all things, by whom also he made the worlds." Now please understand that this is the Word, God's Spirit-produced Son who was with God in the beginning, before He was sent into King David's flesh to be made in the likeness of sinful flesh. Rom 8:3 tells us, "For what the law could not do, in that it was weak through the flesh, God sending his own Son—His Spirit-produced Son—in the likeness of sinful flesh—King David's flesh—and for sin, condemned sin in the flesh." Understand, God sent His own Son—His Word, His Spirit-produced Son—in the likeness of sinful flesh—King David, His begotten son—meaning the Word was God's Son before He sent Him into King David's flesh. Now, by Jehovah's sending His OWN SON, the Word, into flesh, with the flesh being that of King David, we know that this SON is not Jesus Emmanuel but that He is the Word within Jesus Emmanuel. Rom 1:3-4 reads, "Concerning his Son Jesus Christ our Lord—Jesus Emmanuel—which was made of the seed of David according to the flesh; And declared to be the Son of God with power—the Word—according to the spirit of holiness—God's Word of Wisdom—by the resurrection from the dead." Hear! Without the Power of God—the Word—with us, we cannot be His sons. Understand, we are all children of God, but not all of us are sons—women included—of God. See, God sent His OWN SON, and this Son had to be inside of flesh in order to condemn sin in the flesh. Heb 2:11-14 confirms this: "For both he—Jesus Emmanuel—that sanctifieth and they—us—who are sanctified are all of one: for which cause he—Jesus Emmanuel—is not ashamed to call them brethren. Saying, I will declare thy name—God's name and His Word of Wisdom—unto my brethren, in the midst of the church will I sing praise unto thee. And again, I will put my trust in him—the Word. And again, Behold I and the children which God hath given me. Forasmuch then as the children are partakers of flesh and blood, he—the Word, our God—also himself likewise took part of the same—flesh—that through death he—the Word—might destroy him—Satan—that had the power of death, that is, the devil." See, the Word of God was the Power within Jesus Emmanuel, who only received his powers after he was resurrected. This is another picture of the Two that were One and yet are Two.

Heb 1:3 – "Who—the Word—being the brightness of his—Jehovah—glory, and the express image of his—Jehovah—person, and upholding all things by the word of his—Jehovah—power, when he—the Word—had by himself purged our sins, sat down on the right hand of the Majesty on high." This is the Spirit-produced Son—the Word of God, which is God—and the reason why He can by Himself purge our sins. Hebrews 4:12 For the word of God *is* quick, and powerful, and sharper than any twoedged sword, piercing even to the dividing asunder of soul and spirit, and of the joints and marrow, and *is* a discerner of the thoughts and intents of the heart. John further supports this because it is the Word that purges us, and to be purged means to purify, and to purify means to sanctify and it is the Word that sanctifies us for the Word is Truth. John 17:17 reads, "Sanctify them through thy truth: thy word is truth."

Now, we know assuredly that this is the Word who by himself purged our sins, because Jesus Emmanuel cannot do anything on his own without God. We read this in John 5:19: "Then answered Jesus—Emmanuel—and said unto them, Verily, verily, I say unto you, The Son can do nothing of himself, but what he seeth the Father do: for what things soever he doeth, these also doeth the Son likewise." Got it? Of the two, one can do by himself—the Word—and the other can do nothing by himself—Jesus Emmanuel. Because the two are one, the Spirit-produced Son speaks through the potentate Son, and they are the only begotten of Jehovah.

Question: if one can do by Himself—the Lord Jesus Christ our God—and the other can not do anything by himself—Christ Jesus Emmanuel our Lord—tell me, are they the same or are they the Two that were One while on earth and yet are Two?

Please give ear. Both were dead, "the Word by Himself of no effect within the man, and man when he gave up the Ghost." But only the Word—the Lord Jesus Christ our God—had the power to take His and the others—Jesus Emmanuel—life up again, and these two are the firstfruits. 1 Cor. 15:20 reads, "But now is Christ risen from the dead, and become the—one—firstfruits—more than one; two to be exact—of them that slept." Hear! "Of them that slept" is us, meaning we had the firstfruits raised before us and the firstfruits are the Word—our Lord God—and the Author of our faith—Jesus Emmanuel. They are the firstfruits because without the Word, neither Jesus Emmanuel nor us would have the renewed faith in The Word, and without faith we cannot inherit the Kingdom of God. In addition, these firstfruits are both on/at the right hand of Jehovah. This Son, the Word, is seated on the right hand of the Majesty on high because He is the Right Hand of Jehovah, and the potentate Son, our high priest, is seated at that right hand of God on the side of the throne of the Majesty in the heavens. Heb 8:1 states, "Now of the things which we have spoken this is the sum: We have such an high priest, who is set on the right hand of the throne—who is set on the right hand, or side, of the throne—of the Majesty in the heavens." One is seated on the right hand as the Right Hand—the Word—and the other—the potentate Son—is seated at that right hand, which is upon the throne. Ps 80:17 further illustrates this: "Let thy hand—the Word—be upon the man—Jesus Emmanuel—of thy right hand—the Word—upon the son of man—Jesus Emmanuel—whom thou madest strong for thyself—Jehovah."

Now, the Word is Jehovah's Right Hand, and Jesus Emmanuel came to establish Jehovah's Word in us all. Yes, he came to establish Jehovah's Right Hand. We read of this in Ps 89:20-21: "I have found David—Jesus Emmanuel—my servant; with my holy oil have I anointed him: With whom my hand—the Word—shall be established: mine arm—Wisdom—also shall strengthen him." The Word is God's Right Hand because the right hand teaches—see Ps. 45:4; He finds out all of Jehovah's enemies—see Ps 21:8; He breaks into pieces Jehovah enemies—see Ex 15:6 & 12; He upholds us—see Ps. 63:8; ch. 89:13; ch. 139:10; Isa 41:10; He saves—see Ps. 17:7; ch. 20:6; ch. 44:3; ch. 60:5; ch. 138:7.

You see, God's Right Hand—His Word—and His holy arm—His Wisdom—is what got Him the victory: "O sing unto the LORD a new song; for he hath done marvellous things: his right hand, and his holy arm, hath gotten him the victory"—Ps 98:1. God's Right Hand is able to do these things and more because He is the Power and He is full of Jehovah's Wisdom. Ps 48:10 reads, "According to thy name, O God, so is thy praise unto the ends of the earth: thy right hand is full of righteousness." This righteousness that God's Word, His Right Hand, is full of is God's Wisdom—see Jer 33:16—making Him our righteousness as well—see Jer 32:6.

If we abide in the Word, we too have this Power and He—the Word, our Lord God, Jehovah Himself—is at our right hand. Ps 16:8 states, "I have set the LORD always before me: because he is at my right hand, I shall not be moved." That is power! See, God's Word of Wisdom is actually the Right Hand attached to God's right holy arm— God's Wisdom—and the Word is Jehovah's Power—that Right Hand of Power, He who exalted Jesus Emmanuel. Acts 5:31 tells us this: "Him—Jesus Emmanuel—hath God exalted with his right hand—the Word—to be a Prince and a Saviour, for to give repentance to Israel, and forgiveness of sins."

Now, if God's Right Hand of Power is His Word of Power and He exalted Jesus Emmanuel with His Right Hand of Power, how then is Jesus Emmanuel the power of God's Right Hand? This same Power that exalted Jesus Emmanuel is the Power that Jesus Emmanuel is sitting on. Luke 22:69 reads, "Here after shall the Son of man sit on the right hand of the Power of God—God's Word of Wisdom." See, Jesus Emmanuel is on the right hand of the Power of God, which is the Word of God. Again, read Ps 80:17: "Let thy hand—the Word—be upon the man—Jesus Emmanuel—of thy right hand—the Word—upon the son of man whom thou madest strong for thyself." The two that were one while on earth, but are two in heaven. Come on, come on, I hear you again saying God's Word is not His Power. Well again, take a look at Heb 4:12: "For the word of God is quick, and powerful, and sharper than any twoedged sword, piercing even to the dividing asunder of soul and spirit, and of the joints and marrow, and is a discerner of the thoughts and intents of the heart." Moreover, that Power of His Word shall accomplish whatever Jehovah sends it out to do, according to Isa 55:11: "So shall my word be that goeth forth out of my mouth: it shall not return unto me void, but it shall accomplish that which I please, and it shall prosper in the thing whereto I sent it." Now if this is not power, then I do not know what power is!

Note: I use the Father's name, Jehovah, because that is His correct name, according to Ex 6:3: "And I appeared unto Abraham, unto Isaac, and unto Jacob, by the name of God Almighty, but by my name JEHOVAH was I not known to them." I am not of the religion of the Jehovah Witnesses; but I am a Jew. And please understand, I am not of the Jewish religion either, but I am rather a Jew as Jesus Emmanuel said I am, and so are you all who obey and abide in the Word of Jehovah.

Now, to understand better what we just learned in Heb. 1:1-3, we will skip Heb 1:4 and go to verse 5, then come back to verse 4.

Heb 1:5 – "For unto which of the angels said he at any time, Thou art my Son, this day have I begotten thee? And again, I will be to him a Father, and he shall be to me a Son?" Notice here God said "AND AGAIN." "And again, I will be to him a Father, and he shall be to me a Son," which means God had already told him this before. But when, you ask? In Ps 2:7 when he said to King David, "Thou art my Son, this day have I begotten thee."

As we learned a little ways back, God's Word was His Son also before He sent Him into the likeness of sinful flesh. This is why God also said to this SON, "again I will be to him a Father, and he shall be to me a Son?" He said "again" because now the Son—the Word—is being divided outside of the Us—Jehovah—the Male, the Brain—Wisdom—the Female, the Mind—and the Word—the Son, the Spirit-produced Son—as He was brought forth in Heaven by the Female of Jehovah to be sent into flesh. Rev 12:4-5 reads, "And his tail drew the third part of the stars of heaven, and did cast them to the earth: and the dragon stood before the woman—God's Female, Wisdom—which was ready to

247

be delivered, for to devour her child—God's Word of Wisdom—as soon as it was born. And she—God's Female, Wisdom—brought forth a man child—God's Word of Wisdom—who was to rule all nations with a rod of iron: and her child was caught up unto God, and to his throne." This is the dividing of the Spirit-produced Son from the Us. This Son was not given but rather inherited a more excellent name, which He obtained because He is directly from the origin, the source, Jehovah Himself, which is why He was made so much better than the angels—Heb 1:4 – "Being made so much better than the angels, as he hath by inheritance obtained a more excellent name than they."

Incline thy ear, the Word, the Lord our God, by inheritance obtained a more excellent name. It is as Ps 8:9 reads: "O LORD our Lord—the Word—how excellent is thy name in all the earth!" Now, on the other hand, Jesus Emmanuel, like us, was made a little lower than the angels. We read this in Heb 2:7-9: "Thou madest him—us, man—a little lower than the angels; thou crownedst him with glory and honour, and didst set him over the works of thy hands— Also see Gen 1:28. Thou—Jehovah—hast put all things in subjection under his—man—feet. For in that he—Jehovah— put all in subjection under him—man—he—Jehovah—left nothing that is not put under him—man. But now we see not yet all things—sin and death—put under him—man. But we see Jesus—Emmanuel—who was made a little lower than the angels for the suffering of death, crowned with glory and honour; that he by the grace of God—the Word—John 1:14—should taste death for every man." See, God's Word of Wisdom was made SO MUCH BETTER than the angels, and Jesus Emmanuel and we ourselves were made A LITTER LOWER than the angels.

Question: if one was made so much better than the angels—the Lord Jesus Christ our God—and the other were made a little lower that the angels—Christ Jesus Emmanuel our Lord—tell me, are they the same or are they the Two that were One while on earth but are Two? Here is another image of the Two that were One and yet are Two. And Jesus

Emmanuel was given the name—the name of the Word—that is more excellent than any name. Phil 2:9-10 states, "Wherefore God also hath highly exalted him—Jesus Emmanuel—and given him a name, which is above every name. That at the name of Jesus every knee should bow, of things in heaven, and things in earth, and things under the earth." The reason why we shall bow at the name is because, the name is, again, the Father—the name of His Word. Look at Isa. 45:23: "I have sworn by myself, the word is gone out of my mouth in righteousness, and shall not return, That unto me—Jehovah—every knee shall bow, every tongue shall swear." This is the Word's name, the name of the Lord Jesus Christ our God, Him who came in the flesh, which we read of directly in 1 John 4:2: "Hereby know ye the Spirit of God: Every spirit that confesseth that Jesus Christ—the Word—is come in the flesh—in the flesh of David—is of God." Remember, the flesh that He—the Word—came in is King David's; and it is King David's flesh that Jesus Emmanuel was made from. Rom 1:3 confirms this: "Concerning his Son Jesus Christ our Lord, which was made of the seed of David according to the flesh." This is the Two that were One while on earth.

Question: if one by inheritance obtained the more excellent name—Jesus—before He came into David's flesh—the Lord Jesus Christ our God—and the other, by being highly exalted by Jehovah, was given that name which is above every name—Christ Jesus Emmanuel our Lord—again, tell me, are they the same or are they the Two that were One while on earth but are Two?

Again, our God is the Father's Word—the Lord our God. "The Lord God"—hear, we have a Christ Lord—from the bowels of King David, as to the flesh—and we have a Lord God—divided from the Male and Female of God the Father, as to the Spirit. It is the Word of God that we should live by, using the same faith that Jesus Emmanuel had, through the Spirit of Jehovah. Just like Jesus Emmanuel, we too are begotten—through the Spirit of adoption—by the Truth of the Father's Word. James 1:18 tells us this: "Of his own will begat he—Jehovah—us—including Jesus Emmanuel—with the word of truth, that we should be a kind of firstfruits of his creatures." This same Word of Truth begets Jesus Emmanuel as well. To explain this, we will show that God the Father—the Holy Spirit, who is the Creator of evolution—is also the Creator of insemination.

Before man ever learned of artificial insemination, artificial selection, or crossbreeding, Jehovah, the Master Scientist, used them to bring forth His begotten son. First, Jehovah needed bodies—one spiritual and one natural—so He spiritually selected His Spirit-produced Son, His Word, for the spiritual and His begotten son, King David, for the natural. Artificial selection is a process in the breeding of animals/humans and in the cultivation of plants by which the breeder chooses to perpetuate only those forms having certain desirable inheritable characteristics. Then, once God had chosen the bodies, He divided His Word, His Spirit-produced Son, from the Us and used Him to quicken the bowels of King David. Rom 8:10-11 reads, "And if Christ—God's Wisdom, Understanding, Knowledge, and Power—be in you, the body is dead because of sin; but the Spirit—the Word—is life because of righteousness—which is what God's Word is or stands for. But if the Spirit—the Word—of him—Jehovah—that raised up Jesus from the dead dwell in you, he that raised up Christ—Jesus Emmanuel—from the dead shall also quicken your mortal bodies by his Spirit—His Word, Truth, Wisdom, Understanding, Knowledge, and Power—that dwelleth in you." God's Word that He divided from Himself was still with Him while He—the Word—was divided within Jesus Emmanuel, who is of the seed of David. John 7:42 – "Hath not the scripture said, That Christ cometh of the seed of David, and out of the town of Bethlehem, where David was?" That seed—Jesus Emmanuel—which came from David, was made of David's seed, according to the flesh or body, making them the same seed. Rom 1:3-6 states, "Concerning his Son Jesus Christ our Lord, which was made of the seed of David according to the flesh; And declared to be the Son of God with power—the Word—

according to the spirit of holiness, by the resurrection from the dead—by the resurrection from the dead. By whom—and not from whom, who is the Word—we have received grace and apostleship, for obedience to the faith among all nations, for his name. – By whom' means 'through the medium of,' and 'medium' means 'the middle state/man, the intermediate or the acting in between two,' which in this case is the Word and us, which means we received God's grace from God's Word of Wisdom through the Jesus Emmanuel the intermediate.—Among whom—Jesus Emmanuel, with a share for each of or along with whom—are ye also the called of Jesus Christ—the Word." King David is the flesh that the Word quickened when He was made in the flesh. Again, together they—the Word and Jesus Emmanuel—became the only begotten, according to John 1:14 -- "And the Word was made flesh, and dwelt among us, (and we beheld his glory, the glory as of the only begotten of the Father,) full of grace and truth." See, the Word is now begotten of Jehovah, now in the flesh—He who, being made so much better than the angels, hath by inheritance obtained a more excellent name than they. Understand that both the Word—the Lord Jesus Christ our God—and the flesh—Christ Jesus Emmanuel our Lord) are now begotten of God. Moreover, because of this, Jesus Emmanuel our Lord then becomes the soul and body of the Father's Word—the seed of Abraham, the flesh which was begotten from his father David. He—Jesus Emmanuel— was begotten from David when Jehovah raised him the first time from the bowels of King David, and then, along with the Word, God spiritually inseminated them—His embryo—into Mary to bring forth His only Begotten.

To understand this better, we need to explain a little more about this firstbegotten—the Word—because we have in Rev 1:5 the first begotten—Jesus Emmanuel. Please notice the ways in which this word is spelled in both scriptures. In Hebrews 1:6, the Firstbegotten—the Word—is spelled as the one word together—Jehovah and the Word—but in Rev. 1:5, the word is spelled "first begotten," as two separate words— the Word and Jesus Emmanuel—and the two, makes the only

251

Begotten of Jehovah. Therefore, when God said, "thou art my Son, this day have I begotten thee," He was talking to both of them. The difference is, though, that God said this to His Word once, after He had grew and prepared the Lamb to go into the world and suffer the cross. Then, to Jesus Emmanuel, He said it twice, first when he was King David—see Ps. 2:7—and second after he had learned to listen to and obey the Word within him—the Word that led him to be baptized and suffer the cross—see Acts 13:33—the Two that were One while on earth—and being on earth means Jehovah said this to both of them.

Before we look at the following scripture, please note: Hebrews 1:1-14 is all about the Spirit-produced Son. I add Hebrews 1:6 & 7 here to explain this firstbegotten—the Word—because we have in Rev 1:5 the first begotten—Jesus Emmanuel. In addition, this will help us understand more about verses 8-9 of Hebrews 1.

Heb 1:6-7 – "And again, when he bringeth in the firstbegotten into the world, he saith, And let all the angels of God worship him. And of the angels he saith, Who maketh his angels spirits, and his ministers a flame of fire."

Again, please notice the ways this word is spelled in both scriptures. The "Firstbegotten"—the Word—in Hebrews 1:6 is the two words spelled together as one—Jehovah and the Word—but the "first begotten" in Rev. 1:5—the Word and Jesus Emmanuel—is the two words spelled separately as two, and the two make the only begotten son of Jehovah. Therefore, when God said, "thou art my Son, this day have I begotten thee," He was talking to both of them. In addition, throughout the whole Bible we are unable to find any other scriptures, other than these two, that say "Firstbegotten" or "first begotten." We cannot find them anywhere!

We learned earlier that the Word and Jesus Emmanuel are both begotten, both of God—one from the Spirit of God—the Word—and the other—Jesus Emmanuel—by that Spirit of God, from the bowels of King

252

David—the Two that were One while on earth and yet are Two. Hear! the Word is God's firstbegotten, and the same is true of us. Our Word is our firstbegotten. When we get up in the morning, our word is the first to greet us. When we start to think or make a decision, our word is the first to greet us. When it is time to end the day, our word is the first to greet us. Every time we speak, our word is then begotten from us, and the same is the case with God. His Word is His firstbegotten: "In the beginning was the Word" and "God said let there be light and there was light!" You see, He was begotten from Jehovah to bring forth light, and he did so. Prov 18:21 reads, "Death and life are in the power—the Word—of the tongue: and they that love it shall eat the fruit thereof." Moreover, our word is not only our firstbegotten; it is also our lord, our lord god within us, and the same is true of Jehovah. It is our lord god because we live by it; whatever it tells us we will do, be it good or evil. The Word, the Spirit, the Firstbegotten—the Lord Jesus Christ our God—and the soul, the body, the first begotten—Christ Jesus Emmanuel our Lord—the two being one are the Spirit-produced Son speaking through the potentate Son, and they are the only begotten of Jehovah. One is actually seated on the right hand as the Right Hand—the Word—and the other is seated on the right hand of that throne—the potentate Son. Ps 80:17 reads, "Let thy hand—the Word—be upon the man—Jesus Emmanuel—of thy right hand—the Word—upon the son of man—Jesus Emmanuel/us—whom thou madest strong for thyself."

Just so that we are clear on that fact that Jesus Emmanuel—the Lamb—is not actually on the right hand, we should acknowledge the fact that He moved from the right hand of the throne to the middle of that throne. Rev 7:17 states, "For the Lamb which is in the midst of the throne shall feed them, and shall lead them unto living fountains of waters: and God shall wipe away all tears from their eyes." The Word, the Lord God, on the other hand, is at the right hand of Jehovah as the Right Hand, according to Ps 110:1: "The LORD—Jehovah—said unto my Lord—

our Lord God—Sit thou—back—at my right hand, until I make thine enemies thy footstool." Now, the Word is Jehovah's Right Hand and Jesus Emmanuel came to establish Jehovah's Word in us all. Yes, he came to establish Jehovah's hand. Ps 89:20-21 tells us, "I have found David my servant; with my holy oil have I anointed him: With whom my hand shall be established: mine arm also shall strengthen him." You see, God's Right Hand—His Word—and holy arm—His Wisdom, His Spirit—is what got Him the victory. Ps 98:1 reads, "O sing unto the LORD a new song; for he hath done marvellous things: his right hand, and his holy arm, hath gotten him the victory."

This victory is our faith in God's Word, because faith comes by hearing and hearing comes by the Word, which means our faith in the Power of the Word is our faith that gives us the victory to overcome. 1 John 5:4 states, "For whatsoever is born of God—by water, the Word, and by Spirit—the Holy Spirit—overcometh the world: and this is the victory that overcometh the world, even our faith—the hearing that comes by the Word." The right hand is able to do these things and more because He is the Power and He is full of Jehovah's Wisdom. If we abide in the Word, we too have this Power and He—the Word, our Lord God, Jehovah Himself—is at our right hand. Ps 16:8 confirms this: "I have set the LORD always before me: because he is at my right hand, I shall not be moved." See, the Word is actually on the right hand, and the Word is Jehovah's Power—that right hand of Power, He that exalted Jesus Emmanuel.

Take a look at the following scriptures that prove this:

Acts 5:31 – "Him—Jesus Emmanuel—hath God exalted with his right hand to be a Prince and a Saviour, for to give repentance to Israel, and forgiveness of sins."—This Power is the Power that Jesus Emmanuel is sitting on.

Luke 22:69 – "Here after shall the Son of man sit on the right hand of the power of God. See, he is on the right hand of the power of God—God's Word of Wisdom."

Ps 80:17 – "Let thy hand—the Word—be upon the man—Jesus Emmanuel—of thy right hand, upon the son of man whom thou madest strong for thyself."—These are the Two that were One while on earth, but yet were Two, and They are Two in Heaven, but yet They are One as We are One with Them.

Heb 1:8-9 – "But unto the Son—the Spirit-produced Son—he saith, Thy throne, O God, is for ever and ever: a sceptre of righteousness is the sceptre of thy kingdom. Thou hast loved righteousness, and hated iniquity; therefore God, even thy God, hath anointed thee with the oil of gladness above thy fellows."—This throne is the Spirit-produced Son's, because His throne is a scepter of righteousness, which is the Kingdom of Jehovah.

Ps 45:6-7 – "Thy throne, O God, is for ever and ever: the sceptre of thy kingdom is a right sceptre. Thou lovest righteousness, and hatest wickedness: therefore God, thy God, hath anointed thee with the oil of gladness above thy fellows."

Ps 11:7 "For the righteous LORD loveth righteousness; his countenance doth behold the upright. God's Word is our Righteousness;"

Jer 23:5-6 – "Behold, the days come, saith the LORD, that I will raise unto David—Jesus Emmanuel—a righteous Branch, and a King—the Word—shall reign and prosper, and shall execute judgment and justice in the earth. In his days Judah shall be saved, and Israel shall dwell safely: and this is his name whereby he—God's Word—shall be called, THE LORD OUR RIGHTEOUSNESS."

Knowing that this is God's Spirit-produced Son's throne is our proof that Heb. 1:8-9 is not talking about Jesus Emmanuel's throne, because the Word—the Spirit-produced Son, our Lord God—will give him his father David's throne. This is found in Luke 1:32: "He shall be great, and shall be called the Son of the Highest: and the Lord God—the Word—shall give unto him the throne of his father David." Can we digest this? The Word is seated at the right hand of the Father—the power on the throne of truth and righteousness—and Jesus Emmanuel is seated at the right hand of that power of God, on his father David's throne. David's throne is a throne of obedience and faith, as is true of Abraham, as is true of us, because by faith we obey His Word. This faith and obedience is what Jesus Emmanuel came to teach. Everything we must do to remain in the grace of Jehovah we must do through the Spirit—the Word—through faith first—belief—and then through obedience—works. Faith without works is dead. Faith and obedience is what gets us to Jehovah. Believe and obey the Word, and we WILL have eternal life. This faith and obedience is what Abraham and David lived and stood for, just as Jesus Emmanuel did and just as we should.

This, life that they lived was their truth and righteousness in the sight of God. If we live the same, it is our truth and righteousness too. Hear! We get our truth and righteousness from our faith and obedience, and we get our faith and obedience from God's Word of Wisdom. God's righteousness—His Word, Spirit of Wisdom, and Truth—is all Jehovah's. It all comes from Him, and we can only receive them one-way: through the throne of faith and obedience.

This throne is the throne of David's—the one that Jesus Emmanuel/David sits on. This is why Jehovah said, "David should never want a man." NEVER WANT A MAN. NEVER, NEVER, NEVER WANT A MAN. A MAN MEANS ANY MAN OTHER THAN DAVID! Jer 33:14-17 reads, "Behold, the days come, saith the LORD, that I will perform that good thing which I have promised unto the house of Israel and to the house of Judah. In those days, and at that time, will I cause the Branch of righteousness—the Spirit-produced Son—to grow up unto David—Jesus Emmanuel—and he—the Spirit-produced Son—shall execute judgment and righteousness in the land." God said, "I will cause the Branch of righteousness to grow up unto David." Hear: TO GROW UP UNTO, UP UNTO DAVID. And the Branch of righteousness is the Spirit-produced Son and the other Spirits contained within Him, which are the Spirits in

Isaiah 11:2 growing up unto Jesus Emmanuel, King David.

As God's Spirit-produced Son started to grow up unto David, Wisdom took front stage at that point in time, because the child—Jesus Emmanuel—was then growing up, and when a child is growing up, he needs Wisdom to grow. God's Wisdom was the righteousness that grew up within Jesus Emmanuel until he had an understanding of God's righteous Word. Remember, God's Wisdom is always with His Word, and His Word is always with His Wisdom. This is true even though they are divided from Jehovah and are both still with Him. Moreover, this is true even though the three are the US and the US, the three, are one within the fourth—God's Holy Spirit, that one Spirit that we are all made to drink of, the Holy Spirit. The three—the Male—God—His Female— Wisdom—and their Son—the Word—are all our righteousness—Jehovah and His Word—because the Word was God, the righteousness that grew up unto David. Read Jer 23:5-6 again: "Behold, the days come, saith the LORD, that I—Jehovah—will raise unto David a righteous Branch, and a King—the Word—shall reign and prosper, and shall execute judgment and justice in the earth. In his days Judah shall be saved, and Israel shall dwell safely: and this is his name whereby he—the Word—shall be called, THE LORD OUR RIGHTEOUSNESS." We also have Wisdom, the Female of Jehovah—the LORD our righteousness—whom we read of in Jer 33:16: "In those days shall Judah be saved, and Jerusalem shall dwell safely: and this is the name wherewith she—Wisdom—shall be called, The LORD our righteousness." This name wherewith She—Wisdom, the Female of Jehovah—shall be called, the Lord our righteousness.

Jeremiah 33:17 contains the reason why King David should never want a man to sit on his throne. Let us look at this and then we can finish off with Hebrews 1:1-10. Jer. 33:17 reads, "For thus saith the LORD; David shall never want a man to sit upon the throne of the house of Israel." THIS IS WHY NO MAN OTHER THAN KING DAVID

WILL SIT ON HIS THRONE—THE THRONE OF FAITH AND OBEDIENCE. The First—David, King David—and the Last—David, Jesus Emmanuel—the Author—the first David, King David—and the Finisher—the last David, Jesus Emmanuel—the Root—the first David, King David, David himself—and the Offspring—the last David, Jesus Emmanuel, David himself—the other two that is one, the Lamb of Jehovah, the reincarnated Son, the potentate King of kings and Lord of lords, God's spiritual soul made of man, the soul of God for us, the body of God—this is he who will sat on his father's throne, the throne of King David, Christ Jesus Emmanuel, Christ David our Lord Himself.

Question: If Jesus Emmanuel is the Lord God—the Lord Jesus Christ our God, God's Word of Wisdom—how then can he give himself his father David's throne? He cannot, because the Word's Father is Jehovah Himself, not King David. Got it? God's Word of Wisdom, His righteousness within Jesus Emmanuel, the Two that were One while on earth, but yet were Two, and They are Two in Heaven, but yet They are One as We are One with Them the two, the Spirit-produced Son speaking through the Lamb, the begotten son of David's flesh, the Lord Jesus Christ our God, and Christ Jesus Emmanuel our Lord.

These are the two different thrones. The throne of God's Word of Wisdom, our Lord God, is a throne of righteousness, and the throne of Jesus Emmanuel, the faithful witness to God's Word of Wisdom, is a throne of faith and obedience in God's Word of Wisdom. This throne of faith and obedience is what gives us our righteousness—God's Word of Wisdom Himself living within us—all because we chose to believe God's Word of Wisdom.

Now we can finish up with Heb 1:10: "And, Thou, Lord, in the beginning hast laid the foundation of the earth; and the heavens are the works of thine hands." Well we surely know that this is the Word, the Spirit-produced Son within Jesus Emmanuel and not the Begotten Son who created the heavens and the earth. Isa 42:5-6a says, "Thus saith God the

LORD, he that created the heavens, and stretched them out; he that spread forth the earth, and that which cometh out of it; he that giveth breath unto the people upon it, and spirit to them that walk therein. I the LORD have called thee in righteousness, and will hold thine hand, and will keep thee." All of this was done by God's Word of Wisdom, according to John 1:1-4: "In the beginning was the Word, and the Word was with God, and the Word was God. The same was in the beginning with God. All things were made by him; and without him was not any thing made that was made. In him was life; and the life was the light of men."

Question, ask yourself again, who is closer to the truth about the Trinity: Theophilus of Antioch—*the Trinity [Τριάδος] of God, and His Word, and His Wisdom. And the fourth is the type of man who needs light, that so there may be God, the Word, Wisdom, Man*—or Tertullian—*the first to use the Latin words "Trinity," "person," and "substance" to explain that the Father, Son, and Holy Spirit are "one in essence—not one in Person"*?

There you have it: God's Me—the Father, the Male and Female—Myself—the Son, their Word—and I—the body, the Holy Spirit—the Truth and Ultimate Truth about the Trinity's not being in God as to a triune God." With this understanding of God's Wisdom and the role She plays within the Us, we can see that God's Me is His Wisdom.

Please continue on to part two of this work and allow me to introduce you to the Lord and Savior Jesus Christ our God.

References and other copyrights

(1) All Rights Reserved. Copyright Roland Williams 4/7/15
(2) Edited by Brittany Clarke
(3) Wikipedia Encyclopedia ©
(4) Noah Webster Dictionary ©
(5) Easton's Bible Dictionary ©
(6) What Darwin Never Knew (PBS Documentary) ©
(7) New International Bible © 1984
(8) New Living Translation Bible © 2007
(9) English Standard Bible © 2001
(10) New American Standard Bible © 1995
(11) International Standard Bible Encyclopedia © 2008
(12) God's World Translation Bible © 1995
(13) American Standard Version Bible ©
(14) Bible In Basic English Bible ©
(15) Douay-Rheims Bible©
(16) Darby Bible Translation Bible ©
(17) English Revised Version Bible ©
(18) Webster's Bible Translation Bible ©
(19) Weymouth New Testament Bible ©
(20) World English Bible ©
(21) Young's Literal Translation Bible ©
(22) On The Origin Of Species By Charles Darwin © around 1859
(23) New Unger's Bible Dictionary ©1988
(24) The Telegraph Media Group Limited (London) © 2012
(25) Red Bird Nation Blog Spot ©
(26) PC Study Bible © 1993 - 2000
(27) Strong's Greek/Hebrew Dictionary © 1994
(28) Ante-Nicene Fathers, volume 3; chapter III- Sundry Popular Fears and Prejudices. The Doctrine of the Trinity in Unity Rescued from These Misapprehensions ©
(29) Max Planck Institute for Evolutionary Anthropology, Leipzig, Germany (Professor Svante Paabo) ©
(30) Fox News /Fox News.com ©
(31) The Journal Current Biology ©
(32) Oxford University (Dr. Simon Fisher) ©

(33) Oxford Brookes University (Dr. Simon Underdown) ©

(34) Wisegeek.org

(35) Biblehub.com

(36) King James Bible ©

(37) Webster College Dictionary ©